MID-CENTURY MODERN FURNITURE

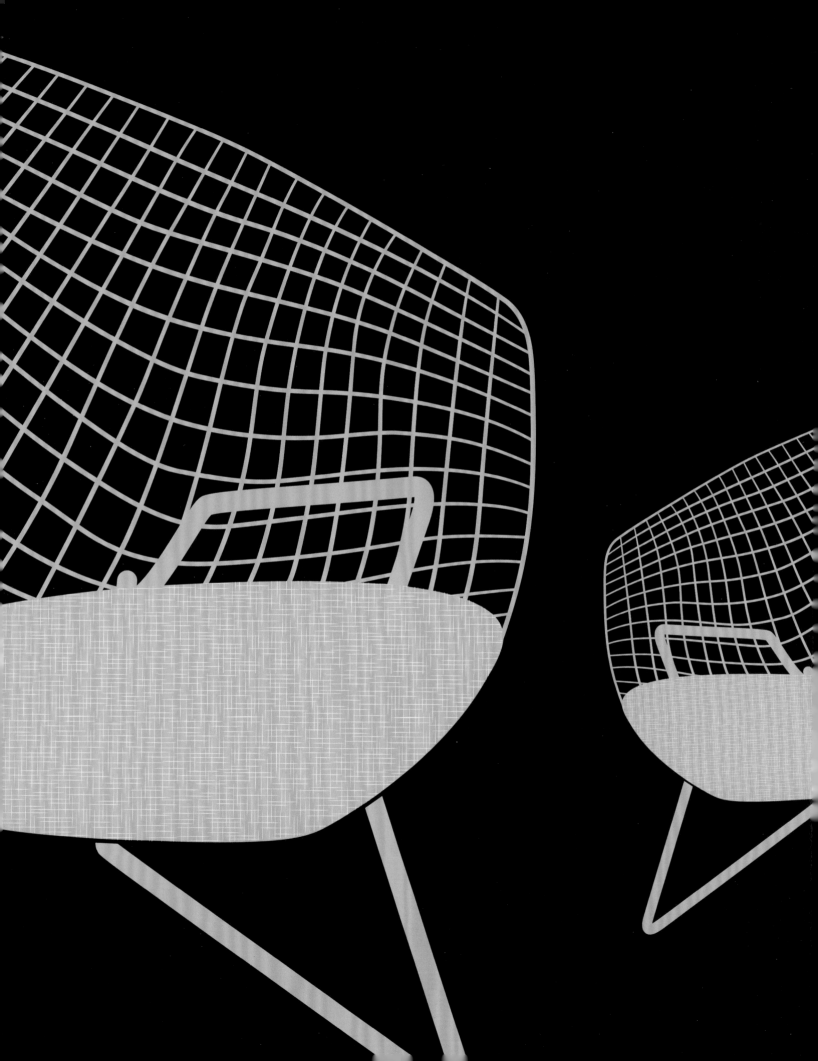

MID-CENTURY MODERN FURNITURE

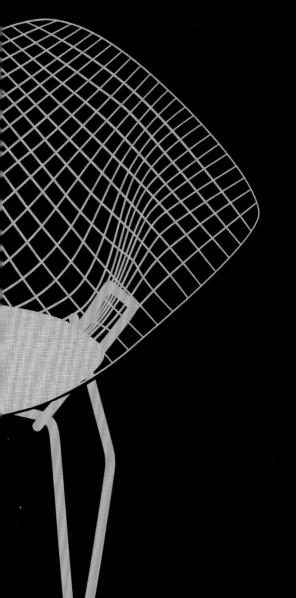

DOMINIC BRADBURY

WITH OVER 450 ILLUSTRATIONS

CONTENTS

INTRODUCTION

BELOW Arne Jacobsen, Model 3605 Drop-Leaf Table, 1955

BOTTOM Hans Wegner, Model GE2 Hammock Chaise Longue, 1967

The mid-century period was the golden age of furniture design. It was a time like no other, when innovation combined with creativity to produce an extraordinary range of furniture with both depth and breadth. Such designs responded to a growing demand for the rounded ingredients of modern living, populating and punctuating not only mid-century houses and apartments, but also high-rise office buildings, corporate headquarters, hotels, resorts and restaurants.

During the late 1940s, 1950s and 1960s, chairs, sofas and seating systems of all kinds were radically reinvented, while designers also devoted themselves to many other staples and typologies, including tables and desks, consoles and credenzas, beds and bedside tables. Furniture designers and makers placed a particular emphasis on versatile chairs and other pieces of furniture that could be moved easily around the home, working equally well in a range of contexts, including spacious modern kitchens and breakfast rooms.

Storage solutions were also a focus of attention, both in homes and offices, as architects and interior designers sought to declutter and refine spaces that were becoming increasingly fluid and open plan. Office furniture was a growth area, with companies like Knoll and Herman Miller developing collections targeted specifically at the corporate market but also with an eye upon the growing trend toward a dedicated study space within private residences. And garden furniture, too, was an important area of interest, with manufacturers producing 'leisure collections' suited for use within the 'outdoor rooms' cropping up around the modern home.

The evolution of mid-century furniture sits within the context of a post-war consumer boom that acted as an important catalyst for modern architecture and design in general. In the USA, the industrial machine that had served the country well during World War II shifted to energetic peacetime production, with American consumers well positioned to enjoy a period of prosperity and growth. In Europe, reconstruction after the devastation of the war years – aided by the Marshall Plan – encouraged not only fresh waves of home building but also provided an impetus for architects,

designers and manufacturers of all kinds. With its workshops and factories relatively unscathed, Scandinavia was especially well placed to take advantage of the post-war renaissance, but the same was true of countries such as Italy and Japan, which managed to recover surprisingly quickly in terms of restarting production while innovating with fresh materials and ways of making.

In some respects, such innovation within the world of furniture design built upon the work of the pioneer modernists of the 1920s and 1930s, including Marcel Breuer, Ludwig Mies van der Rohe, Charlotte Perriand, Eileen Gray and others, who developed early collections using industrially produced 20th-century materials such as tubular steel and chrome, often in combination with dynamic, streamlined shapes and forms. World War II itself had seen rapid advances in the use of factory-made materials such as plywood, laminates and fibreglass, as well as more widespread use of such lighter metals as aluminium. It is also important to remember that the careers of many key innovators – Jean Prouvé, Alvar Aalto, Arne Jacobsen and others – spanned both the pre- and post-war periods, with their groundbreaking work continuing to play a vital part in the development of mid-century furniture.

Advances in terms of materials and methods of production, explored in greater detail in the section of this book devoted to Ways of Making (see pp. 432–39), played a part in addressing key challenges faced by post-war producers and designers. Plywood, plastics and tubular or welded steel enabled furniture designers to create pieces that were lighter than ever before and, therefore, more portable and adaptable. Factory production meant that such furniture was, potentially, cheaper to produce (beyond the research and development phase) and, hence, relatively affordable. There were added benefits in terms of shipping and export, with the gradual rise of the flat pack and self-assembly furniture.

Yet these advances in materials and technology were only one part of the story, with the imaginative and highly creative response of the design community forming the other essential side of the same coin in terms of the rise and rise of mid-century furniture. Designers

and architects embraced such materials, recognizing their potential in terms of adaptability and affordability, while exploring sculptural forms, expressive designs, characterful shapes and playful silhouettes. There is a liberated informality to such pieces that stands in high contrast to the heavy seriousness of most 19th-century furniture, for example, with the possible exception of certain Arts & Crafts designs. There was a joyful quality to so much mid-century design, which is an intrinsic part of its charm, as seen not just in furniture but also textiles, lighting and homeware, not to mention art and graphic design. Even the most illustrious and influential designers, such as Hans Wegner and Arne Jacobsen, revealed a playful side to their personalities within their furniture, as seen in Wegner's Ox Chair (1960, see p. 111) and Jacobsen's Egg Chair (1958, see p. 56).

The continued evolution of plastics into the 1960s saw the use of colour and sculptural lines advance further, with increasing levels of abstraction. Fibreglass and acrylic were used to make shell seats, while polyurethane foam was turned into sculptural shapes, overlaid with upholstered padding, and for the first time injection-moulded plastics were used to make all-in-one designs. Such was the sense of liberation at this time that designers such as Joe Colombo and Verner Panton began to question conventional furniture typologies and developed hybrid designs. Examples are Panton's Living Tower (1968, see p. 223) and Colombo's Tube Chair (1969, see p. 125), which was delivered as a bagged nest of four tubes ready to be shaped at will by the end user.

This was not only the era of hybridization but also of modular seating and shelving systems, which invited consumers to play a part in choosing and moulding a design to suit their space and their lifestyle. In this sense, such designs were partially bespoke, sitting within a wider push toward increased choice for the purchaser in relation to upholstery fabrics and finishing touches. Such malleability was important throughout the period as a whole, with designers and makers seeing opportunities to appeal to fresh markets through the adaptation of existing furniture staples with, for example, alternative bases or configurations that might make them better suited to corporate or commercial use, including settings such as theatres, auditoriums and airports. A number of these themes are explored in more detail within the individual introductions that open the chapters that follow, devoted to specific furniture typologies.

Mid-century originals remain highly collectable and are available via auction sites such as Wright 20, which has been a much-valued partner throughout the development of this book, providing the vast majority of the photography from its archives, which document the wealth of landmark furniture that passes through its doors. But it is also important to note that as a result of the enduring popularity of the period, many pieces featured on these pages are still in production or have been reissued. At the same time, the mid-century movement has become a valued source of reference and inspiration for contemporary designers, helping to ensure that this much-loved aesthetic continues to remain relevant and always rewarding.

Charles & Ray Eames, La Chaise, 1948

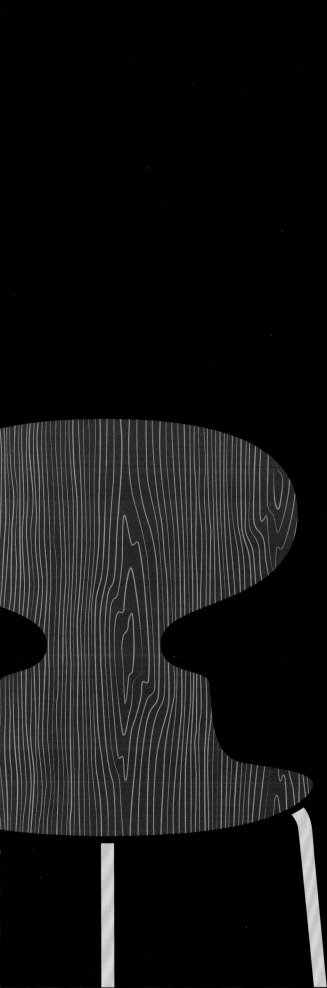

The chair was reworked, reimagined and reinvented as never before during the late 1940s, 1950s and 1960s. It was a period of extraordinary experimentation, during which familiar favourites, such as the wing chair, club chair, lounge chair and dining chair, were transformed as a wave of fresh materials and technological innovations allowed designers to create original, modern designs while exploring sculptural and expressive forms. At the same time, designers and manufacturers sought to address such key challenges as the need for flexible, adaptable seating and furniture suited to modern living, along with the important ambition to provide well-designed pieces that were more affordable and, therefore, accessible to a much wider audience.

The most accomplished furniture designers of the period took past, present and future into consideration in their work. Masters such as Hans Wegner, Finn Juhl, Børge Mogensen and George Nakashima possessed a rich knowledge of both artisanal craftsmanship and historical precedents. Many of the most successful chairs of the period – for example, Wegner's famous Round Chair (1949, see p. 107) or Mogensen's Spanish Chair (1958, see p. 73) – had something of a timeless quality that referenced traditional designs and ways of making.

Mid-century designers also built upon the important work of the pioneer modernists of the 1920s and 1930s, especially in relation to industrially made materials such as tubular steel, laminates and plywood. During the late 1940s and 1950s, designers were able to produce chairs that were light and versatile by using these materials more imaginatively, with plywood in particular embraced by designers including Charles & Ray Eames, Arne Jacobsen and Norman Cherner. The resulting chairs were stackable and foldable, suited to all kinds of contexts, from the domestic through to the commercial, yet were also pleasing in their shape and silhouette.

Designers such as Harry Bertoia, Warren Platner and Ernest Race used tubular steel and welded wire rods to create strong and robust chairs that were also light and easy to move. While the 19th-century chair tended to be a weighty affair, with a substantial wooden frame and often heavily upholstered, the mid-century chair aimed to adapt to multiple settings and situations while allowing light to pass right through their super-light bases. 'If you look at these chairs,' said Bertoia, 'they are mainly made of air'; while designers such as Eero Saarinen vowed to dispense with 'the slum of legs' in favour of single, slimline stems and pedestals, as seen in Saarinen's celebrated Pedestal Collection (see p. 98).

Plastics, including fibreglass, allowed designers to pursue increasingly sculptural and abstract shapes, particularly during the late 1950s and 1960s. Verner Panton's eponymous chair of 1967 (see p. 81) was made using a single piece of injection-moulded plastic to create a light cantilevered chair, comparable to the steel-framed cantilevered seat developed by Ludwig Mies van der Rohe and Marcel Breuer during the inter-war period.

Foam plastics, such as polyurethane foam, were also used to mould and model furniture in ways never possible before, as seen in the expressive and generously upholstered lounge chairs by Marco Zanuso, Arne Jacobsen, Pierre Paulin and others. With their abstract forms, distinctive geometries and bold colours, such pieces echoed the vibrant age of pop art and op art, as well as the futuristic forms of the space age, from Peter Ghyczy's UFO-like Garden Egg Chair (1968, see p. 50) to Eero Aarnio's Ball Chair (1966, see p. 15). Translucent acrylic was used by Charles Hollis Jones, Erwine & Estelle Laverne and others to create ephemeral, see-through chairs with the look of sculpted glass, while 'transformative' pieces such as Gaetano Pesce's Up5 Chair (1969, see p. 84) assumed their final shape only upon release from their vacuum-packed shipping envelopes.

Notably, some of the best known and most respected chair and furniture designers of the period – Charles & Ray Eames, Poul Kjaerholm, Hans Wegner, Gio Ponti and others – embraced many different kinds of modern materials in their work. Such a spirit of openness, along with an acceptance that there were many different solutions to any given design challenge, added to the rich diversity of the era and the profusion of groundbreaking chairs produced during the mid-century period.

FOLLOWING SPREAD The Miller House, Columbus, Indiana, USA, by Eero Saarinen (interiors: Alexander Girard), 1957

Cantilevered Armchair (Model 406)

Alvar Aalto, 1939 Artek

Like many of Alvar Aalto's most famous pieces of furniture, the Cantilevered Armchair (Model 406) was initially designed for a specific architectural and interior project: the Finnish architect's celebrated Villa Mairea, in Noormarkku, designed for patrons Harry and Maire Gullichsen. The chair was, in many ways, a culmination of ideas explored by Aalto during the preceding years, beginning with the Paimio Chair of 1931. Yet, with its innovative use of laminated birch bentwood juxtaposed with a canvas webbing seat and back, the Cantilevered Armchair manages to combine strength and an engaging lightness of touch. The piece was put into production by Artek (the company that Aalto co-founded with the Gullichsens) and can be compared to Aalto's Cantilevered Chaise (c. 1936, see p. 120).

← Ball Chair

Eero Aarnio, 1966 Asko/Eero Aarnio Originals

The Ball Chair, by Finnish designer Eero Aarnio, is one of the most famous mid-century cocoon chairs, creating a womb-like micro-habitat, or a room within a room. Originally made for Aarnio's own home, the piece is constructed of a white fibreglass shell perched upon a single pivoting stem anchored by a circular base plate. The soft, upholstered interior of the chair cradles the occupant while the strong geometrical form of the piece echoes space-age capsules and satellites. The Ball Chair, first released in 1966, can be compared to Aarnio's acrylic Bubble Chair (1968), which is suspended on a chain from the ceiling while also offering a similarly protective cocoon.

Trienna Armchairs

Carl-Axel Acking, 1957 Nordiska Kompaniet

Swedish architect and designer Carl-Axel Acking worked with Gunnar Asplund for many years before founding his own practice in Lund. Alongside architectural projects, such as the Swedish Embassy in Tokyo, Acking designed lighting and furniture, including the elegant Trienna Armchair presented at the Milan triennale in 1957. A robust oak frame combines with a slung-leather seat and back, giving the chair a warm, organic character. Although less well known than some of his Scandinavian contemporaries, Acking created refined and sophisticated furniture that is much coveted by collectors.

↑ Luisa Chairs

Franco Albini, 1955 Poggi/Cassina

Italian architect and designer Franco Albini is generally described
as a rationalist, and pieces such as his LB7 Storage Unit (1957, see
p. 347) certainly adopted a highly logical, systematic and functional
approach. The same is true of Albini's Luisa Chair, which began life
in the late 1930s and was then refined on multiple occasions before
its release by Poggi in 1955. Designed to serve as an elegant but
adaptable dining, desk and multi-use armchair, the Luisa features
soft seat and back pads supported by a distinctive A-shaped walnut
frame on either side. The uppermost section of the frame morphs
into the armrests as well as a holding bar for the backrest; the chair
was awarded a Compasso d'Oro in 1955.

← Margherita Chairs

Franco Albini, 1951 Vittorio Bonacina

During the early 1950s, Albini was invited to design a number of fresh pieces of furniture for Vittorio Bonacina and his family business, which dates back to 1889. The firm specializes in rattan, which Albini embraced in designs that were surprisingly fluid, expressive and organic for an architect seen as a rationalist. The most famous of these light and inviting pieces is the high-backed Margherita lounge chair of 1951, but Albini also designed the Gala Chair (c. 1950). Other mid-century Bonacina designs included Gio Ponti's Continuum (1963) and Joe Colombo's Nastro (1964).

Fiorenza Lounge Chair

Franco Albini, 1952/1956 Arflex

Based on a traditional wing or club chair, the Fiorenza is one of Albini's most characterful pieces yet is also ergonomic and practical. Initially designed in 1952, the chair went through a series of developments, nine in all, as Albini sought to perfect the piece. This version was made in 1956 and features a walnut frame, moulded foam-rubber seating and upholstery, while the legs are straighter than the cross-shaped formation often seen on the Fiorenza. The profile of the chair, with its outstretched and open arms, brings to mind Hans Wegner's famous Papa Bear Chair (1951, see p. 109).

Mies Chair & Ottoman

Archizoom Associati, 1969 Poltronova

The Mies Chair, designed by avant-garde Italian collective Archizoom Associati, can be seen either as an iconoclastic critique of modernist architecture and design, exemplified by Ludwig Mies van der Rohe, or as a gentle tongue-in-cheek homage to Mies; or both. Certainly, the chair – designed by Andrea Branzi, Gilberto Corretti, Paolo Deganello and Massimo Morozzi – is suitably architectural, juxtaposing the chrome-plated steel triangles that form the frame of the chair with its rectangular ottoman, which features its own concealed lighting. Yet the collective opted for a slung-rubber sheet for the seat, giving it an almost deckchair-like quality, and added cowhide cushions to each piece, subverting the purity of line. Archizoom also turned its subversive attention to the sofa, as seen in their Safari Sectional Seating (1967, see p. 194).

GA Chairs →

Hans Bellmann, 1952 Horgenglarus

After founding his own studio in Zurich in 1946, designer and architect Hans Bellmann produced a number of designs for Knoll, such as his Tripod Table (1947, see p. 249), as well as working with Swiss furniture maker Horgenglarus. The collaboration with Horgenglarus resulted in two of Bellmann's most famous designs, beginning with the One-Point (or Einpunkt) Chair of 1951, made of a single piece of birch ply connected to steel legs with one fixing. This was followed by the better-known GA Chair, featuring a seat and back made of two separate pieces of bent plywood, placed side by side, with a clear line of separation between the two. This unusual pairing gives the piece an original and distinctive character.

Sled Chairs

Ward Bennett, 1966 Brickel Associates/Geiger

During the 1960s, American sculptor-turned-designer Ward Bennett began a long and highly creative collaboration with Brickel Associates. The relationship resulted in many of Bennett's best-known and most innovative designs, including the Scissor Chair (1968) and the Sled Chair of 1966. The latter has an X-shaped, tubular-steel base set on sled-like runners, along with a seat and back originally made of wicker and often topped with a leatherette cushion. One of the most pleasing details is the pair of side handles (or low-slung armrests), which are also playfully reminiscent of sled design. Along with a number of other Bennett designs, the piece is still produced today by Geiger, who acquired Brickel in 1993.

Diamond Chair (Model 421) & Ottoman →

Harry Bertoia, 1952 Knoll

As both sculptor and furniture designer, Harry Bertoia saw clear links between his two professions: 'When you get right down to it,' he said, 'the chairs are studies in space, form and metal too.' Florence Knoll, who Bertoia first met at the Cranbrook Academy of Art in Michigan, embraced such thinking and offered Bertoia free rein to develop a collection of furniture. The most famous piece in Bertoia's suitably sculptural collection produced by Knoll is the Diamond Chair, which uses a lattice of welded steel wire rods and a slimline steel base, giving the piece an extraordinary lightness. Colourful pads float upon the diamond-shaped seat and back, with the chair becoming a familiar and friendly icon of mid-century design.

Bird Chair (Model 423) & Ottoman

Harry Bertoia, 1952 Knoll

Assisted by designer Richard Schultz, Bertoia developed not only the Diamond Chair (above) but also a complementary range of Knoll chairs, which made full and imaginative use of interlaced, steel wire rods. These included the Side Chair (Model 420), a Child's Chair (Model 425) and a Bar Stool (Model 428), all within a sequence simply known as the Bertoia Collection, and marketed through a series of landmark advertisements created by graphic designer and photographer Herbert Matter. The most playful and biomorphic design in the collection is the Bird Chair (or High Back Diamond Chair, Model 423), usually paired with a matching ottoman (Model 424).

Tripod Chairs

Max Bill, 1949 Horgenglarus

Given his famous preoccupation with processes of reduction that pared
down an object, or a typeface, to its purest form, it is (perhaps) not
such a surprise that Max Bill designed a chair with three legs rather
than four. The Tripod Chair, or Three-Legged Chair, has a neat triptych
of beechwood legs, and a beech plywood seat and backrest. Alternative
versions of the piece show contrasting chair legs in a darker stain
or choice of wood, while a matching dining table was also produced
around the same time. The piece can be compared with Max Bill and
Hans Gugelot's Ulmer Hocker Stool (1954, see p. 159), a masterclass
in functionalist minimalism.

Bellevue Chairs →

André Bloc, 1951 Limited edition

During the 1950s and 1960s, artist, sculptor and magazine editor André
Bloc commissioned an extraordinary sequence of avant-garde modernist
houses, beginning with Bellevue, his home in Meudon to the southwest
of Paris. Bloc designed a number of pieces of furniture for the house,
including this Bellevue Chair, which explores the sculptural possibilities
offered by moulded plywood. The beech ply forms a long, continuous
ribbon, or wave, flowing down from the high backrest to the seat and
then dipping down toward the floor, with the enamelled-steel legs
almost disappearing behind the wooden surface of the chair. Ultimately,
the Bellevue Chair was considered too complex for mass production
with only a limited number of pieces produced during the 1950s.

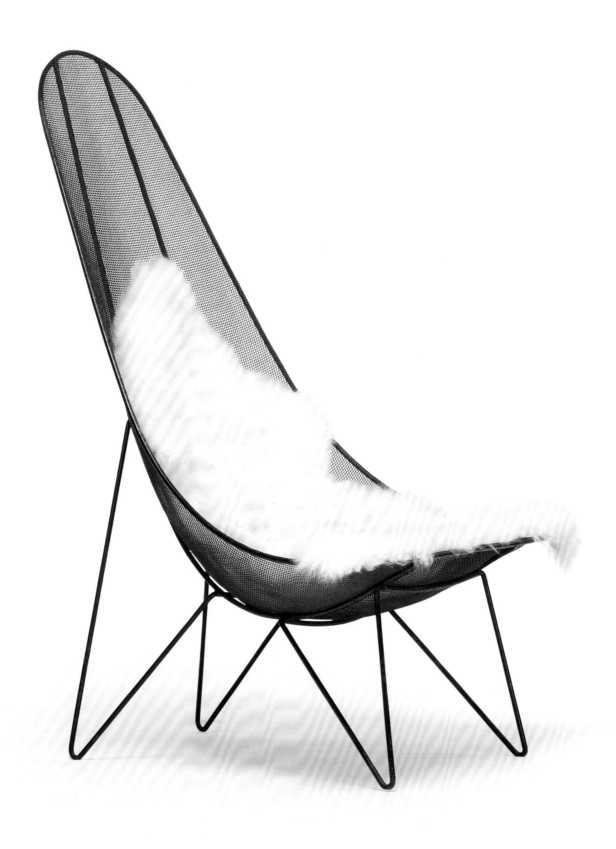

← Scoop Chair

Sol Bloom, 1950 New Dimensions Furniture

During the 1950s, American designer Sol Bloom created an innovative sequence of designs for New York-based company New Dimensions Furniture, using a combination of lightweight, enamelled-steel frames combined with lattices of wire mesh or expanded metal. The resulting pieces included a catch-it-all, a magazine rack and this Scoop Chair, where the use of mesh for the seat and back gives the piece a light and translucent quality. A matching Scoop Settee was also produced at the same time; the robust character of the materials makes the pieces well suited to use on terraces and patios.

Bowl Chair

Lina Bo Bardi, 1951 Arper

The Bowl Chair is the most famous and joyful chair produced by Italian-born, Brazilian architect Lina Bo Bardi. Rejecting the linear forms and rich timbers prevalent in Brazil at the time, Bo Bardi embraced a different kind of geometry with her upholstered half orb resting on a steel circular support with four slim legs. Sometimes upholstered in leather but more commonly seen in bright colours and with twin cushion pads nestling within its neat hemisphere, the Bowl Chair is both playful and delightful. It also represents an early example of the many eggs and spheres adopted by mid-century furniture designers during the 1950s and 1960s.

Butterfly Chairs

Antonio Bonet, Juan Kurchan & Jorge Ferrari Hardoy, 1938
Artek-Pascoe/Knoll

The much-imitated Butterfly Chair dates back to the late 1930s, when Spanish architect Antonio Bonet designed the piece in Buenos Aires with his Argentinian colleagues Juan Kurchan and Jorge Ferrari Hardoy. In 1940, curator Edgar Kaufmann Jr admired the chair and presented one to the Museum of Modern Art in New York while sending another to his father's landmark house, Fallingwater. The design – also known as the BKF Chair after its inventors – captured the public imagination from then on, with its engaging combination of lightweight steel frame and leather (or canvas) slung seat. Light and portable, the piece was suited to indoor or outdoor use, with countless copies produced over the decades.

Model P31 Chairs

Osvaldo Borsani, 1957 Tecno

There was considerable breadth and depth to the extensive collection of pieces that Osvaldo Borsani designed for Tecno, the Italian firm that he co-founded in 1953. The adjustable P40 Folding Lounge Chair and D70 Sofa (1954, see p. 199) were designed to be adaptable, while others demonstrated a spirit of experimentation through the character of their chosen materials. Such is the case with Borsani's three-legged plywood chair, the P31, which combines a sturdy steel frame with a plywood seat and separate backrest made of mahogany plywood with its expressive grain. The piece can be compared with Max Bill's Tripod Chair of 1949 (see p. 22).

Scandia Dining Chairs

Hans Brattrud, 1957 Hove Møbler

Norwegian architect and designer Hans Brattrud developed his
first ideas for the Scandia series while he was still a student at
the National College of Art & Design in Oslo. The sequence began,
in 1957, with a stackable dining chair consisting of a lightweight,
chrome-plated steel base and curvaceous strips of rosewood ply,
laid side by side, which collectively form a continuous seat and back.
Following the success of the dining chair, similar principles and
aesthetics were applied to a broader Scandia collection, including
a high-backed lounge chair, a swivel chair and a junior version
of the dining chair.

Lounge Chair

Franco Campo & Carlo Graffi, 1951 Apelli & Varesio

Franco Campo and Carlo Graffi worked with and studied under
Carlo Mollino, with comparisons often made between the furniture
created by the two Italian designers and their mentor. There were
similarities, with many of Campo & Graffi's pieces (also produced
by Apelli & Varesio in Turin) adopting fluid and biomorphic
forms in a manner associated with Mollino. This engaging Lounge
Chair of 1951 is made of sculpted pieces of acero, held together
with brass fixings, and topped with segmented cushions and back
pads. Other influential and highly collectable Campo & Graffi
designs include the Millepiedi Dining Table of 1952.

Model 683 Dining Chairs

Carlo de Carli, 1954 Cassina

One of the great mid-century Italian polymaths, who drew lines
of connection between multiple design disciplines, Carlo de Carli
embraced architecture, interiors, furniture and much more besides.
Within the field of furniture, de Carli was both prolific and influential,
designing a number of landmark pieces for Cassina. These included
the elegant Model 683 Dining Chair, a combination of a slimline oak
frame and legs with a mahogany ply seat and backrest, held together
with brass fastenings. This refined piece was awarded a Compasso
d'Oro in 1954.

Primate Seat

Achille Castiglioni, 1970 Zanotta

Many of Achille Castiglioni's most adventurous and playful furniture
designs challenged convention while purposefully raising questions
about how they might be used and enjoyed. Such was the case with
the Primate, which has been described variously as a chair or as
a kneeling stool yet almost defies categorization. The piece invites
a meditative position, with knees placed on the lower pad of the
Primate and the backside supported by the uppermost pad. Compact
and intriguing, the Primate remains in production today. It brings
to mind other seats and stools designed by the Castiglioni Brothers,
including the Mezzadro Stool (1957, see p. 161).

← Cherner Armchair

Norman Cherner, 1958 Plycraft/Cherner Chair Company

American architectural and furniture designer Norman Cherner specialized in prefabricated housing during the 1940s before moving into furniture design. His most famous designs, simply known as the Cherner Dining Chair and Armchair, made imaginative use of plywood and were originally developed in association with Plycraft. The Cherner Dining Chair adopted a silhouette comparable with Arne Jacobsen's iconic Series 7 Chair (1955, see p. 54), but it was the brilliant addition of a twisting ribbon of walnut ply to create the armchair that made the design sing out. The Cherner Armchair, which has also been compared with George Nelson's Pretzel Chair (1952, see p. 78), is still in production today.

Lounge Chair

Luigi Colani, *c.* 1968 Kusch + Co

Within the field of furniture design, innovative German polymath Luigi Colani is best known for his Modular Seating Units (*c.* 1970, see p. 200) and his experimental plastic furniture suited to outdoor use. This Lounge Chair, produced in a limited edition by Kusch + Co, offers a crimson hemisphere floating in a lightweight, chrome-plated steel cradle. Graphic, colourful and playful, the piece can be compared with the bubble chairs and egg-shaped seats that were so popular during the pop-art period.

← Elda Armchair no. 1005

Joe Colombo, 1963 Comfort/Fratelli Longhi

For a designer whose career spanned just two decades and who died tragically young on his 41st birthday, Joe Colombo contributed an extraordinary amount to furniture design. A prime example is his groundbreaking Elda Armchair – a reinvention of the club chair – which made use of boat-building expertise to create its enveloping fibreglass shell with a low seat and high back. The shell's upholstered leather interior, comparable to a fine sports car, gives the chair a luxurious quality. The pièce de résistance is its turntable base that allows the occupant of the Elda – named after Colombo's wife – to swivel at will.

Universale Chair (Model 4867)

Joe Colombo, 1967 Kartell

Despite his sophisticated playboy image and the luxurious character of some of his designs, including the Elda Armchair (opposite), Colombo was also a believer in democratic design. His Universale Chair, developed in conjunction with Kartell, was the result of an ambitious project to produce an affordable chair suited to a wide range of uses, whether indoors or outdoors. After many experiments with injection-moulded plastics, Colombo and Kartell settled upon a design using a standardized seating unit made in one piece but with interchangeable legs that allowed the height of the chair to be adjusted as required. The stackable Universale was initially made of ABS plastic and then polypropylene, which was more robust.

Royal Festival Hall Lounge Chair (Model 658)

Robin Day, 1951 Hille

During the late 1940s, long-established and family-owned British furniture-making firm Hille embraced progressive modernist design after Rosamind and Leslie Julius, the heads of the company, visited the USA and noted the work of Charles & Ray Eames. They began collaborating with designer Robin Day on a new collection of furniture that explored the possibilities of plywood in particular, as seen in the Q Rod Chair of 1953 and this Lounge Chair originally designed – along with a small number of other pieces – for the newly completed Royal Festival Hall on the South Bank in London. The walnut plywood back plate morphs into the outstretched wings that form the armrests, creating a dynamic design that Hille then put into wider production.

Polypropylene Armchair

Robin Day, 1967 Hille

Following the success of Day's early pieces for Hille during the 1950s,
the collaboration continued with the development of a collection
made using injection-moulded plastics. In the early 1960s, Hille
and Day settled on polypropylene to form a robust seat and backrest
in a single piece, which was then attached to tubular-steel legs.
Hille released Day's Polypropylene Chair in 1963/64, followed a few
years later by the Polypropylene Armchair. Affordable, stackable
and hard-wearing, the chairs were produced in the millions for
home and export markets, including a Series E Chair (1971) aimed
at schools, with a hole in the back of the seat to make it easier to
carry from place to place.

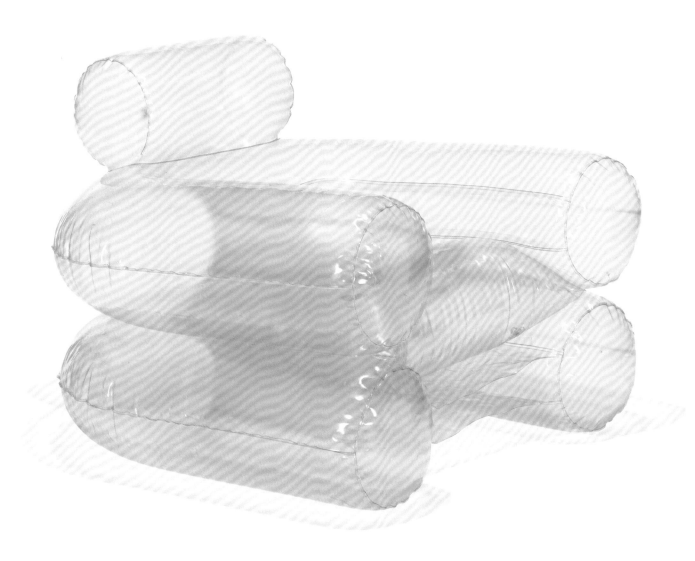

Blow

Jonathan De Pas, Donato D'Urbino, Paolo Lomazzi & Carla Scolari, 1967 Zanotta

In 1966, Jonathan De Pas, Donato D'Urbino and Paolo Lomazzi formed a design collective in Milan known as DDL Studio. One of their earliest and most recognizable designs (in association with Carla Scolari) reinvented the idea of the chair, using super-light PVC plastic to create an inflatable armchair, known as Blow. The low-cost chair was delivered in its compact form and its four distinct air compartments were then inflated at home, with its bulbous rings reminiscent of Eileen Gray's famous Bibendum Armchair of 1926. Blow, which came with its own puncture kit, could be used indoors or outdoors.

Joe

Jonathan De Pas, Donato D'Urbino & Paolo Lomazzi, 1970
Poltronova

During the late 1960s and early 1970s, furniture – and seating in particular – explored abstraction in increasingly radical forms. A key example is the Joe lounge chair, designed by DDL Studio, which takes the form of a giant baseball glove and is named in honour of legendary American baseball star Joe DiMaggio. The piece has a metal framework, polyurethane padding and a leather coat, with hidden castors attached to the base to allow the seat to be moved around. Still produced by Poltronova, the chair is now made in a choice of colours.

Rattan Lounge Chairs

Nanna & Jørgen Ditzel, 1950 Ludvig Pontoppidan

Mid-century furniture by Danish designers Nanna & Jørgen Ditzel explored, for the most part, a combination of organic materials and sculptural forms. This was true of pieces such as their wicker Hanging Chair (1957) and Nanna's Toadstools (1962, see p. 162), as well as this Rattan Lounge Chair. The piece combines a teak or ash frame with a bucket seat, made of woven rattan, lending the chair both texture and warmth of tone. The reassuring, enveloping shape also corresponds with a number of other Ditzel chair designs from the period.

Ring Chairs

Nanna & Jørgen Ditzel, 1958 Kolds Savvaerk/Artek

Circular shapes reappear again and again in both Nanna Ditzel's jewelry and the furniture designed in collaboration with her husband, Jørgen Ditzel, including a child's high chair (Paul Kold Møbler, 1955) where the uppermost section of the piece is a protective wooden ring. The Ring Chair of 1958 comprises four tapered teak posts supporting an upholstered seat cushion and a matching upholstered ring, which wraps around the occupant like a sturdy belt. The piece was later reissued by Artek under the name Sausage Chair to reference the shape of this belt-like bolster.

LCW (Lounge Chair Wood)

Charles & Ray Eames, 1945 Evans Products Company/
Herman Miller/Vitra

Charles & Ray Eames's LCW (Lounge Chair Wood) can be seen as
the culmination of the designers' experiments with plywood furniture
dating back to the early 1940s. Many of these early designs used
relatively complex single pieces of moulded ply, which were difficult to
manufacture in large volumes. With the LCW, the Eameses opted for
a handful of component parts consisting of three bent laminate pieces
that form the legs and a spine, plus two pieces of moulded ply for the
seat and back plate, held together with screws and discreetly placed
rubber shock absorbers. This methodology not only allowed the LCW
to be factory produced but also enabled variations, as seen in the
DCW (Dining Chair Wood) and then the LCM (Lounge Chair Metal).

DAR (Dining Armchair Rod)

Charles & Ray Eames, 1951 Herman Miller

Following the success of their plywood chair collection (opposite), Charles & Ray Eames collaborated with Herman Miller on ideas for another low-cost and factory-produced collection, which became known as the 'Plastic Group'. Experiments with fibreglass led to the idea of a moulded shell seat, which could then be fitted with a choice of different legs and bases. One of the most famous pieces within the range is the DAR (Dining Armchair Rod): a sinuous shell floating on a base of steel wire rods often compared to a miniature version of the Eiffel Tower. Other associated pieces include the RAR (Rocking Armchair Rod), while the designers' innovative work with fibreglass also led to the evolution of La Chaise (1948, see p. 127).

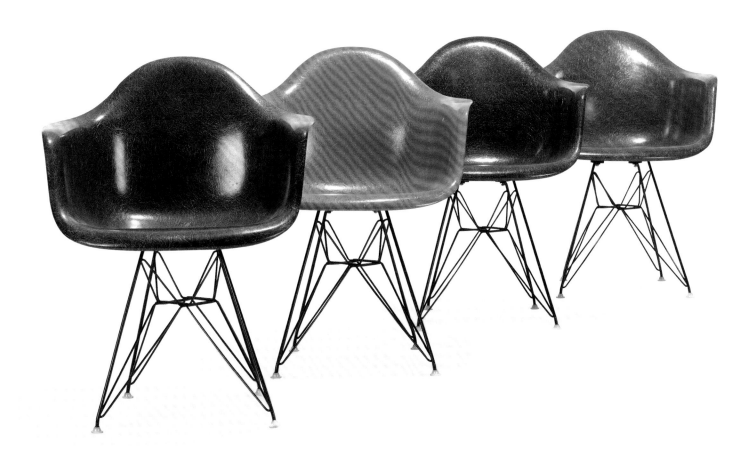

Wire Chairs

Charles & Ray Eames, 1951 Herman Miller/Vitra

During the late 1940s and early 1950s, Charles & Ray Eames made extensive and imaginative use of wire-rod bases for their plywood and fibreglass chair collections. Attracted by the sculptural possibilities of this affordable and industrially produced material, the designers developed a dedicated collection of wire mesh chairs for Herman Miller. The most famous of these is known as the Wire Chair, or DKR-2, or sometimes the Eiffel Tower Chair after its base (also used on the DAR, see p. 43). The Wire Chair features a two-piece pad, or 'bikini', that softens the piece but – as with the earlier collections of plywood and fibreglass chairs – the design could also be adapted with options for different legs and seat pads. Steel wire rods were also used to great effect for the Eames's ETR, or Elliptical Table Rod (1951, see p. 259).

Eames Lounge Chair (Model 670)
& Ottoman

Charles & Ray Eames, 1956 Herman Miller/Vitra

In some respects, Charles & Ray Eames's iconic Lounge Chair (Model 670) can be seen as an evolution of design principles explored in the LCW plywood chair (1945, see p. 42) and associated pieces. Here, again, after much deliberation over their unique version of a club chair, the designers opted to produce the piece using three complementary segments of moulded ply for the seat, backrest and headrest, held together by a metal spine. Yet, the Lounge Chair is also a far more luxurious piece than anything they had designed before, with its leather upholstered cushions and a swivelling, five-star aluminium base. A matching Ottoman (Model 671) adopts a similar aesthetic but has one ply shell, a single cushion and a fixed, four-star base. The Lounge Chair has been in continuous production since 1956.

Aluminium Group Lounge Chair (Model 681)

Charles & Ray Eames, 1958 Herman Miller

Following on from plywood, fibreglass and wire rods, aluminium was the fourth modern and industrially produced material explored by Charles & Ray Eames. Aluminium offers the advantages of being lightweight but super strong, making it well suited to furniture, with the designers developing a collection known as the 'Aluminium Group' from 1957 onward. Early members of this family, which mostly featured distinctive star-shaped bases and a single support stem, include the Model 681 Lounge Chair, which was also produced with arms (Model 682), and the Time-Life Chair (1960). The Billy Wilder Chaise (1968, see p. 128) also has an aluminium frame.

SE69 Chair →

Egon Eiermann, 1952 Wilde + Spieth

During the late 1940s and 1950s, German architect and designer Egon Eiermann worked on a collection of plywood furniture for Wilde + Spieth, which – like Charles & Ray Eames's plywood chairs (see p. 42) – was intended to be both affordable and flexible in terms of its use. Among this collection was the SE68 Chair (1950), with four tubular-steel legs and a plywood seat and back, followed by this variant, the three-legged SE69. A number of Eiermann's designs are still produced by Wilde + Spieth, including the SE68 and the SE18 Folding Chair (1952).

Lamino Lounge Chair

Yngve Ekström, 1956 Swedese

'To have designed one good chair might not be a bad life's work', said Swedish designer Yngve Ekström. The chair in question is the Lamino Lounge Chair, which became a firm favourite across Scandinavia and beyond during the mid-century period. The sinuous, ergonomic classic is made of laminated bentwood with a high-backed seat upholstered in leather or sheepskin, enhancing the chair's natural, organic warmth. The Lamino is shipped in three pieces, with the purchaser given a custom tool to attach the legs to the seat. Still in production, the Lamino became a hugely successful staple for Swedese, the furniture company co-founded by Ekström himself.

Bird Armchairs →

Preben Fabricius & Jørgen Kastholm, 1964 Alfred Kill

The sculptural shapes and forms explored by Fabricius and Kastholm often stepped into the rich world of the biomorphic. A key example is the Bird Armchair of 1964, featuring a bird-like, winged seat set upon a single stem anchored in a steel tripod base. Usually finished in leather, the chair was also produced with a high back and an option for castors. The piece can be compared with Fabricius and Kastholm's Grasshopper Chaise Longue released by Alfred Kill a few years later (c. 1968, see p. 129).

Scimitar Chair

Preben Fabricius & Jørgen Kastholm, 1962 Ivan Schlechter

Danish designer Preben Fabricius worked with Finn Juhl before joining forces with architect and designer Jørgen Kastholm, whom he had first met while studying interior architecture in Copenhagen. One of their most famous designs is undoubtedly the Scimitar Chair, which features a distinctive crescent-shaped steel base that gives the piece its name, along with an upholstered leather seat. Fabricius and Kastholm revisited the crescent motif in their Scimitar Coffee Table (c. 1968, see p. 260), also produced by Ivan Schlechter.

Model 831 Lounge Chairs

Gianfranco Frattini, 1955 Cassina

Milanese architect and designer Gianfranco Frattini collaborated with Gio Ponti and Livio Castiglioni, while also designing furniture for many Italian producers, including Cassina. These Model 831 Lounge Chairs sit high among Frattini's standout pieces for Cassina, featuring A-shaped walnut legs supporting the frame and plywood wings that serve as armrests. The piece, which could be delivered to customers in sections and easily assembled, has a leather-upholstered base seat and back cushion. Other Frattini designs for Cassina include the Model 780 Nesting Tables (1966, see p. 261).

Garden Egg Chair →

Peter Ghyczy, 1968 Reuter Products/VEB Schwarzheide/ Ghyczy Novo

During the late 1960s, Hungarian-born designer, architect and engineer Peter Ghyczy was asked to develop a fresh line of plastic pieces for Reuter Products in West Germany. The most famous result of these experiments is the Garden Egg Chair: a flip-top shell seat made of fibreglass. With the top firmly closed, the lozenge is watertight enough to leave outside, but when open it reveals a padded seat, with back support provided by the open lid. The brightly coloured, UFO-shaped design, which was initially produced by VEB Schwarzheide in East Germany and later by Ghyczy's own company, can be compared with other pop-inspired plastic classics such as Eero Aarnio's Pastilli Chair (1967, see p. 121).

Model 66301 Lounge Chair

Alexander Girard, 1967 Herman Miller

One of the great American polymaths of the mid-century period, Alexander Girard had a rich and varied portfolio that embraced architecture, interiors, textiles, furniture and exhibition curation. During the mid-1960s, he was well placed to meet an ambitious commission from Braniff Airways to reinvent every aspect of the airline's corporate identity, including its offices and airport lounges. This led to an extensive collection of furniture (see pp. 204, 263 and 308), which was then put into production for one year only by Herman Miller, where Girard was head of the textile division. Highlights included Girard's lounge chairs, particularly Model 66301 with its extended wing-like armrests flowing outward from the seat and giving the piece a bird-like form; the seat cushion, as seen here, is upholstered in one of Girard's textile designs.

Tonneau Chairs

Pierre Guariche, 1954 Steiner

During the 1950s, Pierre Guariche established himself as one of the
most inventive and original modern French designers, with collections
of both furniture and lighting. One of his most famous designs is the
Tonneau Chair, widely regarded as the first mass-produced plywood
chair made in France, and developed in conjunction with Steiner
furniture. The Tonneau, which translates as 'barrel', features a rounded,
lacquered-ply shell seat with a cushion pad and a circular aperture
that doubles as a carry aid, set on four lightweight steel legs. Guariche's
G10 Lounge Chair (1954) for Airborne International also made use
of plywood for its wing-like armrests in its earliest incarnation.

AX Armchairs

Peter Hvidt & Orla Mølgaard-Nielsen, 1947 Fritz Hansen

The AX Armchair is one of the most innovative and successful pieces of furniture by Danish designers Peter Hvidt and Orla Mølgaard-Nielsen. The chair is an early exemplar in terms of its use of plywood, as seen in the teak ply seat and separate backrest, combined with a laminated beech frame, including curvaceous bentwood armrests. More than this, the AX – produced by Fritz Hansen – could be delivered flat packed and ready for assembly by the buyer. The elegant AX led on to a sequence of associated designs, including a version with a padded leather seat, a side chair, a sofa and also AX tables (see p. 265). Other influential Hvidt & Mølgaard-Nelsen designs for Fritz Hansen include the laminated teak and cane X Chair of 1958.

Model 3100 Ant Chairs →

Arne Jacobsen, 1952 Fritz Hansen

Although Arne Jacobsen's iconic Ant Chair was designed in response to a specific architectural and interior commission, it became the perfect solution to a broader challenge of creating a light, affordable, elegant and stackable modern chair. Jacobsen had kept just such a challenge in mind since noting Charles & Ray Eames's early plywood chairs. Asked to design a canteen chair for his repeat client, Danish pharmaceutical company Novo, Jacobsen took the opportunity to work closely with Fritz Hansen on the first mass-produced plywood chair made with a single piece of moulded ply. The breakthrough came with the nipped, ant-like waist of the chair that allowed the ply to be folded without damaging the structural integrity of the piece, with tubular-steel legs providing support. Originally produced with three legs, the Ant went on to sell in its millions.

Series 7 Chairs (Model 3107) →

Arne Jacobsen, 1955 Fritz Hansen

Having found such a powerful solution to the problem of how to create a moulded plywood seat and back in one single piece (opposite top), Jacobsen and Fritz Hansen did not rest on their laurels. They went on to refine their ideas, developing the landmark Series 7 Chair, or the 'Sevener'. In this design, the seat is more rounded and the backrest splays as it rises to create an inviting V-shaped form. With four tubular-steel legs, the chair is more stable than its predecessor, while the design of the seat shell allows for various bases, including the Model 3117 Desk Chair on wheels and the Model 3207 Sevener Armchair. Still beloved, still selling in its millions, the Series 7 Chair is one of the most widely imitated furniture designs ever created.

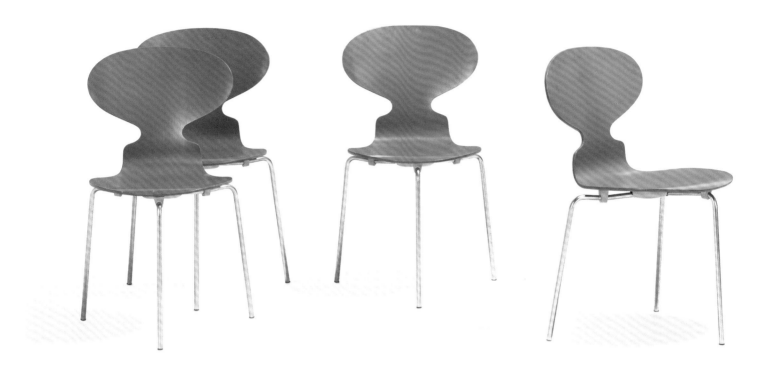

Model 3316 Egg Chair & Ottoman

Arne Jacobsen, 1958 Fritz Hansen

Along with the Swan Chair and Sofa (1958, see p. 207), Jacobsen's instantly recognizable Egg Chair is one of many mid-century classics that emerged from the commission to design the architecture and interiors of the SAS Royal Hotel in Copenhagen. As with the Ant and Series 7 plywood chairs (see p. 54), part of the refined beauty of Jacobsen's design lay in the way that he created such a cohesive design with a single sculpted seat floating on a swivel stem supported by a discreet four-armed aluminium base. In the case of the Egg, Jacobsen embraced the possibilities offered by plastics, using injection-moulded polystyrene (EPS) to create the structural outline of the piece, which was then upholstered either in textiles or, later on, leather. The Egg famously provides an enveloping and secure space within a space.

Model 3208 Seagull Chair →

Arne Jacobsen, 1969 Fritz Hansen

'A chair is a three-dimensional thing, like a sculpture', Jacobsen once said, pointing to the way in which he combined mastery of both form and function. His finest pieces, which have stood the test of time, are both ergonomic and full of artistic invention, as seen in his more biomorphic designs such as the Egg Chair (below) and the endearing Series 8 Seagull, one of the last but most delightful pieces in Jacobsen's extensive portfolio and originally designed for the Danmarks Nationalbank. In many respects, the essential form of the plywood Seagull owes much to the Sevener (1955, see p. 54), but the additions of leather upholstery and distinctive gull-wing armrests help set it apart. The Series 8 designs, now known as the Lily, have been re-released by Fritz Hansen.

Laminated Chair

Grete Jalk, 1963 Poul Jeppesen

Following on from the innovative laminated wood and plywood chairs developed during the 1940s and 1950s by Arne Jacobsen, Charles & Ray Eames and others, designers began stretching the possibilities of such materials to the limit. A prime example is Danish designer Grete Jalk, who used teak laminate to create this origami-like design for Poul Jeppesen, simply known as the Laminated Chair but also referred to as the GJ (Grete Jalk) Chair, the Rest Chair and the Model 9-1 Chair. The piece comprises a pair of ingenious folds of laminated wood, conjoined at a discreet point toward the rear of the chair. The complexities of the design meant that it was not produced in large numbers, but the chair can be compared to Jalk's laminated Nesting Tables (see p. 267), produced by Poul Jeppesen in the same year.

Model 92 Scissor Chair →

Pierre Jeanneret, 1948 Knoll

In the 1920s, architect and designer Pierre Jeanneret worked with Le Corbusier (his cousin) and colleague Charlotte Perriand on a small but highly influential collection of steel-framed furniture that included the iconic LC2 and LC3 'Grand Confort' armchairs and the LC4 recliner. During the post-war years, Hans and Florence Knoll noted Jeanneret's work and asked him to contribute designs for the Knoll collection. The result is the Model 92 Scissor Chair, with its scissor legs and frame in birch, and upholstered seat and back cushions supported by canvas straps.

Chandigarh Lounge Chair ↓

Pierre Jeanneret, *c.* 1957 Limited edition

During the 1950s, Jeanneret collaborated with Le Corbusier on the ambitious design of the new administrative centre for the Punjab, India, at Chandigarh. He served as chief architect but also worked on the interiors of the buildings and houses at Chandigarh, as well as designing an extensive portfolio of furniture that is now highly collectable. One of the most famous of these pieces, made locally and largely using teak, was Jeanneret's Lounge Chair, with its X-shaped sides supporting an additional cross bar that serves as an armrest as well as the wooden frame to hold the cane seat and back, with the option for a seat cushion. Variants on this design form part of an extensive family of Chandigarh furniture, which includes stools (see p. 169), tables (see p. 268), beds (see p. 403) and desks (see p. 360).

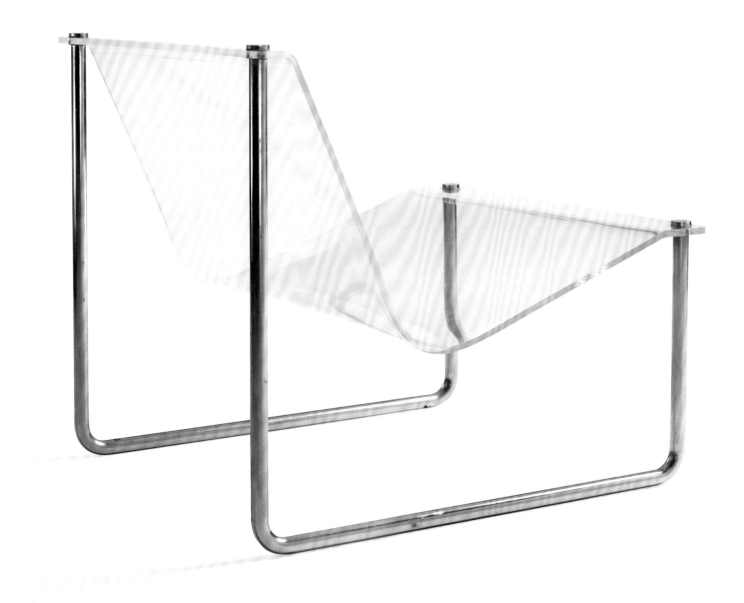

← Sling Chair

Charles Hollis Jones, *c.* 1968 CHJ Designs

Much of the furniture and lighting designed by Charles Hollis Jones during the 1960s and 1970s made extensive use of acrylic. The material offered the kind of translucency and lightness of touch provided by glass, yet at that time it was much safer, stronger and better suited to the production of furniture. One of the most remarkable results of Jones's many experiments with acrylic is his Sling Chair, which features a thin wave of acrylic, forming the combined seat and back, set on a pair of U-shaped, chrome-plated tubular-steel supports. Jones consulted aircraft engineers, who used acrylic for aeroplane windows, to advise on the structural integrity of the design, which was produced in limited editions by Jones's own company.

Egyptian Chairs

Finn Juhl, 1949 Niels Vodder

Danish designer Finn Juhl first began collaborating with master cabinetmaker Niels Vodder during the 1930s, when Juhl was still a student. Their working relationship spanned thirty years, with Juhl and Vodder perfecting what became known as the 'teak style', using crafted timber in modern, expressive forms. A key example is the Egyptian Chair, which featured in the designer's own home and is partly inspired by historical precedents. The teak frame has a distinctive, angled back support, which meets the high vertical leg supports to the rear of the piece, while the seat and backrest are upholstered in either textiles or leather.

Chieftain Chair

Finn Juhl, 1949 Niels Vodder/Baker Furniture

Juhl's Chieftain Chair is one of the many successful pieces that
emerged from the designer's creative partnership with Danish
furniture maker Niels Vodder. The original armchair, dating from
the late 1940s, is made of teak and features an upholstered seat,
a high backrest and suitably throne-like armrests, also finished
in leather or suede. The Chieftain is one of a number of key designs
that Juhl later reworked for release by Baker Furniture in the USA
from the early 1950s onward, with changes to the timber (largely
walnut) and alternative options and colour tones for the upholstery,
creating a somewhat lighter piece overall.

Contour Lounge Chairs

Vladimir Kagan, 1954 Kagan-Dreyfuss

As the name might suggest, the Contour Lounge Chair encapsulates
a gift for expressive, sculptural forms that made American designer
Vladimir Kagan so successful during the post-war period. The sloping
legs and angled, wrap-around walnut armrests suggest a sense of
dynamism, contrasting with the relaxed, ergonomic character
of the continuous seat and backrest. A key piece in Kagan's collection,
the Contour was produced in a number of variations, including a
high-backed version, a multi-position version and a version with
a concealed, pull-out footrest; a Contour Sofa was also released.

Model T-3010 Rattan Round Chair

Isamu Kenmochi, 1965 Yamakawa Rattan

Japanese architect and designer Isamu Kenmochi was one of a number of mid-century designers who revisited traditional crafts and materials, while also adopting fresh forms and innovative ideas. Kenmochi famously made best use of indigenous materials such as bamboo, cedar and rattan, as seen in his landmark Rattan Round Chair produced by Yamakawa Rattan, who asked him to develop a range of new pieces. The rounded and enveloping form of the chair manages to feel organic and modern at one and the same time, with its success leading on to a small family of similar pieces, including a sofa, stool and planter.

PK0 Chair

Poul Kjaerholm, 1952 Fritz Hansen

Danish master Poul Kjaerholm's material of choice was steel, which he considered just as noble and poetic as such natural materials as wood and leather. Yet there were notable instances when the designer experimented with other materials, as evidenced by the extraordinary PK0 Chair. Kjaerholm had hoped to create a chair using a single piece of plywood, yet eventually settled for a chair made of just two harmoniously conjoined elements: one consisting of the rounded seat with two side legs and the other the splayed backrest with one forward leg. Kjaerholm lacquered the seat black, creating a graphic and sculptural object. To his disappointment, Fritz Hansen was focused on the development of Arne Jacobsen's Ant Chair (see p. 54), and it was not until 1997 that the PK0 was eventually put into production.

PK22 Chairs

Poul Kjaerholm, 1956 E. Kold Christensen/Fritz Hansen

The 1950s was a period of powerful creativity for Kjaerholm, with the designer developing a series of innovative pieces in conjunction with E. Kold Christensen. The most iconic of these is the PK22 Chair of 1956, which saw Kjaerholm perfecting a steel-framed structure pared down to just six key components held together by machine screws. Two pairs of legs are connected to two cross bars, supporting side frames that are then fitted with continuous seats and backs in either cane, canvas or leather. It is the juxtaposition of an industrial material with an organic, natural material that makes the PK22 so appealing, along with its essential minimalism. Later designs include the PK31/1 Lounge Chair, which was created as a modular piece (1958, see the PK31/3 Sofa, p. 213).

Model 132 Chair

Donald Knorr, 1948 Knoll

The Model 132 Chair by Donald Knorr was the fruit of a search
for a well-designed, mass-produced and affordable chair, which won
a commendation at the Museum of Modern Art's low-cost furniture
design competition of 1949 in New York. Knorr began his architectural
and design career working for Eliel and Eero Saarinen before
opening his own studio and developing initial ideas for the conical
seat of the Model 132 using plastics. When this proved too costly and
technically challenging, Knorr switched to an enamelled-steel seat
and slim legs. The chair was produced in a choice of colours but was
discontinued in the early 1950s due to steel restrictions as a result
of the Korean War.

Karuselli Lounge Chair & Ottoman

Yrjö Kukkapuro, 1964 Haimi/Avarte

During the early 1960s, Finnish furniture designer Yrjö Kukkapuro began experimenting with plastics and fibreglass while maintaining an enduring focus on the importance of ergonomics. The most famous of Kukkapuro's fibreglass chairs is the Karuselli – or 'Carousel' – Lounge Chair of 1964, which features a fibreglass shell seat perched on a steel suspension bracket and pedestal. This combination of elements allows the seat to swivel but also tilt within the bracket, winning admiration from Gio Ponti, who published the chair on the cover of *Domus* magazine. Other Kukkapuro designs include the Saturn Easy Chair of 1966, also produced by Haimi, while the Karuselli was later reissued by Avarte.

Daffodil Chair

Erwine & Estelle Laverne, 1957 Laverne International

During the late 1930s, American husband-and-wife design team Erwine
& Estelle Laverne founded their own studio in New York, going on
to establish their own production unit and open a showroom. Their
most famous creations use translucent acrylic (or Lucite) within a
range dating from the 1950s and known as the Invisible Group. The
Lavernes employed moulded acrylic to create a sequence of chairs with
biomorphic forms, including the Daffodil, the Lily (1957), the Lotus
(1958), the Buttercup (1960) and the Tulip (1960). The chairs are
united by their ephemeral lightness, but were also marketed as hard-
wearing and robust pieces of furniture. The designers' use of acrylic
can be compared to the work of Charles Hollis Jones (see p. 61).

Planner Group Model 1503 Dining Chairs

Paul McCobb, 1949 Winchendon

Along with a number of his mid-century contemporaries, designer
Paul McCobb wanted to make good design more affordable and, in
doing so, appeal to a wider audience. Having established his own design
studio in New York in 1945, McCobb developed the Planner Group:
a comprehensive collection of well-designed and well-made pieces for
the home, mass-produced to keep costs down. Produced by Winchendon,
the collection includes these elegant maple or birch dining chairs with
characterful rounded backrests. The Winchendon range also includes
McCobb's Planner Group Desk (1952, see p. 367).

Selene Chair

Vico Magistretti, 1968 Artemide/Heller

During the early 1960s, Italian architect and designer Vico Magistretti began working with Artemide on ideas for a moulded-plastic chair suited to mass production. Given the technical difficulties of producing a chair made of a single piece of plastic, the collaboration spanned nearly a decade, with Magistretti working closely with Artemide's engineers to refine the design of the stackable Selene Chair, particularly the S-shaped cross section of the leg, which gives the piece extra strength and resilience. The chair, later reissued by Heller, was a particular success and formed one of a small family of associated Magistretti–Artemide designs that included the Gaudi and Vicario chairs (both 1971), also made of moulded plastic.

Lounge Chairs

Børge Mogensen, 1949 Erhard Rasmussen

After studying at the Royal Danish Academy of Fine Arts under the mentorship of master designer Kaare Klint, Børge Mogensen became famous for his modern reworkings of vernacular themes, as seen in his Hunting Chair and Spanish Chair (opposite). But there was also a more experimental side to his work, with plywood in particular being a source of fascination. Mogensen designed a number of pieces for Erhard Rasmussen that made use of ply, sometimes in combination with laminates and bentwood. One of the most innovative and original of these pieces is this Lounge Chair from 1949, with an oak frame, a teak seat and a teardrop back.

Hunting Chair →

Børge Mogensen, 1950 Erhard Rasmussen/Fredericia

Historical precedents and vernacular furniture designs were always a source of inspiration for Mogensen, as seen in his modern reinterpretations of spoke-back chairs and settees, club chairs and rocking chairs. One of the most engaging of these 20th-century reworkings of familiar staples is Mogensen's Hunting Chair. Its low-slung oak (or teak) frame is combined with a leather seat and back support held in place by belt-like straps. As with a number of Mogensen's designs of the 1950s, the piece was initially developed for Erhard Rasmussen and later produced by Fredericia.

Spanish Chair 2226 →

Børge Mogensen, 1958 Erhard Rasmussen/Fredericia

Mogensen became fascinated with traditional Spanish rustic chairs on a family holiday to Andalusia in 1958. Upon his return to Denmark, he designed his own Spanish Chair using an oak frame with broad armrests (wide enough for a drink or book) and a leather seat and back tensioned with discreet straps. Beautifully crafted yet simply made, the chair was more expensive than many of Mogensen's more 'democratic' designs, which drew some criticism, yet still became one of his successful and recognizable designs. Mogensen designed a complementary coffee table (527), also made of oak.

Tipo B Chair

Carlo Mollino, 1950 Limited edition

The highly collectable furniture designed by Italian mid-century master Carlo Mollino combines biomorphic influences, dynamic lines and expressive originality. Such ingredients come together in this extraordinary piece designed as part of a wedding gift for Lisa Ponti, daughter of Gio Ponti, along with another five chairs, a sofa and two armchairs. With a lightweight brass frame and a cloven seat and backrest, the piece achieved nearly $350,000 at a Wright auction in 2019.

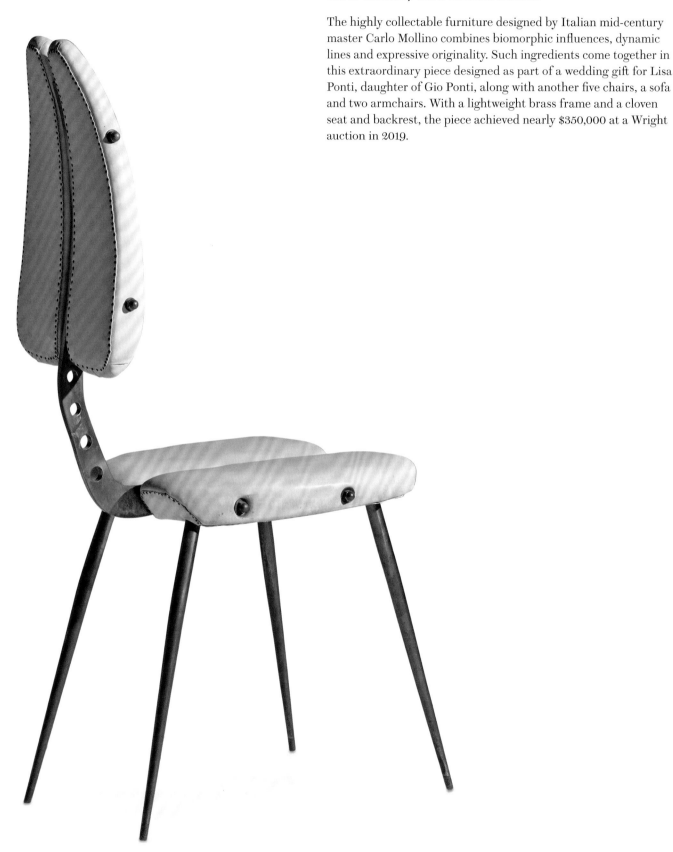

RAI Auditorium Chair

Carlo Mollino, 1951 Limited edition

In the early 1950s, Mollino was commissioned by Italy's national public broadcasting company, RAI (Radiotelevisione Italiana), to design the interiors of a theatre auditorium in his native Turin. The interiors were sumptuous and colourful, as was the furniture, evidenced by Mollino's RAI Auditorium Chair. The high-sided armchair has a brass base supporting a plywood frame coated in foam padding upholstered in red velvet, and could be arranged separately or in rows, with folding seats to offer protection when not in use. The collection brings to mind Mollino's range for the Lutrario Hall in Turin (see p. 175).

Casa del Sole Side Chair

Carlo Mollino, 1953 Ettore Canali

As well as working as a designer and architect, the flamboyant Mollino was also a photographer, a racing-car driver and an accomplished skier, with a passion for both speed and the mountains. During the late 1940s, Mollino was asked to design an apartment building in the Alpine resort of Cervinia, in the Valle d'Aosta, a commission that included the architecture, interiors and furniture. The collection included this side chair used in the apartments and the building's restaurant, made of oak and brass by Ettore Canali. The distinctive cloven backrest echoes other Mollino designs, such as the Tipo B Chair (opposite), yet was inspired by the idea of two skis resting vertically side by side.

Conoid Chairs

George Nakashima, 1960 Nakashima Studio

Master woodworker, craftsman and designer George Nakashima
fused multiple influences in his work, particularly those drawn
from artisanal Japanese and Shaker traditions, while maintaining
a devotion to modernity. His furniture, largely made at his own
workshops in New Hope, Pennsylvania, was also inspired by his love
of the inherent character of his favourite woods. This is seen in his
famous Conoid Chair, first produced in the early 1960s and part
of a 'Conoid' collection named after the distinctive Conoid Studio
(1959) built at New Hope to Nakashima's own design. The particular
Conoid Chairs pictured date from around 1970 and are made of
American black walnut and hickory.

Coconut Chairs Model 5569

George Nelson, 1955 Herman Miller/Vitra

The Coconut Chair is one of the most famous furniture designs produced by George Nelson for Herman Miller during his long tenure as the company's design director (1946–65). It is, arguably, one of the purest Nelson pieces in terms of its geometrical precision: the seat and back are reduced down to one triangular shell – reminiscent of a coconut segment – sitting on a steel frame supported by three slim legs. Originally the shell seat had a steel foundation coated in polyurethane foam, which was upholstered in a choice of vividly coloured textiles or leather, but in later production the steel was switched for fibreglass to make the chair lighter. A matching footstool was released in 1958.

Pretzel Chair Model 5890

George Nelson, 1952 Herman Miller/De Padova/Vitra

As the design director of Herman Miller, as well as a designer in his
own right, George Nelson was actively engaged in the development
of furniture and products made of such modern materials as plastics,
steel and wire rods, and plywood. The super-light and elegantly
sculptural Pretzel Chair was originally developed in 1952, using
a combination of laminated bentwood and ply, but proved complex
to produce in large volumes. Plycraft, who went on to produce the
comparable Cherner Armchair (1958, see p. 33), was commissioned
to make the Pretzel for Herman Miller in 1957–58, with subsequent
reissues by De Padova and Vitra.

Alta Lounge Chairs

Oscar Niemeyer, *c.* 1971 Mobilier de France/Tendo Brasileira/Móveis Tepperman

As well as his decidedly dynamic landmark buildings, Brazilian architect Oscar Niemeyer designed a number of pieces of furniture during the late 1960s and 1970s. The Marquesa Bench (*c.* 1974) and the Rio Chaise Longue (*c.* 1978) suggest Niemeyer's love of curvaceous shapes and forms, as does the Alta Lounge Chair that uses a curving band of steel, like a partially coiled spring, to support both the seat base and the back cushion. The two cushions are amply padded and coated in faux leather. Originally produced in France, where the Alta graced Niemeyer's Parisian headquarters for the French Communist Party, later production shifted to Brazil.

K3 Heart Cone Chair

Verner Panton, 1959 Plus-linje/Vitra

Having previously worked with Arne Jacobsen, Verner Panton
opened his own design studio in 1955, finding fame a few years later
with his Cone chair sequence, or the K Series as it was widely known.
The sequence began with the K1, or original Cone Chair, of 1958,
with a conical seat perched by its point on an aluminium base, and
developed with Danish furniture maker Plus-linje. The initial success
of K1 led to other additions, including the K2 Wire Cone Chair and
then the most famous of the series, the K3 Heart Cone Chair, where
the steel-framed, foam-coated and upholstered seat splays upward
into a pair of wings. Seen from the front, the chair assumes a vivid
heart-like shape, particularly when coated in red upholstery.

Panton Chair

Verner Panton, 1967 Vitra

Following on from the K Series (opposite), Panton began work on an ambitious project to design a cantilevered, one-piece chair. This brief led to the evolution, with Thonet, of the S-Chair (1965), made of a folded ribbon of laminated wood, and, eventually, to what became known as the Panton Chair, produced by Vitra. Panton worked closely with Vitra's founder, Willi Fehlbaum, on the development of the groundbreaking plastic chair and the technology required to make it. Finally, in 1967, they succeeded in producing the first model using cold-pressed, fibreglass-reinforced polyester. In 1970, Vitra switched to an injection-moulded plastic, with further refinements made over subsequent years. The Panton Chair speaks of the future but is also playful and hard-wearing.

Ribbon Chairs Model 582

Pierre Paulin, 1966 Artifort

The Ribbon Chair is one of the most famous and successful pieces
by French sculptor-turned-furniture-designer Pierre Paulin. It
was one of a series of dynamic, pop-art designs by Paulin for Dutch
furniture maker Artifort, which also included such pieces as the
Tulip Chair (1965), the ABCD Sofa (1968, see p. 224) and the
Tongue chaise longue (c. 1969, see p. 142). The Ribbon is constructed
from a loop of tubular steel, comparable to a Möbius strip, that
is then padded, brightly upholstered and set on a wooden plinth.
The striking geometrical precision of the piece helped to make it a
standout design of the 1960s.

Les Arcs Dining Chairs →

Charlotte Perriand, c. 1970 Dal Vera

During the 1960s, French designer Charlotte Perriand worked on
an ambitious project to create a new ski resort in the French Savoie,
known as Les Arcs. The scheme embraced multiple apartment
buildings perched on the mountainside, with Perriand's work
spanning architecture, interiors and furniture. Pieces included the
Les Arcs Stool (c. 1968, see p. 180) and these dining chairs, made
in Italy with a tubular-steel frame supporting a one-piece, slung-
leather seat and back. Most sources suggest Dal Vera as the original
manufacturers, although some also point to production by Cassina.

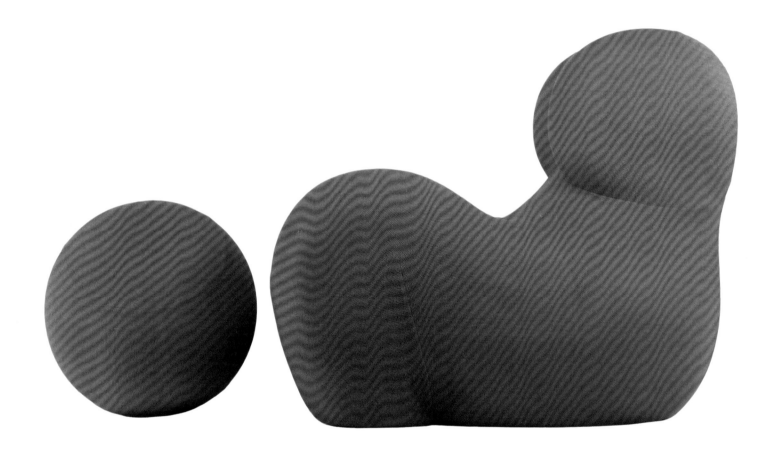

Up5 Chair & Ottoman

Gaetano Pesce, 1969 C&B Italia/B&B Italia

The Up5 Chair, authored by Italian designer Gaetano Pesce, sits among
a handful of mid-century pieces that can claim to have truly reinvented
the typology in a radical way. It was a 'transformative' piece that came
vacuum-packed in PVC wrapping, with the polyurethane chair only
expanding and growing on contact with the air. Once fully formed,
the curvaceous and enveloping shape of the armchair – also known
as La Mamma or Donna – reveals itself, while a round ottoman (Up6)
was also designed to sit alongside the piece in a mother and child
formation. The Up5 can be compared with other transformative pieces
such as DDL Studio's inflatable Blow armchair of 1967 (see p. 38).

DSC Series Chair (Model DSC 106)

Giancarlo Piretti, 1965 Castelli

After his studies at the Istituto Statale d'Arte in Bologna, Giancarlo Piretti began working with Cesare Castelli's furniture-making company, eventually becoming its director of research and design. Piretti's work with Castelli was focused on adaptability and affordability, with the evolution of chairs and other furniture suited to mass production. One of Piretti's most famous designs is the DSC 106 Chair, which has a standardized set of parts revolving around a pair of cast-aluminium side fixings that support a moulded-plastic seat and back, as well as providing sockets for the legs. The chair was purposefully made to be easily adapted into row seating suited to theatres and other venues, while other elements – such as armrests and mini, folding tabletops – could also be added.

Plia Folding Chair

Giancarlo Piretti, 1970 Castelli

Following on from the success of Castelli's DSC Series (left), Piretti continued to develop new ideas for the Bologna-based company founded upon principles of versatility and affordability. He began to explore designs for lightweight folding chairs, which led to the evolution of two famous models: the Plona – with an aluminium frame supporting a slung-leather seat – and also the best-selling Plia. The Plia makes use of a slim aluminium frame combined with a transparent acrylic seat and backrest, enhancing the sense of lightness. Importantly, the easily portable chair can be stored flat or stacked in an X-shaped formation.

Platner Collection Lounge Chairs

Warren Platner, 1966 Knoll

Knoll's iconic Platner Collection of furniture, released in 1966, offers a prime example of the way in which mid-century designers stepped firmly away from the heavy-lift furniture of previous centuries and embraced pieces that were light in every sense. The architect and designer used 'wheatsheaf' bases of welded steel rods to create his matching collection of chairs and tables (see p. 290). The Platner chairs included a dining chair, an armchair and this high-backed lounge chair, with padded upholstery for the seat and back (plus a matching cushion) over the steel framework. Even with the upholstery, the base remains translucent and gives the piece an ephemeral quality.

Executive Chairs

Charles Pollock, 1965 Knoll

During the post-war period, Florence Knoll placed particular importance upon the growing marketplace for innovative modern furniture for office and executive use. She invited designer Charles Pollock, who had previously worked with George Nelson, to explore ideas for a new office chair suited to mass production, leading to the development of his streamlined Executive Chair, often referred to as the Pollock Chair. The swivel chair, set on a four-armed star base with or without castors, has a moulded-plastic shell seat with the option of plastic armrests, while the leather upholstery is limited to a single, continuous seat and back pad, making the piece more affordable and easier to produce than previous designs. Along with the Model 657 Sling Chair (1960), it was one of a number of successful Pollock designs for Knoll.

Model 807 Distex Lounge Chair

Gio Ponti, 1953 Cassina

Given all that the great Italian polymath achieved as an architect, designer, educator and magazine editor, it is extraordinary just how prolific Gio Ponti was when it came to furniture design. His chairs, in particular, are not only innovative but also characterful, as seen in his collaborations with Cassina. One of his first designs was the Distex Lounge Chair: a tubular-brass framework and legs, with the seat, back and armrests elegantly upholstered. The piece, which appeared in Ponti's own home, was also produced with a number of variations that featured similarly dynamic profiles. Other key Ponti designs include the Diamond lounge chair and matching sofa (1953, see p. 226).

Model 699 Superleggera →

Gio Ponti, 1957 Cassina

While Ponti's lounge chairs, such as the Distex (below), speak of exuberant dynamism and ergonomic comfort, his dining chairs form part of a very different project. The ambition here was to produce a versatile and lightweight ladder-back dining chair that would be decidedly modern but would also draw on historical precedents. The first step was the Leggera ('light') of 1952 (Model 646), followed a few years later by the Model 699 Superleggera ('superlight') chair with its lighter ash frame, tapered legs and cane seat (originally produced in the traditional manner by artisans in Chiavari). The chair became an Italian mid-century classic and is still produced by Cassina.

Sling Chair

Harvey Probber, 1948 Harvey Probber

New York-based designer Harvey Probber launched his own
manufacturing company in 1945, followed by showrooms across
the USA. Probber's work was often expressive, incorporating colour
and pattern, but also innovative and even experimental, as seen
in his Sling Chair of 1948. The piece, sometimes referred to as the
Suspension Chair, features a frame made of laminated birch gently
supporting the upholstered seat cushion that floats between the
bentwood. The piece appeared in the 'Useful Objects' exhibition
of 1948 held at the Museum of Modern Art and helped establish
Probber's reputation.

Antony Chair

Jean Prouvé, 1954 Ateliers Jean Prouvé/Galerie Steph
Simon/Vitra

Many of Jean Prouvé's most famous pieces of furniture, such as
the Standard Chair (1934), date from the 1930s when the engineer
and 'constructeur' devoted much of his energy to the development
of affordable, factory-made furniture. The Antony Chair of 1954
was one of Prouvé's last pieces of furniture and was designed for
the interiors of the Cité Universitaire in Antony, near Paris, using
a lacquered-steel frame and a single curved sheet of beech plywood
for the seat and back. Initially made by Prouvé's own workshop
(later by Galerie Steph Simon and then Vitra), the chair is one of a
number of Antony pieces, which also includes a daybed (see p. 425)
and the Compas Desk (1953, see p. 383).

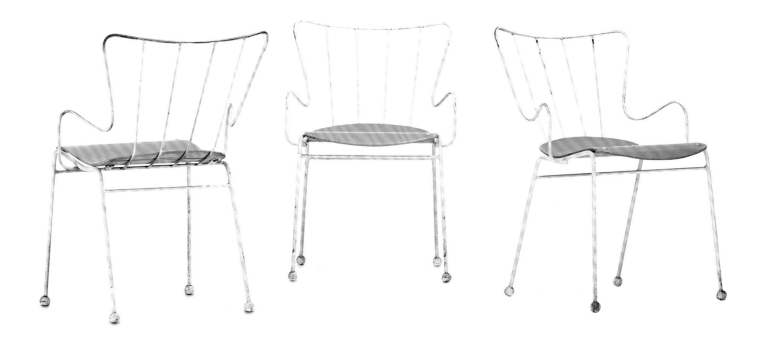

← Stokke Lounge Chair

Jens Quistgaard, 1965 Nissen

Danish designer Jens Quistgaard is best known for his collections of flatware and homeware, including his famous Dansk teak ice bucket of 1960. But there were also many pieces of furniture, such as his Dansk Stool (*c.* 1970, see p. 182) and this elegant lounge chair produced by Richard Nissen. The distinctive piece features a framework of rosewood sticks, or 'stokke', neatly held together by four chrome-plated steel braces, while suede for the seat and backrest adds to the organic character of the piece. Nissen also produced a matching square table and a circular coffee table, again featuring Quistgaard's crafted timber batons.

Antelope Chairs

Ernest Race, 1950 Race Furniture

The Antelope Chair and matching bench were originally designed by Ernest Race for the 1951 Festival of Britain, intended for outdoor use on the terraces of the South Bank around the Royal Festival Hall (designed by Leslie Martin). Race used lightweight, bent-steel rods for the framework and high back, which echoed a traditional Windsor chair but in a clearly modern medium. The sculptural, white enamelled-steel outline contrasts with colourful seats made of plywood, while the rounded ball feet add another playful touch. The Antelope is part of a zoomorphic series by Race that also includes the Springbok (1951), the Heron (1955) and the Flamingo (1957).

Zwaan Armchair

Gerrit Rietveld, 1958 Artifort

While Gerrit Rietveld was a pioneering modernist architect and
designer best known for his work between the wars, for example,
his iconic Red Blue Chair (1918) and his Zig-Zag Chair (1932), he
continued his influential work during the mid-century period. This
resulted in fresh pieces of furniture, such as Rietveld's designs for
the interiors of the 'Ideal Flat', presented within the Dutch Pavilion
at the 1958 World's Fair held in Brussels. The upholstered Zwaan
Armchair features a dynamic profile with two projecting armrests
facing forward like a pair of pointers. This characterful design also
has echoes of Rietveld's classic Utrecht Chair, first produced by
Metz & Co. during the 1930s and then reissued in the 1960s.

Model 654L Risom Lounge Chair

Jens Risom, 1941 Knoll

Danish-born designer Jens Risom moved to the USA in 1939, soon after completing his studies in Copenhagen. Having met Hans Knoll, the designer went on to develop one of the first collections for the eponymous furniture company. The range included a number of chairs that combined modern, sculptural lines with webbed seats and backs. Webbing was a readily available material that was also used by such other Knoll designers as Ralph Rapson (see p. 142) and Abel Sorenson (see p. 295) during the 1940s. The most engaging of the Risom designs is, arguably, the Model 654L Lounge Chair, which offers a curvaceous silhouette and natural materials in true Danish style. Following the success of his Knoll collection, Risom went on to found his own furniture company in 1946.

Sheriff Armchair & Ottoman ↓

Sergio Rodrigues, 1961 ISA

With his love of indigenous natural materials, artisanal craftsmanship and playful forms, Sergio Rodrigues established himself as one of the most successful and internationally renowned mid-century Brazilian designers. His best-known chair is undoubtedly the Sheriff Armchair, with its combination of rosewood frame and leather upholstery that envelops the frame while folding over the sides and back. It began life in the late 1950s as the Mole (Portuguese for 'soft') Lounge Chair produced by Brazilian company Oca, which Rodrigues co-founded. Later, the chair was renamed and production switched to Italian company ISA, who marketed the chair internationally. The Sheriff is the most famous of a series of throne-like chairs designed by Rodrigues, which also includes the Tonico Lounge Chair and matching sofa (see p. 229) of 1963.

↑ Grasshopper Chairs (Model 61U) & Ottoman

Eero Saarinen, 1946 Knoll

Renowned American architect Eero Saarinen first got to know Florence Knoll at the Cranbrook Academy of Art, where she was a student and he was briefly a tutor. During the 1940s, Knoll invited her friend and colleague to contribute designs to the furniture company she ran with her husband, Hans Knoll. Among the most famous of these early designs is the Grasshopper Chair that uses a pair of continuous, bentwood laminate ribbons to form the feet, base and armrests while supporting the curvaceous, upholstered seat and back. In 1948, Knoll released Saarinen's Womb Chair followed by a matching settee (see p. 231).

Pedestal Side Chairs (Model 151U)

Eero Saarinen, 1956 Knoll

One of the characteristics of traditional furniture that Saarinen objected to, along with a number of his contemporaries, was the 'slum of legs'. His famous solution is the Pedestal Collection for Knoll, where the legs are replaced with a single stem set upon a round base. The series includes a Pedestal Table (1957, see p. 293), coffee table, stool, armchair and the Pedestal Side Chair (Model 151U), commonly known as the Tulip Chair. Made of a moulded-fibreglass shell seat and a circular aluminium base, the piece was either upholstered or came with a circular seat cushion; swivel versions of the Tulip Chair were also produced.

Model 5016 Teiza Chair →

Junzo Sakakura, 1957 Tendo Mokko

During the mid-century period, designers sought to reduce the number of different ingredients within a piece of furniture to achieve purity of form and ease of manufacture. Such was the case with the Teiza Chair designed by Japanese architect Junzo Sakakura, who worked in Le Corbusier's Parisian studio during the 1930s before returning to his native Japan. The chair features two cross-braced side supports in laminated wood forming the legs and holding the rounded seat and back pad, both of which are upholstered. Low-slung and evenly balanced, the piece is well suited to Japanese tatami rooms.

Domus Stacking Chairs

Ilmari Tapiovaara, 1946 Keravan Puuteollisuus/Artek

Finnish designer Ilmari Tapiovaara immersed himself in the world of modern furniture, working for Artek and then Asko before establishing his own design studio in Helsinki. One of his earliest and most successful designs is this stacking chair, initially produced for student accommodation at Helsinki's Domus Academica. With a birch-laminate frame and a matching plywood seat and back plate, the chair is both robust and stackable. It was initially produced in Finland by Keravan Puuteollisuus, distributed in the USA by Knoll and later reissued by Artek. Other pieces in the Domus collection include a high-backed armchair and a desk.

Rauma-Repola Chairs →

Ilmari Tapiovaara, *c.* 1955 Limited edition

While Ilmari Tapiovaara's furniture from the 1940s was designed with a focus on function and utility, his work became more expressive during the 1950s. There was the Dolphin Chaise (1955, see p. 147), the Pirkka Collection (1956, see p. 183) and also this characterful lounge chair designed for the headquarters and offices of Rauma-Repola, a Finnish conglomerate with interests in forestry and shipping. The framework is, suitably enough, made from intersecting batons of oak that support a webbed-leather lattice used to create the seat and backrest.

Cadeira de Três Pés
(Three-Legged Chair)

Joaquim Tenreiro, *c.* 1947 Tenreiro Móveis e Decorações

Joaquim Tenreiro was one of Brazil's most accomplished and well-known mid-century furniture designers. He famously explored and expressed the natural beauty of Brazilian hardwoods in his furniture, which included credenzas (see p. 334) and tables (see p. 298). In the late 1940s and 1950s, he combined various woods, such as amendoim and imbuia, to create laminated stools and chairs in which the striped pattern came purely from these organic materials. Chief among these pieces is his beautifully crafted Cadeira de Três Pés, made using five different hardwoods by Tenreiro's own workshop.

← Model EJ-5 Corona Chair

Poul Volther, 1964 Erik Jørgensen

The Corona Chair speaks of an era obsessed with the space race and moon shots. The most famous piece created by Danish designer Poul Volther, the Corona Chair has four elliptical pads with a lunar quality: diminishing in size they climb up the crisp steel frame from the seat toward the smallest pad at the summit of the high back. Still produced today by Erik Jørgensen, the swivelling Corona comes with either leather-upholstered pads or fabric upholstery in a choice of colours.

Model OW149 Colonial Chairs

Ole Wanscher, 1949 Poul Jeppesen/Carl Hansen & Søn

The erudite and academic son of an art historian, Danish furniture designer Ole Wanscher was influenced by historical forms and precedents, as seen in his Egyptian Stool (1960, see p. 185) and many other designs, including the Colonial Chair. One of a handful of elegant Wanscher lounge chairs and armchairs from the mid-century period, the piece has a rosewood frame and a woven rattan seat, usually combined with two loose, leather-upholstered cushions for the seat and back. As well as working with Poul Jeppesen, Wanscher designed furniture for Fritz Hansen.

← Model JH550 Peacock Chair
Hans Wegner, 1947 Johannes Hansen/PP Møbler

Danish master designer Hans Wegner emerged from a deep-rooted craft tradition and, after serving a long apprenticeship as a cabinetmaker and studying furniture design, went on to work with many of the country's leading producers, including Johannes Hansen, Carl Hansen & Søn, Fritz Hansen and PP Møbler. From the 1940s onward, Wegner created an extraordinary number of iconic and instantly recognizable designs, including the Peacock Chair of 1947. Made of ash and teak, along with a paper-cord seat, the Peacock is one of a number of early Wegner pieces that sought to reinvent the traditional, spindle-backed Windsor chair. In this case, the high back and fan-shaped, peacock-feather spindles bring a unique and engaging character to the chair.

Model FH1936 Shell Chair
Hans Wegner, 1948 Fritz Hansen

There is a tendency to see Wegner as a purist, but his positive commitment to innovation and experimentation helps to set him apart, even within the illustrious context of Danish mid-century modernism. During the late 1940s, at a time when he was developing pieces inspired by historical precedents, Wegner also became fascinated by one of the most modern materials available: plywood. He began developing ideas for affordable 'shell chairs', made from sheets of ply, which led to this early Shell Chair (and a matching bench and table) produced by Fritz Hansen. A beech frame complements a curvaceous seat and a crescent-shaped backrest in moulded teak plywood. The piece proved more expensive to manufacture than initially hoped, but Wegner continued to pursue ideas for other shell chairs, including a 'two-part shell chair' for Johannes Hansen, also known as the Smiling Chair (1963).

← Model JH503 Round Chair

Hans Wegner, 1949 Johannes Hansen/PP Møbler

Like the Peacock Chair (see p. 105), the Round Chair referenced historical precedents and is one of a number of Wegner designs from the late 1940s based on traditional Chinese chairs. Through a process 'of purification and of simplification', Wegner eventually developed the Round Chair with an elegant oak frame and rounded back, as well as a cane seat. The piece became known simply as 'The Chair' after featuring in the televised 1960 debate between American presidential candidates John F. Kennedy and Richard Nixon. It is also perhaps the most famous of a family of rounded chairs perfected by Wegner during the 1950s and early 1960s.

Model CH24 Wishbone Chairs

Hans Wegner, 1950 Carl Hansen & Søn

While Wegner's Round Chair (opposite) was lauded to the point that it became known simply as 'The Chair', it has – arguably – been overtaken in terms of its landmark status by the designer's Wishbone Chair, also known as the Y Chair, which has become a familiar friend and a staple within the homes of appreciative design aficionados. The piece can be seen as a further refinement of Wegner's Chinese and rounded chairs, with its crafted oak frame and paper-cord seat, yet the Y-shaped back support adds a fresh and engaging element to the composition. The initial reception to the chair was relatively subdued, yet it gradually established itself as a design classic and has remained in continuous production by Carl Hansen & Søn.

Model GE225 Flag Halyard Chair

Hans Wegner, 1950 Getama/PP Møbler

Wegner's extensive portfolio exhibits not just innovation and
inventiveness, but also openness to fresh materials and ways of
making. A case in point is the Flag Halyard Chair of 1950, which
makes use of a steel frame combined with a seat and back made
of 250m of flag halyard, the flagline rope commonly used by
sailors. The piece is finished with a brightly coloured head cushion,
resembling a sailor's kit bag or even a life preserver, plus a sheepskin
draped over the chair that softens the piece and adds another
textural ingredient.

Model AP19 Papa Bear Chair & Ottoman

Hans Wegner, 1951 A. P. Stolen/Carl Hansen & Søn

Although Wegner immersed himself in the artisanal craft tradition
and the history of furniture design, there was also a more playful
and expressive strand to his work that evolved over time. He gradually
embraced the challenge of designing upholstered furniture, developing
one of the most beloved takes on the wing chair in the form of the
Papa Bear Chair. In some respects, the form of the piece came from
ergonomics, with the pair of projecting 'paws' making it easier to get
in and out of the chair, but commentators also noted its endearing
zoomorphic character. A few years later, in 1954, Wegner designed the
slightly smaller Model AP28 Chair, which became known as the Mama
Bear Chair, although the two pieces have distinctive personalities.

← Model AP46 Ox Chairs

Hans Wegner, 1960 A. P. Stolen

Over time, Wegner became more interested in sculptural forms and expressive statements. The apotheosis of this strand in his work is the Ox Chair of 1960, which expanded upon his work in the field of upholstered wing chairs and armchairs while creating one of the most striking mid-century silhouettes. Discreet tubular-steel legs support the bull-like body of the chair, with its arms and projecting horns ending in rounded ovals. When seen dressed in dark leather, the piece assumes the character of a minotaur reaching outward. Tellingly, the Ox became one of Wegner's favourite designs and featured prominently in his own home.

Model 5499 Lounge Chairs

Edward Wormley, *c.* 1949 Dunbar

Prolific mid-century American designer Edward Wormley created a broad range of chairs of all shapes and sizes during his long tenure as chief designer for furniture maker Dunbar. The Wormley collection was inventive and imaginative but also diverse, with his experiments in shape and form taking him in many different directions. One of his most refined chairs is the Model 5499, with its angled seat contrasting with the rectangular outline of the dark mahogany frame and armrests. Despite the breadth of Wormley's output, the quality of his furniture has made it increasingly collectable.

← Model 9019 Nikke Chairs

Tapio Wirkkala, 1958 Asko

Finnish designer Tapio Wirkkala investigated the particular characteristics of the many different materials that he worked with, expressing them in ways that were both modern and imaginative. This was true of his glassware, ceramics and flatware, but also his furniture, such as his stackable Nikke Chair produced by Asko. Rather than using a uniform piece of plywood in combination with a simple set of tubular-steel legs, Wirkkala opted for a curvaceous seat and back made of a single, slim piece of laminate timber combining birch and teak, with the resulting pattern lending the chair its unique personality. The Nikke Chair can be compared with Wirkkala's Model 9016 Coffee Table (see p. 298), also produced by Asko in 1958.

Veranda Armchair

Jorge Zalszupin, 1959 L'Atelier

Polish-born architect and designer Jorge Zalszupin arrived in Brazil
in 1949 and established his own furniture company, L'Atelier, ten
years later. His early work fused the influence of Danish design,
in particular, with a love of Brazilian materials and craftsmanship,
as seen in his Dinamarquesa ('Danish Girl') chair of 1959 and the
Veranda Armchair, released around the same time. The relaxed
Veranda Armchair features four vertical jacaranda corner posts
helping to support the frame, while the seat, armrests and backrest
are all in slung leather, lending the piece the look and feel of an
elegant, modern safari or campaign chair.

Senior Armchairs

Marco Zanuso, 1951 Arflex

During the 1950s, Italian architect and designer Marco Zanuso played a key role in the development of Arflex, the Milan-based furniture maker established in 1950. The foundation pieces for the company were a series of characterful armchairs made of upholstered foam rubber, which ensured that the chairs were comfortable but could also be sculpted into expressive forms. High among these landmark armchairs stands the Senior Armchair of 1951, whose curvaceous seat and high back form a distinctive and continuous wave resting on four discreet brass legs. The Senior can be compared to the Lady Chair and matching sofa (see p. 237), also released in 1951.

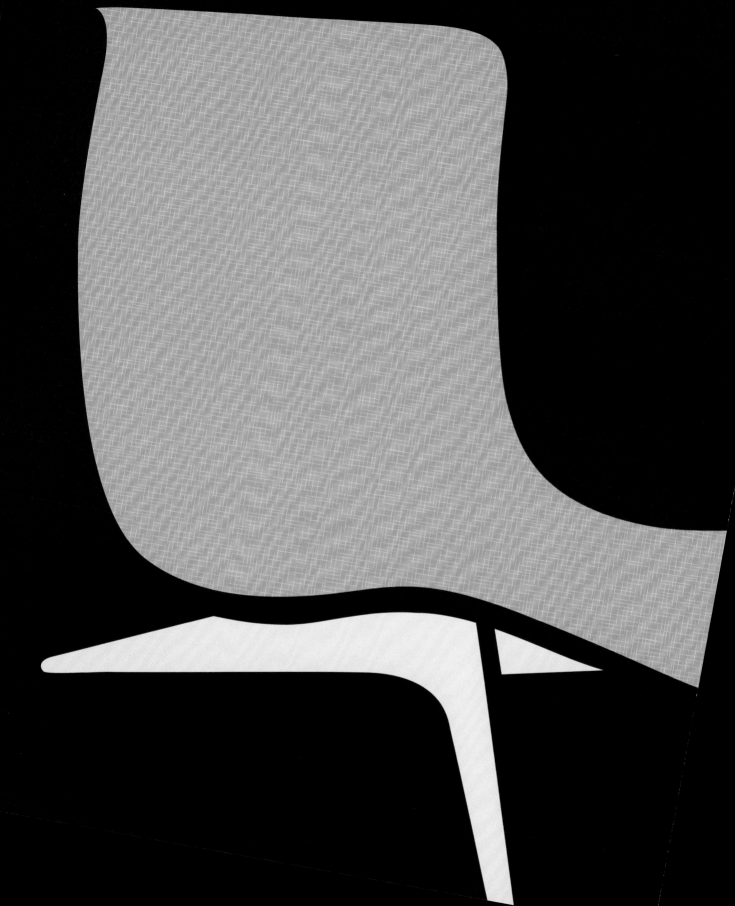

CHAISES
LONGUES

CHAISES LONGUES
RECLINERS
ROCKING CHAIRS

During the mid-century period there was a significant process of hybridization within the field of furniture. It was seen, for example, in the rise of modular and sectional seating systems that challenged the accepted view of what a sofa or a chair should look like. It was also seen within the world of the chaise longue and the recliner, which stretched and morphed during the 1950s and especially through the 1960s.

The long chair was, in itself, a kind of hybrid to start with, somewhere between a lounger and a daybed. During the early modernist period between World War I and II, designers and architects such as Le Corbusier, Charlotte Perriand, Alvar Aalto and Marcel Breuer were drawn to the long chair, transforming it into a thoroughly contemporary piece of furniture using materials such as tubular steel, plywood, and steamed and bent laminated wood. After World War II, this process continued and gathered pace, helped by advances in ways of making, as seen in pieces by Bruno Mathsson, Ernest Race, Hans Wegner and others who used such organic materials in fresh and original ways.

Yet it was, arguably, the rapid rise of plastics that saw the process of hybridization accelerate, combined with a push toward increasingly sculptural and abstract forms. During the late 1940s, Charles & Ray Eames created their iconic La Chaise (1948, see p. 127), with Eero Aarnio and Charles Zublena also using the material during the 1960s to create colourful, pop-art pieces that were robust enough to be used outdoors.

Polyurethane foam and other plastics were increasingly drawn on to create low-slung forms with sinuous seat pads, as seen in sculpted pieces by Olivier Mourgue and Pierre Paulin. Super-light but super-strong steel frames were coated in layers of foam and then wrapped in brightly coloured upholstery or slip covers, with the resulting designs tying in well with the relaxed and casual character of the period, which also saw the ascendance of the conversation pit and the floor cushion. The push toward abstraction saw the arrival of experimental recliners such as Joe Colombo's Tube Chair (1969, see p. 125), consisting of a nest of tubes that arrived in a bag and could be arranged at will into the shape of a recliner.

It was notable how designers and producers also turned their attention to the outdoors during the mid-century period. Some, including Ernest Race and Hans Wegner, invented innovative deckchairs suited to land or sea. Others, such as Richard Schultz, created entire collections for outdoor and leisure use with such pieces well suited to the poolside, terrace or garden.

Willy Guhl famously used another modern material, namely cement fibreboard, to create his iconic Garden Chair of 1954 (see p. 130), which was also a rocking chair. Rockers, too, were reinvented for modern living and not just by Guhl but also by Ralph Rapson, Gae Aulenti, Edward Wormley and others. They sat well with the push toward the playful, yet also referenced a traditional and familiar favourite.

FOLLOWING SPREAD The Butterfly House, Carmel, California, USA, by Frank Wynkoop (restoration: Jamie Bush), 1951

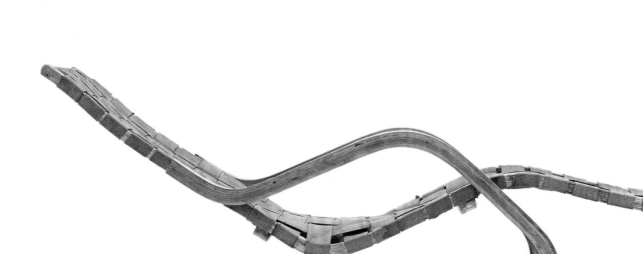

Cantilevered Chaise (Model 39)

Alvar Aalto, *c.* 1936 Artek

The highly influential Model 39 Cantilevered Chaise by Alvar Aalto
was a pre-war design with a positively mid-century modern look
and feel to it. This experimental and avant-garde piece was made
by Artek, co-founded by Aalto himself, using pieces of laminated,
bentwood birch that morph elegantly from armrests into parallel,
ski-style legs while supporting the webbed canvas (or leather) seat.
Marcel Breuer was exploring similar ideas and materials at the
same point in time, with his Isokon Long Chair released in 1936.

Pastilli Chair

Eero Aarnio, 1967 Asko/Adelta

The Pastilli Chair is an extraordinary hybrid, which can be used indoors or outside for reclining, lounging or rocking. Made of two conjoined pieces of shining fibreglass, usually brightly coloured, Eero Aarnio's Pastilli (also known as the Pastil, Pastille or Gyro Chair) is also a playful, pop-art sculpture, brilliantly in tune with the informal, iconoclastic spirit of the 1960s. Following on from the success of the Pastilli, Aarnio went on to design the Tomato Lounge Chair (1972), produced by Asko, based on the same principles and also made of sculpted fibreglass. Both pieces have a boat-like quality, resembling abstract pedaloes minus the pedals.

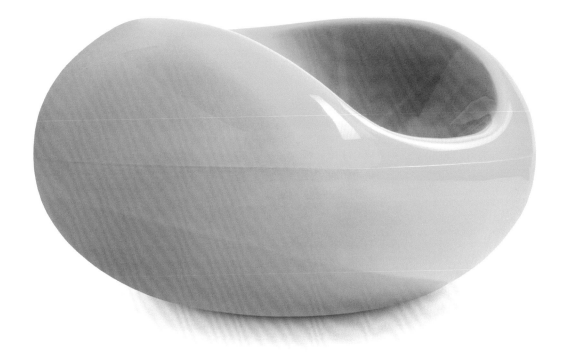

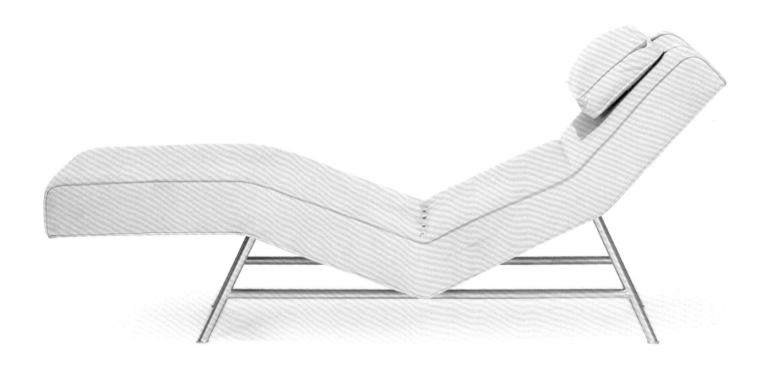

← Sgarsul

Gae Aulenti, 1962 Poltronova/Stendig

A number of mid-century designers were drawn to the rocking chair, partly because its intrinsically informal and playful character was so well suited to the spirit of the times. Along with Hans Wegner, Sam Maloof and others, Gae Aulenti reimagined the rocker while referencing, in particular, the late-19th-century, bentwood rocking chairs produced by Thonet. Aulenti and Poltronova also made use of bentwood loops, using them in the form of two interconnecting and overlapping teardrops that support a comfortable vinyl- or leather-upholstered seat and headrest. The Sgarsul was produced in a number of different colourways.

Fred Chaise Longue Model 1231-400

Milo Baughman, *c.* 1953 Thayer Coggin

The Fred Chaise Longue has the look and feel of the archetypal psychiatrist's couch. It was one of the earliest of Milo Baughman's many designs for furniture maker Thayer Coggin, forming a lynchpin piece within a working relationship that spanned five decades. 'Fred' features a wedge-shaped, tubular-steel frame and leg base supporting an ergonomically designed, upholstered seat that mirrors the shape of the reclining patient. One of a small number of chaises longues designed by Baughman for Thayer Coggin, Fred is the only model still produced by the firm today, and is available in a range of finishes and upholstery choices.

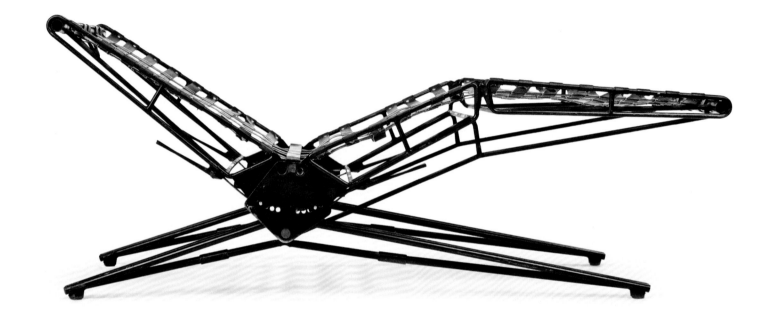

L77 Lounger/Daybed

Osvaldo Borsani, 1956 Tecno

Flexibility and versatility were built into many of Osvaldo Borsani's early designs for Tecno, the Italian furniture company that he founded with his brother. Hybrid pieces such as the D70 Sofa (1954, see p. 199) and the P40 Folding Lounge Chair employed adjustable locking mechanisms to allow the pieces to be securely used in various positions. The same is true of the L77 Lounger or Daybed, which features a folding steel framework and upholstered cushions perched on four tensile steel legs, with the choice of using the piece as a recliner or locking it flat to serve as a daybed.

Tube Chair

Joe Colombo, 1969 Flexform/Vitra

Italian designer Joe Colombo famously challenged conventional stereotypes when it came to furniture, while exploring designs that could adapt and change according to the needs and wishes of the end user. His 'polymorphic' pieces include the Tube Chair, which was delivered as a bagged nest of four plastic tubes wrapped in foam and coated in vinyl or fabric. The piece came with simple fixings to arrange and secure the tubes in various configurations; it was most commonly used as a recliner. Similarly, Colombo's Multi Chair for Sormani, released a year later, consisted of two units connected by a leather strap and could also be arranged in a choice of configurations.

Fulbright Chaise Longue

Edward Durell Stone, 1945 Fulbright Industries

Although Edward Durell Stone was best known for his architectural
work, including such major cultural projects as the Museum of
Modern Art in New York (1939), he also designed a number of pieces
of furniture for Fulbright during the post-war period. Chief among
the most characterful of these pieces is this curvaceous chaise
longue, with an oak frame and a seat of woven oak veneer. Durell
Stone also designed lounge chairs and a settee using the same
combination of materials, as well as an oak console table and stool.

La Chaise

Charles & Ray Eames, 1948 Vitra

The origins of La Chaise date back to the 1940s when Charles & Ray Eames began experimenting with fibreglass (or glass fibre-reinforced plastic) and developed a fresh family of affordable shell chairs. Many of these early designs, including the DAR (1951, see p. 43) and DAX (Dining Height Armchair X-Base, 1951), were put into production during the 1950s, with the exception of La Chaise. The piece was named in honour of sculptor Gaston Lachaise and his work, *Floating Figure*, which was first shown in 1937 at the Museum of Modern Art, New York. It helped to inspire the unforgettable sculptural form of the reclining chair, with its flowing fibreglass seat supported by steel struts and an X-shaped wooden base. But the complex shape of the piece meant that only prototypes were created during the 1940s, with full production (by Vitra) only beginning in the 1990s.

Billy Wilder Chaise

Charles & Ray Eames, 1968 Herman Miller/Vitra

The Billy Wilder Chaise takes its name from the famous Hollywood film director, best known for *Sunset Boulevard* (1950) and *Some Like It Hot* (1959), who once suggested to Charles & Ray Eames that it would be wonderful to have a chaise longue in his office for an afternoon power nap. It took the designers some years to oblige but, in 1968, they produced their famous solution, also known as the Eames Chaise and, more prosaically, the Model ES106 Soft Pad Chaise. An aluminium base, with cross braces for additional strength, supports an ergonomically shaped recliner with six interlinked upholstered cushions plus two smaller matching pillows. The Eameses presented Billy Wilder with one of the first pieces off the production line.

Grasshopper Chaise Longue

Preben Fabricius & Jørgen Kastholm, *c.* 1968 Alfred Kill

The Grasshopper Chaise, by Danish design team Preben Fabricius and Jørgen Kastholm, has a suitably dynamic and biomorphic quality. Its slim and sculptural steel legs double as armrests while supporting the V-shaped frame of the seat itself, which is wrapped in canvas and tied at the rear like a corset. A soft, segmented cushion upholstered in leather sits upon the canvas, with an additional head cushion strapped to the back of the chair; these organic materials gently soften the slender steelwork. The piece should not be confused with Eero Saarinen's similarly zoomorphic Grasshopper Chair for Knoll (1946, see p. 97).

Garden Chairs

Willy Guhl, 1954 Eternit

The Garden Chair by Swiss designer Willy (Wilhelm) Guhl is a prime example of experimentation generated by fresh, industrially produced materials during the post-war period. In this case, the material was cement fibreboard produced by Eternit, used primarily as a building and roofing material. The manufacturer was looking for inventive uses for its fibrated concrete and Guhl obliged, looping the freshly made board into the shape of a rocking chair, which then set while forming a super-strong and robust piece of furniture well suited to outdoor and garden use. Guhl also designed a stool using the same material and even a dog house, but it was his Garden Chair, also known as the Loop Chair, that became a mid-century icon.

Contour Chaise Longue →

Vladimir Kagan, c. 1958 Kagan-Dreyfuss

'Chairs are uniquely the best expression of design', said New York-based designer Vladimir Kagan, whose focus on sinuous lines and biomorphic shapes was well suited to the chaise longue. Kagan designed a number of chaises longues and recliners during his long career, including this one-armed Contour Chaise Longue from the late 1950s. Also known as the VK Chaise, it features a sculptural aluminium base and a curvaceous, upholstered reclining seat. Two one-armed chaises could also be placed side-by-side to create a more substantial reclining sofa.

Model 177LS Chaise Longue →

Vladimir Kagan, c. 1959 Kagan-Dreyfuss

Kagan's furniture characteristically combined sculptural forms and high craftsmanship, as seen in this 177LS Chaise with a walnut frame, produced by his own workshop during the late 1950s. With its distinctive, sinuous shape, the 177LS is a recognizably Kagan-esque design, comparable to the Contour Chaise (opposite top) and the Erica Chaise Longue (c. 1970). During the 1970s, Kagan also experimented with more linear geometrical designs, as seen in the Omnibus Chaise.

Sun Chaises

Hendrik Van Keppel & Taylor Green, *c.* 1950
Van-Keppel-Green (VKG)

During the 1930s, Van Keppel and Green formed a design partnership in Los Angeles and opened their eponymous VKG store in the city. Among their best-known designs were a matching lounge chair and ottoman, which featured in Julius Shulman's iconic images of Pierre Koenig's Case Study House #22, and were recently reissued as the 'Case Study Lounge Chair and Ottoman' by Modernica. Their subsequent Sun Chaise features a similar combination of a lightweight, tubular-steel frame and robust plastic cording, which is stretched across the frame. As with the Case Study Chair, the Sun Chaise is well suited to outdoor living in California and on the West Coast.

PK24 Chaise Longue

Poul Kjaerholm, 1965 E. Kold Christensen/Fritz Hansen

Poul Kjaerholm called the PK24 Chaise, a design in three parts, his 'hammock chair'. The moniker speaks of the lightness of the piece, but also of the way in which the ergonomic wicker seat floats loosely on the simplest of stainless-steel bases, with gravity and the weight of the occupant helping to hold these two distinct elements together. A round neck pillow, similarly, is kept in position only by a slender steel counterweight attached by slim straps and draped over the summit of the chaise. At the same time, the PK24 offers a pleasing and vibrant contrast between the industrial quality of the super-slim steel base and the organic warmth of the crafted rattan seat.

Model C-4700 Chaises Longues

Walter Lamb, *c.* 1952 Brown Jordan

American designer Walter Lamb took an imaginative response to restrictions on materials during and just after World War II: he began experimenting with surplus bronze tubing, released onto the market by the US Navy, using it to create a collection of outdoor furniture. Lamb's highly successful post-war collection for Brown Jordan included chairs, ottomans and tables made from a combination of lightweight, tubular-bronze frames and hard-wearing seats made of materials such as canvas and leather. As seen in the Model C-4700 Chaise Longue, ribbons of cotton cord are held taut by the bronze frame, forming the supporting seat and backrest. Much of Lamb's Brown Jordan collection remains in production, now using aluminium frames.

Pernilla Long Chair

Bruno Mathsson, 1944 Firma Karl Mathsson

Focusing on natural materials and ergonomic forms, Bruno Mathsson developed a sequence of highly original seating designs during the 1930s and 1940s, including his Pernilla collection. There was a number of variations on the original Pernilla Lounge Chair, but all shared the same vocabulary of a bentwood beech frame and webbed seating (made of jute or hemp or occasionally leather). One of the most pleasing versions is the Pernilla Long Chair, which mirrors and supports the entire body, with a loose pillow at the head and a curving footrest at the base; this version features two wheels, instead of the rear legs, for ease of movement. There was also a three-seater Pernilla Settee.

Whist Chaise Longue

Olivier Mourgue, 1964 Airborne International

French designer Olivier Mourgue was one of the most radical and experimental designers who came to fame during the 1960s. His approach had a decidedly futuristic, sci-fi quality, as seen in his furniture, lighting and other work. Yet, at the same time, he showed an ergonomic consideration, with pieces such as the Whist Chaise Longue – in chrome-plated steel with a leather-upholstered seat – carefully contoured to accommodate the reclining occupant. The piece famously appeared in the 1967 James Bond film, *You Only Live Twice*.

Djinn Chaise Longue

Olivier Mourgue, *c.* 1965 Airborne International

Along with such contemporaries as Verner Panton and Pierre Paulin, Mourgue was fascinated by the possibilities offered by plastics on the one hand and pop-art-inspired abstraction on the other. The most famous fruit of these preoccupations was his Djinn collection, which used steel frames coated in brightly upholstered polyurethane foam to create striking sculptural forms. There is a Djinn chair, settee and bench, along with the Djinn Chaise Longue, which – like the Whist (opposite) – adopts a suitably ergonomic form. The Djinn collection was futuristic and cinematic enough to make a film appearance, starring in Stanley Kubrick's *2001: A Space Odyssey* (1968).

Long Chair

George Nakashima, 1951 Nakashima Studio

As one might expect from a master craftsman with a love for the inherent character of his favourite woods, George Nakashima fashioned his famous Long Chair out of American black walnut. Choice cuts were used for the frame of the recliner as well as the elongated single arm, which doubles as a useful surface for holding drinks or books. For the seat and back support, Nakashima chose another natural material: webbed canvas held taut by the wooden framework. Webbed seating was widely used by other mid-century furniture designers, including Alvar Aalto (see pp. 14 and 120).

Chrome Base Chaise Model 5490

George Nelson, 1956 Herman Miller

George Nelson's micro collection of luxurious chrome-based furniture has been described as a response to Ludwig Mies van der Rohe's Barcelona Chairs, produced by Knoll. Working with associate Irving Harper, Nelson created a set of three designs that featured a refined chrome-plated frame. A low-backed lounge chair was never put into production but the Model 5469 high-backed lounge chair and this Chaise Longue Model 5490 were both released by Herman Miller. With its pleasing and curvaceous padded seat cushion, the chaise is arguably the most successful design of Nelson's chrome group and is now a collectable rarity.

← Model 001 Chaise Longue

Antti & Vuokko Nurmesniemi, *c.* 1970 Vuokko

In 1956, Finnish furniture and product designer Antti Nurmesniemi established his own design studio in Helsinki. He often worked in conjunction with his wife, textile designer Vuokko Eskolin-Nurmesniemi, particularly after her departure from Marimekko in 1960. Their collaborations included this chaise longue, featuring chrome-plated steel legs and support, with a sinuous seat and high backrest in polyurethane. It is upholstered in a distinctive striped textile by Vuokko Nurmesniemi in black and white (there was a black and red version, too). The couple also designed a matching lounge chair in the same striped fabric.

Relax Chaise

Pierre Paulin, 1968 Artifort

French sculptor and designer Pierre Paulin famously challenged conventional furniture typologies, developing hybrid designs and radical forms. A key example is the Relax Chaise of 1968, sometimes known as the Face-to-Face Seating Unit. The Relax is essentially two conjoined recliners, fused at the centre, which allow two occupants to enjoy the same piece at one time. With a steel frame coated in foam and upholstered (seen here in a Kvadrat Tempo fabric), the chaise sat well with the casual and informal character of interiors of the 1960s.

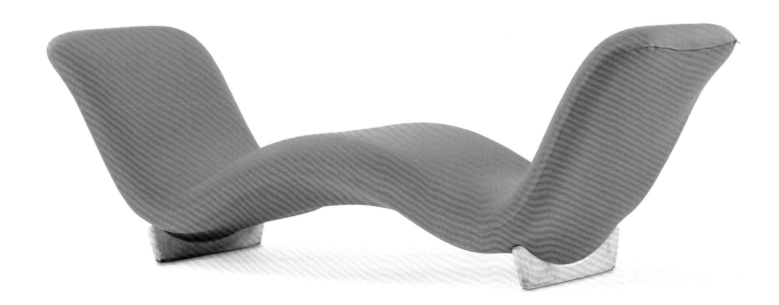

Tongue

Pierre Paulin, *c.* 1969 Artifort

Along with the work of contemporaries such as Verner Panton and Olivier Mourgue, Paulin's work encapsulated a pop-art aesthetic that sat well with the liberated character of the times. This was seen in such pieces as the Relax Chaise (1968, see p. 141) and the Tongue, both of which adopted fluid forms. Again, Paulin used a metal frame coated in polyurethane foam to create the eye-catching, elongated form of the Tongue, which could be described as a radical recliner. Rather than using fixed upholstery, the piece has a slipcover that unzips for cleaning but also to enable alternative colour choices.

Model 657 Rocking Chair →

Ralph Rapson, 1945 Knoll/Rapson-Inc.

Designer and architect Ralph Rapson was one of a number of post-war designers (along with Hans Wegner, Sam Maloof and others) drawn to the idea of reinventing a familiar friend for a new era. The 'Rapson Line' of furniture that he developed for Knoll during the 1940s included the Model 657 Rocking Chair with a birch frame and a choice of either a webbed or upholstered seat and back; a variant with a higher back support was also produced by Knoll. Many of Rapson's rocking-chair designs have been reissued by Rapson-Inc.

Neptune Chair

Ernest Race, 1954 Race Furniture

As one might guess from the name, the Neptune was developed by Ernest Race for use as a deckchair. It formed part of a commission from P&O's Orient Line to create a number of robust and stowable designs suitable for use at sea. Race noted that laminated timber had been used by the boat-building industry for some time and opted for a frame of laminated beech, or mahogany, with a plywood seat back and footrest, within a design that was both elegant and functional. The P&O project also led to the evolution of the folding Cormorant Chair (1959), using a similar combination of laminated timber and plywood.

Chaises Longues

T. H. Robsjohn-Gibbings, *c.* 1955 Widdicomb

English-born interior and furniture designer T. H. Robsjohn-Gibbings settled in Manhattan in 1936, opening a showroom and studio with such well-known clients as Doris Duke and Walter Annenberg. Robsjohn-Gibbings's furniture often traced its roots to traditional and classical designs, as seen in his Klini Chaise of 1961. His collection for Widdicomb included pieces that were more mid-century modern in their character yet luxurious in feel, as seen in this Chaise Longue made of painted walnut, with brass legs and suede upholstery.

Leisure Collection Chaise Longue

Richard Schultz, 1966 Knoll

Having previously worked as an assistant to Harry Bertoia and
then as a respected designer in his own right, Richard Schultz was
invited by Florence Knoll to come up with an elegant, functional and
decidedly modern collection of outdoor furniture. Schultz readily
obliged, creating a classic range of aluminium-framed pieces known
as the Leisure Collection, or the '1966 Collection', after its year of
release. It included chairs and tables, yet one of the most distinctive
elements was this Chaise Longue, with its pair of back wheels for
easy portability around the pool terrace or garden, and an adjustable
backrest that could also be placed in a horizontal position.

← Dolphin Chaises

Ilmari Tapiovaara, 1955 Skanno

Finnish designer Ilmari Tapiovaara has been described as primarily a 'functionalist'. Yet he also showed a respect for craftsmanship, natural materials and sculptural forms, as seen in, for example, his Pirkka Chair and Stool (1956, see p. 183). One of Tapiovaara's most expressive designs is his Dolphin (or 'Pyöriäinen') Chaise of 1955, with its engaging biomorphic form ingeniously constructed from a stained oak frame and curvaceous seat and back pads, both upholstered in leather. The design of the Dolphin proved that furniture could be both functional and expressive at the same time.

Chaise Longue

Arne Vodder, *c.* 1950 Bovirke

Danish designer and architect Arne Vodder, who studied under Finn Juhl at the Royal Danish Academy of Fine Arts, was drawn to warm, natural materials and finely crafted compositions. One of his most engaging designs of the early 1950s was this chaise, manufactured by Bovirke, which features a sinuous beech frame combined with gentle, ergonomic support provided by a lattice of intertwined leather strips. The integrated mini-table, in teak with a slender brass mount, is a delightful addition. Many of Vodder's mid-century chairs and sofas feature a combination of wood and leather, lending them an engaging organic character.

Folding Pincer Chaise Longue

Hans Wegner, 1956 Johannes Hansen

Danish master Hans Wegner designed a number of long chairs
during the 1950s, including the Long Dolphin Chair (1950), which
referenced the deckchair and was produced in both folding and
non-folding versions. Six years later, Wegner returned to the
concept of the ideal deckchair and designed the Pincer Chair and
Chaise Longue, which can be seen as an evolution of the Dolphin.
The chaise has an oak frame and webbed canvas seating, while
the addition of two small wheels to the rear legs means that it can
easily be moved from place to place, as well as folded and stored.

Model GE2 Hammock Chaise Longue

Hans Wegner, 1967 Getama

'A chair isn't finished until someone sits in it', Hans Wegner once said. Certainly, pieces such as the Hammock Chaise Longue offer an open and tempting invitation to do just that, with its elegant and ergonomic laminated oak frame combined with its hammock-style seating support. While early sketches of Wegner's playful design suggest outdoor use, the Hammock Chaise was certainly refined enough to be taken indoors and was also promoted as an enticing addition to a living room setting.

← Model 4873 Listen-To-Me Chaise

Edward Wormley, 1948 Dunbar

During his long tenure as design director of Dunbar, American Edward Wormley conceived a number of long chairs and recliners. Such pieces adopted a variety of aesthetic styles and materials, yet among the most successful, pared down and refined of Wormley's pieces is the Listen-To-Me, designed during the late 1940s. The chaise features a beautifully crafted and curvaceous framework of laminated maple and cherry, reinforced with slim steel and brass struts, supporting a padded cushion moulded to the contours of the body. It is one of the most collectable pieces in Wormley's Dunbar seating range.

← Adjustable Rocking Chaise

Edward Wormley, 1961 Dunbar

Wormley's portfolio for Dunbar, spanning forty years, encompassed an eclectic and diverse output, ranging from the conservative to the experimental. This Rocking Chaise from the early 1960s combines the ambition to revisit the rocker with an homage to the late-19th-century bentwood rocking chairs designed and produced by Austrian furniture maker Thonet. Wormley, too, used a lacquered bentwood frame and a cane seat support for his rocker, while paring down the flourishes seen in its historical predecessor. He also made the piece adjustable, with the option of three different positions for the back of the chair.

Fibreglass Chaises Longues

Charles Zublena, *c.* 1965 Editions Les Plastiques de Bourgogne

Charles Zublena was born in Italy but settled in France in 1930, where he completed his studies and established himself as a designer. He came to prominence during the 1960s when he began experimenting with fibreglass and other plastics, producing abstract pieces that inhabited the borderland between furniture and sculpture. Among these pieces were fibreglass recliners for Club Med, well suited to poolside and beach use, and which were seen in many European resorts during the 1960s and 1970s. Other Zublena seating designs explored rounded, bowl-like forms, resulting in pieces comparable to Eero Aarnio's Pastilli Chair (1967, see p. 121).

STOOLS

LOW STOOLS

BAR STOOLS

It may be one of the smallest and most compact pieces of furniture, yet the modest stool managed to make a big impression during the mid-century period. As a typology, the playful and characterful stool sat well within the spirit of the age, and as a relatively affordable investment offered a neat entry point into the world of modern design. The versatility of the stool also made it a temptation, serving so many different uses and functions, as well as being portable.

For post-war designers, the versatile nature of the stool was certainly a key part of its allure. Max Bill and Hans Gugelot's famous Ulmer Hocker Stool (1954, see p. 159), for example, was originally used at the Hochschule für Gestaltung, the design school in the German town of Ulm, not just as a seat but also as a low table and as a plinth for displaying sculptures and artworks. Students were even encouraged to tip the stool upside down and use it as a carry-all to take their books and art materials around the campus.

Similarly, a number of mid-century designers were drawn to the idea of reimagining the traditional folding stool, which has a long history stretching back into antiquity. Ole Wanscher and Poul Hundevad developed their own folding stools during the post-war period (see pp. 185 and 166), while Poul Kjaerholm's sublime PK91 Folding Stool of 1961 (see p. 171) is, arguably, what some might call a 'category killer', meaning that it is hard to see how the design could ever be bettered. Stacking stools were also popular during the period and for similar reasons: they could easily be brought into use and then stored away, while often doubling as side tables. Florence Knoll, Arne Jacobsen, Alvar Aalto, Rud Thygesen and others all produced their own versions of compact, stackable stools.

A number of mid-century designs, like the folding stool, were reworkings of traditional staples. Charlotte Perriand's Les Arcs Stool (c. 1968, see p. 180), for instance, also known as the Tabouret Stool, has been described as a 20th-century version of an Alpine milking stool. Antti Nurmesniemi's hugely successful Sauna Stool

(1952, see p. 179) was, again, a reimagining of a familiar friend but one that resonated widely throughout the Nordic countries in particular.

Some mid-century stools were essentially miniature versions of larger chairs or even sofas, as was the case with Vladimir Kagan's Unicorn Stool of 1963 (see p. 170). The Pirkka Stool (1956, see page 183), by Ilmari Tapiovaara, played the part of little brother to the Pirkka Chair, as well as to a matching table and bench, yet was no less delightful because of it.

What is most remarkable is how, in the right hands, the humble stool became an icon in its own right. Perhaps because of its inherent modesty of scale, the stool invited a sculptural treatment, as seen in Eero Aarnio's Mushroom Stool (1961, see p. 158) or Charles & Ray Eames's Time-Life Stool (1960, see p. 163). For sculptors Isamu Noguchi and Sori Yanagi, the stool offered the perfect opportunity to create a piece that was expressive and beautiful, as well as functional, as seen in the former's Rudder and Rocking Stools (1944 and 1955, see pp. 177 and 179) and the latter's Elephant and Butterfly Stools (1954 and 1956, see p. 187).

FOLLOWING SPREAD The Frank House, Fire Island, New York, USA, by Andrew Geller (restoration: Larson & Paul Architects), 1958

Mushroom Double Stools →

Eero Aarnio, 1961 Asko/Eero Aarnio Originals

Finnish designer Eero Aarnio made innovative and inventive use
of plastics in many of his most famous designs, such as the Ball
Chair of 1966 (see p. 15) and the Pastilli Chair of 1967 (see p. 121).
Yet Aarnio's Mushroom Stools were inspired by woven baskets
turned upside down, and made use of wicker, or rattan, one of
the most natural and traditional materials available. Also known
as the Juttujakkara, or Story Stool, the pieces were produced either
as single mushrooms or as taller double mushrooms (seen here).
Aarnio designed a matching lounge chair and ottoman using
wicker in similarly sculptural shapes. The Mushroom Stool is now
available from Eero Aarnio Originals.

← X-Leg Stool (Model 601)
Alvar Aalto, 1954 Artek

The most famous stools designed by Finnish architect Alvar Aalto date back to the 1930s and include the laminated birch L-Leg Stool (Model 60, 1933) produced by Artek, and the stools with plywood tops and tubular steel bases designed for the Paimio Sanatorium (1932, manufactured by O. Y. Huonekalu). However, the Finnish master also designed inventive mid-century stools, including this X-Leg, or 'Fan-Leg', Stool from 1954, manufactured by Artek using birch with a leather-coated seat. A round stacking version was released in the early 1950s alongside Aalto's X-Legs Table (see p. 244).

Ulmer Hocker Stools
Max Bill & Hans Gugelot, 1954 HfG/Zanotta/Vitra

Inspired by traditional drafting stools, designers Max Bill and Hans Gugelot created this simple but ingenious piece of lightweight furniture for the Hochschule für Gestaltung (HfG): the design school in Ulm, Germany, co-founded by Bill, who also worked on the architecture of the campus, completed in 1955. The stool, originally manufactured in the HfG's own workshops, comprises three planks of spruce forming a simple U-shaped stool, strengthened by a rounded cross-bracing rod. The stool is so strong that it can be tipped onto its side and still used as a low seat, but is also versatile enough to double as a side table or plinth. The Ulmer Hocker Stool could even be inverted, and the rounded rod used by students as a handle, to carry books and drawing materials around the campus. Zanotta began producing the piece in the 1970s under the name Sgabillo.

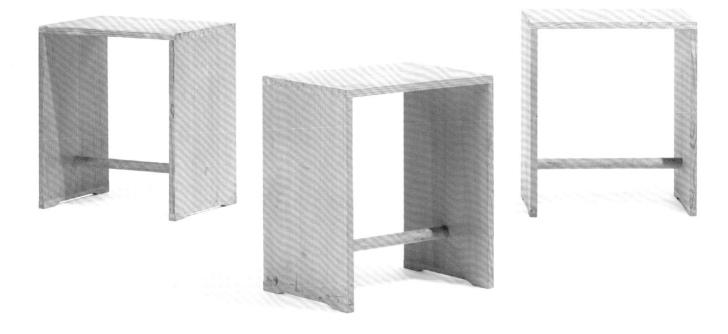

← Mezzadro Stool

Achille & Pier Giacomo Castiglioni, 1957 Zanotta

Along with a number of the Castiglioni brothers' most radical furniture and lighting designs, the 1957 Mezzadro Stool challenged convention, tradition and accepted wisdom. The stool is made of three interconnected but very different elements: a colourful tractor seat made of enamelled steel supported by a simple cantilevered steel bar, which is, in turn, stabilized by a wooden foot running at right angles to the bar. The surprising combination of such disparate ingredients within the triptych made the Mezzadro so decidedly avant-garde that it was not put into production until the 1970s, when it slotted into the super-strong strand of postmodern Italian design. The Mezzadro can be compared with the Castiglioni brothers' equally eye-catching Sella Stool (1957), which featured an adjustable bicycle seat set upon a slender pole anchored within a rocking base.

Birillo Bar Stools

Joe Colombo, 1970 Zanotta

The Birillo Bar Stool is one of a small collection of interrelated designs by Joe Colombo, which also includes a matching office chair. The pieces share the same design vocabulary and aesthetic, with each seat perched on a chunky stainless-steel stem set in a distinctive base that not only supports the seat above but also allows it to swivel by 360 degrees. The Birillo Bar Stool is the most famous piece in the series and features a leather or vinyl seat pad and a small button-shaped backrest. Characteristically for Colombo, the design and finish had a futuristic, space-age quality.

Toadstools (Trisse Stools)

Nanna Ditzel, 1962 Kolds Savvaerk/Snedkergaarden

In her furniture, Danish designer Nanna Ditzel was often drawn toward a combination of natural materials and biomorphic forms, as seen in her famous wicker Hanging Chair, or Egg Chair, of 1957, and her rounded rattan and ash Rattan Lounge Chair (1950, see p. 40). The same is true of her Toadstools, produced by Kolds Savvaerk in beech, along with a matching round table. Both pieces, and a complementary bar stool, are still made by Danish manufacturer Snedkergaarden, together with other key Ditzel designs.

Time-Life Stools

Charles & Ray Eames, 1960 Herman Miller

Made of solid, crafted walnut, the Time-Life Stool is an unusual
and distinctive piece in the extensive Eames portfolio. Also known as
the Walnut Stool or simply the Eames Stool, it was one of a number
of designs for the interiors of the Time & Life Building (1271 Avenue
of the Americas, 1960) designed by architect Wallace Harrison
and home to Time Inc, publishers of *Life* magazine among others.
While many designs by Eames famously made use of fresh materials
such as plywood, fibreglass and tubular steel, the Time-Life Stool
comprises a solid piece of turned timber, lending it weight and
substance. Other Eames designs for the building included the Time-
Life Chair and matching Ottoman (1960), as well as furniture for
La Fonda del Sol, the restaurant housed in the skyscraper (see p. 259).

Three-Legged Seiver Stool

Wharton Esherick, 1960 Bespoke

During the late 1950s and early 1960s, Pennsylvania-based artist, sculptor and furniture maker Wharton Esherick was asked to design the interiors and furniture for the Villanova home of Lawrence and Alice Seiver. The commission eventually resulted in a highly significant collection of original pieces, made at Esherick's Malvern studio, that included chairs, a sofa, tables and this three-legged stool in walnut and hickory. As with much of the Seiver furniture, rounded edges soften the piece and enhance the organic character of the design.

Bar Stools

Piero Fornasetti, *c.* 1960 Fornasetti Milano

Celebrated mid-century Milanese artist and designer Piero
Fornasetti was much admired for his extraordinarily imaginative
approach to interiors, furniture, ceramics and decorative art,
drawing on a multitude of references and infused with touches
of the surreal. These bar stools are a case in point, combining
a tapered, sculptural form with a rubber coating over the steel legs
and frame to create intriguing cactus-like bumps and undulations
over the surface of the metal. Around twenty of these stools were
made in the 1960s, including these black stools with a nylon cord
seat, but also a red version with a black leather seat.

Bar Stools

Piet Hein, 1971 Fritz Hansen

As evidenced by his famous Superellipse Table (1964, see p. 263), Piet Hein's furniture combines both art and science. The Danish designer studied not only the arts but also maths and physics, with many of his pieces having a solid foundation in terms of their expert engineering. This is true of Hein's Bar Stool for Fritz Hansen, which combines a cast-aluminium, circular base with chrome-plated steel rods supporting a leather-coated button seat. The needs of the user are carefully considered, with a neat ring of steel about a third of the way up to serve as the sitter's footrest.

Guldhoj Folding Stool →

Poul Hundevad, *c.* 1948 Poul Hundevad

Although not as well known as some of his Danish contemporaries, Poul Hundevad was a much-respected designer and cabinetmaker who – like Kaare Klint and Børge Mogensen – fused respectful references to the past with a devotion to modernity. This was expressed, in particular, through a concern for flexible and functional furniture, as seen in one of Hundevad's most famous designs: the Guldhoj Folding Stool. Inspired by an historic wooden piece found in a burial mound near the Danish town of Vamdrup, the stool was originally made by Hundevad's own workshops with an oak frame and leather seat. This light, portable and pared-down design fitted neatly with the trend toward versatile seating in the 1950s and 1960s.

Dot Stools

Arne Jacobsen, 1954 Fritz Hansen

During the 1950s and 1960s, a number of manufacturers and makers produced versions of stacking and nesting stools that could easily be moved from place to place or neatly stored away. One of the most delightful of these designs is Arne Jacobsen's Dot Stool, manufactured by Fritz Hansen, with three tubular steel legs supporting a round 'dot' of teak. As well as being light and portable, the stools can be stacked when not in use. Mid-century designers such as Florence Knoll also produced their own versions of compact, stacking stools (see p. 173).

Chandigarh College
of Architecture Stools

Pierre Jeanneret, *c.* 1960 Limited edition

Among the many pieces of furniture that Pierre Jeanneret designed for the new Indian administrative centre of Chandigarh was a series of stools primarily intended for academic use. They included teak and cane stools for Punjab University and these high seats for the Chandigarh College of Architecture. Three steel legs are reinforced by a strengthening ring toward the lower portion of the stool (which also serves as a footrest) and are topped by a thick teak disc. As well as these scholarly stools, Jeanneret designed sets of box stools and sewing stools for private residences at the new provincial capital.

Unicorn Stool

Vladimir Kagan, 1963 Limited edition

While Vladimir Kagan might be best known for his dynamic and sinuous sofas (see pp. 210–12), the New York–based designer also created a number of seductive stools during the 1950s and 1960s, which were – in their own way – also rich in imagination and ambition. These were characteristically sculptural pieces, even though smaller in scale than much of Kagan's other work, and included the Unicorn Stool of 1963. A miniature version of Kagan's Unicorn Chair and Sofa, the stool features the same distinctive V-shaped aluminium base but is teamed with a tractor-like seat, seen here with leopard-print upholstery.

PK91 Folding Stools

Poul Kjaerholm, 1961 E. Kold Christensen/Fritz Hansen

As one might expect of Danish master Poul Kjaerholm, his modern interpretation of a folding stool is elegant, refined and pared down to a point of pleasing purity. Instead of using wood for the frame of the stool, Kjaerholm opted for two overlapping rectangular frames of chrome-plated steel, which pivot neatly at the point of intersection. The lower portion of these rectangles forms the base, while the upper strips anchor the seat of leather or canvas, which is held taut when the stool is open. Kjaerholm twisted the side bars of the frame, enhancing its strength but also creating a delightful sculptural dimension to the piece, which is still produced today.

← Hairpin Stacking Stool

Florence Knoll, 1948 Knoll

Along with many other mid-century furniture companies, Knoll added a number of stools to its collection during the post-war period. Hans and Florence Knoll commissioned a webbed stool by Jens Risom (*c*. 1947) and a bar stool by Henry Kann (1947), as well as the Hairpin Stacking Stool designed by Florence Knoll herself. Named after its characterful 'hairpin' legs in enamelled bent metal, the stacking stool features a round wooden top in birch, with options introduced later for laminated seats in black, white or maple. Some years later, Knoll added Eero Saarinen's Pedestal Stool (1957) and Isamu Noguchi's Rocking Stool (1955, see p. 179) to its range.

Model 1306 Stools

Paul McCobb, 1954 Calvin

The prolific Paul McCobb designed a number of stools during the mid-century period, including the Model 1305 Stool produced as part of the Linear Group by Custom Craft (1951). This Model 1306 Stool, manufactured by Calvin, adopts a similar shape and form to its predecessor but is more refined in its choice of materials and upholstery. The legs are in brass, with X-shaped cross bracing, while the seat cushions are comfortably plump; both the 1305 and 1306 were produced with various options for upholstery fabrics and patterns.

Four Seasons Bar Stools

Ludwig Mies van der Rohe & Philip Johnson, 1958
Treitel Gratz/Knoll

The Four Seasons once occupied the ground floor of the Seagram
Building, the iconic Manhattan skyscraper designed by Ludwig
Mies van der Rohe and Philip Johnson, both of whom also worked
on the interiors of this landmark restaurant. The furniture at the
Four Seasons was largely designed by Mies and Johnson themselves,
along with colleagues and contemporaries such as Eero Saarinen.
The collection included this cantilevered bar stool used in the
Grill Room, manufactured with a chrome-plated steel base featuring
an integrated footrest and a square seat upholstered in leather.
Following the closure of the restaurant in 2016, the contents of
the Four Seasons were sold at auction.

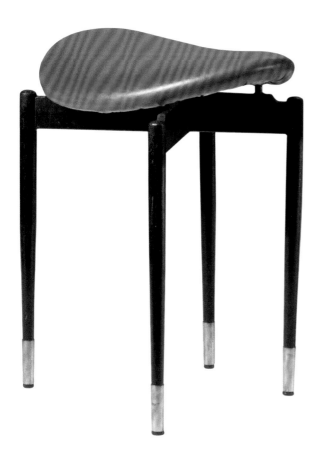

Lutrario Hall Stools

Carlo Mollino, 1959 Doro

During the late 1950s, entrepreneur Attilio Lutrario commissioned
the multi-talented Italian maestro Carlo Mollino to design the
interiors and furniture for his dance hall and cinema in Turin.
The Lutrario Roi Collection included armchairs with black
enamelled steel frames and red vinyl upholstery for the seat cushions
and backrests, along with these matching stools. Mollino's Lutrario
Hall Stools are suitably theatrical, with an X-shaped steel frame and
four legs tipped with brass, while the rounded ruby-red seat is
somewhat reminiscent of a luxurious saddle.

← Perch Stool Model 64940

George Nelson, 1964 Herman Miller

George Nelson and his associates designed a small number of stools for Herman Miller during the 1950s and 1960s, including the Pedestal Stool of 1954 (made to match the Pedestal tables, models 5451–5453), which could also be used as vanity units or jewelry cabinets. One of the most innovative Nelson stools is this Perch Stool, with an aluminium X-shaped base set on castors, and a ring-shaped footrest around the central stem that holds a Naugahyde-coated seat plus a slim upholstered cross bar to support the back. This highly flexible and adaptable design can be compared to Herman Miller's Roll-Back Chair (1976), designed by Ray Wilkes and intended principally for office use.

Model IN-22 Rudder Stool

Isamu Noguchi, 1944 Herman Miller/Vitra

'Everything is sculpture', Isamu Noguchi once said. 'Any idea without hindrance born into space, I consider sculpture.' Certainly, the designer and artist created unique pieces of furniture with their own abstract character and sculptural beauty. This included Noguchi's stools, which might be small but are full of invention, as is the case with the Model IN-22 Rudder Stool, sometimes known as the Fin Stool, with its combination of a fin-like wooden support, two steel legs and a lacquered timber seat. The design of the piece is closely related to Noguchi's IN-52 Rudder Coffee Table, released by Herman Miller in the same year.

← Model 86T Rocking Stool

Isamu Noguchi, 1955 Knoll

Just as Noguchi's Rudder Stool (see p. 177) is closely related to his Rudder Table, the sculptor's Rocking Stool is a sister piece to his Cyclone Dining Table for Knoll (see p. 287). Like the Cyclone, the Rocking Stool features a 'whirlwind' of overlapping and intersecting chrome-plated steel rods that form a supporting structural link between the round wooden base and top. The Rocking Stool originally came in either teak or walnut and in two different heights (85T and 86T), while the seat is indented thus creating a neat inversion of the rounded base plate.

Sauna Stool

Antti Nurmesniemi, 1952 G. Soderstrom

Finnish furniture and product designer Antti Nurmesniemi proved that it was more than possible to make a big impression with a stool. It helped that the piece in question was related to the sauna, which has long played an important part in Nordic lifestyles. Nurmesniemi was originally commissioned to create a sauna stool for the Palace Hotel in Helsinki and came up with a distinctive design in birch and teak, featuring a horseshoe-shaped seat supported by four legs. Both functional and beautifully crafted, with a pleasing organic character, the piece became iconic in its own right; an alternative but lesser-known version was also produced with a solid wooden button seat (shown here).

Les Arcs Stool

Charlotte Perriand, *c.* 1968 Limited edition/Cassina

Charlotte Perriand is much respected for her innovative and
experimental work with 20th-century materials and modern ways of
making. The designer's Model 308 Tripod Stool of 1952, for example,
combines steel legs with an oak seat and was produced by Ateliers
Jean Prouvé (and André Chetaille). Yet during the 1960s Perriand
created a number of stools for the French modern mountain resort
of Les Arcs and the Hôtel le Doron in Méribel that were more rustic
in character and referenced traditional Alpine stools. They included
an oak stool with a rush seat and this modern take on a milking stool,
with a circular pine seat supported by three fin-like legs. Also known
as the Tabouret Stool, the piece was recently reissued by Cassina.

Bar Stools

Gio Ponti & Gianfranco Frattini, *c.* 1960 Cassina

Various architectural and interior commissions for hotel projects
encouraged the evolution of multiple pieces of furniture designed
by the great Milanese polymath, Gio Ponti. They include sofas
(see p. 226), armchairs, beds (see p. 421) and these bar stools,
designed in conjunction with colleague and occasional collaborator
Gianfranco Frattini. These characterful pieces, made by Cassina,
have walnut frames, brass detailing and thick padded cushions
upholstered in dark vinyl. The stools pictured come from the Hotel
Parco dei Principi in Rome but were also put to good use at the
Royal Hotel in Naples.

Dansk Stool

Jens Quistgaard, *c.* 1970 Dansk

Danish artist and designer Jens Quistgaard trained in sculpture, silversmithing, ceramics and carpentry. After co-founding Dansk in 1954, he drew on these various skills and talents while exploring, in particular, the intrinsic character of his chosen materials. This teak tripod stool is evidence of his approach, where the texture and grain of the wood complement its sculptural outline. Much later, in 2004, Quistgaard designed the limited-edition Sculptor's Stool to mark a major retrospective of his work. Once again, his chosen material was teak.

Pirkka Stools

Ilmari Tapiovaara, 1956 Laukaan Puu

During the mid-1950s designer Ilmari Tapiovaara created a
collection of furniture for Finnish producer Laukaan Puu. The range
included a chair, table and bench, all made with dark and splayed
lacquered wooden legs combined with seats and tabletops consisting
of two conjoined and rounded pieces of pine. The same principles
apply to the Pirkka Stool, which is, arguably, one of the most
delightful pieces in the set. Here, the open seam between the twin
pine pieces that form the seat is widened toward the centre to create
a neatly integrated carry handle that makes the piece easily portable.

← Olesen Stools

Rud Thygesen, *c.* 1971 Magnus Olesen

Danish designer Rud Thygesen formed a long-standing and successful partnership with Johnny Sørensen in 1966 after the two met at the Danish School of Arts, Crafts and Design. Together, they designed furniture for Botium, Thams Møbler and others, although one of Thygesen's best-known pieces is this solo design for Magnus Olesen. The stool has a graphic effect with three laminated oak legs in a natural finish meeting a dark circle of lacquered timber, with a hole at the centre creating a donut-shaped seat. When not in use, the stools can be stacked neatly and stored away.

Egyptian Stool

Ole Wanscher, 1960 A. J. Iversen Snedkermester

Like his mentor, Kaare Klint, Danish designer Ole Wanscher was fascinated by historical influences. His furniture referenced English, Greek and Egyptian precedents, as seen in the Egyptian Stool produced by A. J. Iversen Snedkermester. This is Wanscher's much admired version of a traditional folding stool, made of either cherry wood, teak or rosewood folding legs and a simple leather seat. When closed, the rounded pieces of the conjoined base double as a carry handle. Wanscher's Egyptian Stool can be compared with other mid-century folding stools designed by Poul Hundevad (see p. 166), Poul Kjaerholm (see p. 171) and others.

Model JH539 Stools

Hans Wegner, 1953 Johannes Hansen

Danish master designer Hans Wegner created a small number
of stools during the post-war period. They included the Model
JH539 Stool of 1953, with its gently splayed teak legs and matching
dipped frame holding a seat made of woven cane; integrated handles
at either side of the piece make it easily portable. The design of the
stool had much in common with the Model PP120 Stool released a
year later by PP Møbler and initially intended as a companion piece
to the Papa Bear Chair (1951, see p. 109), serving as a footstool. The
PP120, still produced today, features a similar shape and form but
with an upholstered seat designed to match that of its parent piece.

Butterfly Stools

Sori Yanagi, 1956 Tendo Mokko/Vitra

Japanese designer Sori Yanagi famously combined biomorphic,
sculptural forms with an experimental approach to materials.
In 1954, Yanagi released his Elephant Stool, made of fibreglass,
followed two years later by one of the most recognizable and
seductive stools of the mid-century period: the Butterfly. Made
of two matching wings of rosewood plywood held together by
discreet brass fixings, the stool is delightful in both its simplicity
and its inviting shape. Some years later, in 1974, Yanagi released
a third stool known as the Monjiro, after the broad, rounded hat
worn by a character of the same name in a well-known Japanese
television series.

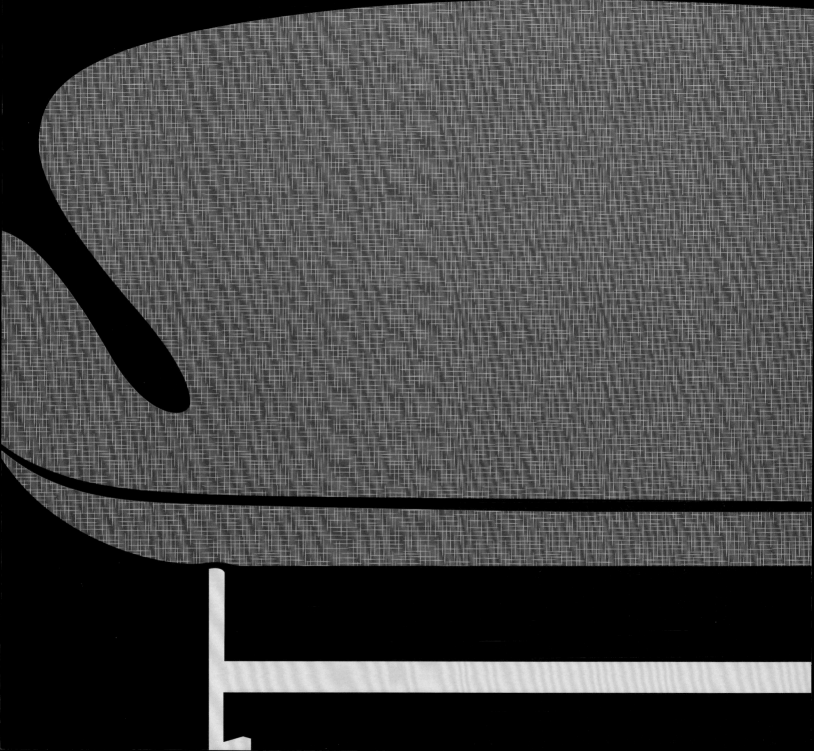

SOFAS

SOFAS
BENCHES
MODULAR SEATING

Sofa design was one of the key sectors in furniture production that experienced radical and profound changes during the mid-century period. Some of these changes overlapped with shifts within the world of the chair and seating in general, certainly as far as experimentation with materials was concerned. Yet, at the same time, post-war designers also began to rethink the shape, form and function of sofas and settees, while stepping away from traditional staples and ways of making.

Particularly well suited to the growing interest in sculptural and dynamic forms, sofa design often drew upon zoomorphic and biomorphic points of reference and inspiration. Some designers, such as Sergio Rodrigues, George Nakashima, Joaquim Tenreiro and Børge Mogensen, focused on largely natural and organic materials while pursuing innovative compositions and structural solutions. Peter Hvidt and Orla Mølgaard-Nielsen, for example, designed the Model FD 451 Sofa & Daybed using teak and cane (*c.* 1956, see p. 205), including fold-down armrests that transformed into pillow bases. In the UK, Lucian Ercolani concentrated on natural materials, particularly timber and bentwood, to create a fresh set of designs inspired by familiar favourites such as the Windsor Chair (see p. 203).

Other designers and architects were increasingly attracted by the fresh possibilities offered by plastics of various kinds, including fibreglass, moulded polystyrene and polyurethane foam. These materials presented opportunities to create pieces that were both lightweight and dynamic in form, often using complementary materials such as tubular steel or plywood to provide structure and rigidity while keeping the seating adaptable and easy to move.

Among those drawn to these innovative and malleable materials were influential designers Arne Jacobsen, Eero Saarinen and Marco Zanuso, who saw the chance to create organic and ergonomic shapes while making the most of these soft and flexible materials. The fact that a number of iconic mid-century chairs were also launched as sofas – such as Saarinen's Womb Chair and Settee (1950, see p. 231), Zanuso's Lady Chair and Sofa (1951, see p. 237) and Jacobsen's Swan Chair and

Sofa (1958, see p. 207) – points to the inherent adaptability of these designs and the materials used to produce them.

By the late 1950s and early 1960s, designers such as Pierre Paulin and Verner Panton were using moulded plastics, such as polystyrene and polyurethane, to create pioneering seating systems characterized by their eye-catching abstract forms and vivid use of pop-art colours in their upholstery and outer coats. Many of these pieces were also modular, including Archizoom's Safari system (1967, see p. 194), Verner Panton's Living Tower (1968, see p. 223) and Luigi Colani's Modular Seating Units (c. 1970, see p. 200). The most ambitious of these systems framed a space within a space, or a 'livingscape' as Archizoom described it, bringing a sense of drama and theatre to the home. The most avant-garde inventions had the look and feel of art installations as much as conventional pieces of furniture.

By the early 1960s, a new generation of sectional seating systems was coming into existence that offered consumers a growing level of flexibility in configuration and enjoyment. This was a period of rapid evolution in terms of adaptable seating systems of all kinds, evidenced by Mario Bellini's Camaleonda (1971, see p. 195) and Dieter Rams's 620 Chair Programme (1962, see p. 228), which offered the consumer numerous choices in terms of size and format.

Increasingly, producers and manufacturers provided buyers with a range of options when it came to the choice of sofa size, as well as upholstery materials and colourways. Poul Kjaerholm's PK31 series, for example, was designed in such a way that individual PK31 chairs could easily be combined to create two- or three-seater sofas (see p. 213). The ability to 'tailor' these options according to the needs of the end user, and of the room or space in question, formed an important element of the bespoke while still making best use of a standardized and readily available set of parts to ensure that these pieces remained relatively affordable.

FOLLOWING SPREAD The Miller House, Columbus, Indiana, USA, by Eero Saarinen (interiors: Alexander Girard), 1957

↑ Safari Sectional Seating

Archizoom Associati, 1967 Poltronova

The Florentine collective of young architects known as Archizoom
Associati described the Safari Sectional Sofa 'as an imperial piece
within the sordidness of your own home'. It was one of the earliest
'livingscapes' designed by the radical group, which was founded
in 1966, and made a characteristically bold statement in terms
of both its scale and vividly patterned upholstery. One of a number
of ambitious and flamboyant multi-sectional sofas that were
significant enough to become a room within a room, the piece is
composed of a combination of one- and two-seater units made from
fibreglass coated in foam padding and a patterned faux-fur covering.

↓ Camaleonda Modular Sofa

Mario Bellini, 1971 B&B Italia

The name Camaleonda, Italian architect Mario Bellini explained, came from a fusion of two words: 'camaleonte' ('chameleon'), and 'onda' ('wave'). It is an apt description of a unique modular sofa design that can adapt and change within multiple configurations, yet also creates a poetic and repeated rhythm within a space. The system is founded on standard units, made of polyurethane coated in fabric, which can easily be bound together using fitted carabiners; while cushions and armrests can also be hooked on in the same way. These individual units can be used as ottomans, single chairs or as part of a much larger seating system, according to the needs of the space; the Camaleonda was recently reissued by B&B Italia.

DS-600 Organic Sofa

Ueli Berger, Eleanora Peduzzi-Riva & Heinz Ulrich, 1972 de Sede

The DS-600 Organic Sofa produced by Swiss furniture company de Sede is one of the most ambitious and dramatic sectional seating systems of the late 1960s and early 1970s. Designed by artist Ueli Berger and his colleagues Eleanora Peduzzi-Riva and Heinz Ulrich, the DS-600 is composed of a series of slim leather-coated seating modules that combine in organic, fluid shapes with as many as forty units or more. Also known as the Tatzelwurm Sofa, after a mythical Alpine creature, it is still produced by de Sede and now includes armrest modules to bookend the piece.

Slat Bench →

Harry Bertoia, 1952 Knoll

Artist, sculptor and designer Harry Bertoia developed the Slat Bench at around the same time as his famous steel wire and rod chairs, also produced by Knoll. While the bench may not be as well known as Bertoia's Diamond Chair (1952, see p. 20), it has become a familiar classic in its own right and remains in production. Bertoia created two bases at either end of the piece using U-shaped steel rods combined with fused Y-shaped supports, which hold the wooden slats of the bench top. Vintage pieces tend to be in ash, while white- and black-finished slatted tops are produced today along with optional bench cushions.

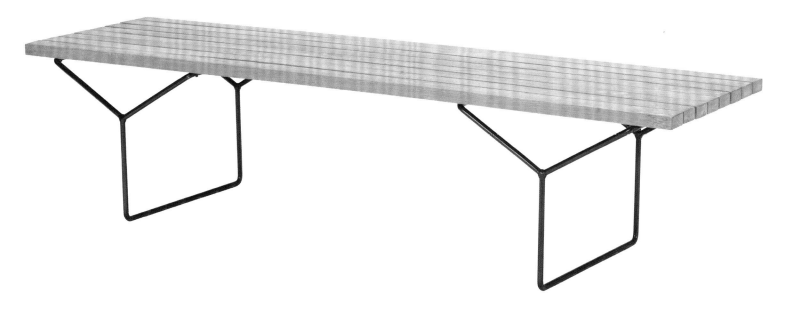

Settee

Lina Bo Bardi, *c.* 1950 Pau-Brasil

Italian-born, Brazilian-based architect Lina Bo Bardi designed
a number of chairs and sofas with a strong Franco-Italian influence
during the 1950s and 1960s. Among them is this sofa with a South
American peroba rosa timber frame featuring splayed legs and
cantilevered, or projecting, armrests, together with an upholstered
base and back cushions. Bo Bardi also designed a lounge chair in
a similar style, as well as a scissor-legged chair comparable to the
work of Pierre Jeanneret.

D70 Sofa

Osvaldo Borsani, 1954 Tecno

The D70 Sofa, designed by Osvaldo Borsani, was one of the key
early pieces that helped to launch Tecno, the Italian furniture
brand that Borsani co-founded with his twin brother, Fulgenzio.
First shown at the Milan Triennale in 1954, the D70 features a
rugged tubular-steel frame supporting an upholstered seat and
back in matching rectangular shapes and rounded edges.
The innovation lies in the way that the angle of the two planes can
be adjusted and folded flat, using a secure locking system, so that
the piece transforms into a sofa bed. A similar locking system
was applied to the P40 Reclining Lounge Chair, launched a year
later in 1955.

Modular Seating Units

Luigi Colani, *c.* **1970** Rosenthal Studio Line

Polymath designer Luigi Colani was one of a number of designers
who explored the idea of ambitious modular seating systems during
the late 1960s and early 1970s. Working with German furniture
producers Rosenthal, Colani developed this sectional system, which
creates a theatrical space within a space, almost like a stage set.
Sculpted and upholstered blocks of polyurethane foam, the modules
include seating units, corner units, floor cushions and headrests,
as well as small side tables, also designed by Colani.

Piumino Sofa

Jonathan De Pas, Donato D'Urbino & Paolo Lomazzi, 1970

Dall'Oca

Seating by the radical Milanese design collective DDL Studio and its members Jonathan De Pas, Donato D'Urbino and Paolo Lomazzi repeatedly challenged the idea of what seating should look like, as seen in their Blow and Joe chairs (1967 and 1970, see pp. 38–9). The Piumino Sofa presents the outline of a settee that looks as though it has been draped with a loose quilt (or 'piumino'). Yet this quilt is actually made of leather and fitted, although so rich in folds and texture that it lends the piece a character that is theatrical, somewhat subversive and organic all at the same time.

Model S-73 Sofa Compact

Charles & Ray Eames, 1954 Herman Miller/Vitra

Despite the extraordinary range and diversity of Charles & Ray Eames's portfolio, sofas played a relatively small part. The first and most successful of just three designs put into production is the Model S-73 Sofa Compact, comprising steel legs and frame, an upholstered polyurethane foam seat and a double cushion pad for the high back-rest, designed in such a way that it can be folded down for shipping. The S-73 was launched with a brief introductory film by the designers and targeted at both residential and commercial markets. Ten years later, in 1964, the couple launched a second armless sofa, the Model 3473 Sofa, which has much in common with the Sofa Compact and can be seen as a further refinement of the design.

Loveseat

Lucian Ercolani, 1956 Ercol/L. Ercolani

Ercol, the British furniture company founded by Italian-born designer and entrepreneur Lucian Ercolani, dates back to the 1920s but came to prominence during the 1950s with a collection of modern pieces designed by Ercolani himself. These designs, sometimes known as the Windsor Collection, were influenced by traditional pieces, such as the Windsor Chair and Shaker-style furniture, as well as mid-century reference points. Modern in feel and well made, many of Ercolani's designs featured solid timber frames and spindle backs, including his much-admired Loveseat of 1956. A version of this classic is still produced today.

Model 66303 Sofa

Alexander Girard, 1967 Herman Miller

During the 1950s and 1960s, designer Alexander Girard balanced
work for Herman Miller – directing the textile department and
contributing designs – with a range of other commissions. One of the
most ambitious of these was an ongoing project with Braniff Airways,
for whom he created a comprehensive corporate identity programme.
This included a 1965 range of airline lounge furniture developed in
conjunction with Herman Miller Special Projects Division (see pp.
52, 263 and 308). Two years later, Herman Miller put this collection
into production. One of the most accomplished designs is the Model
66303 Sofa, with an aluminium frame and curvaceous wing-like
armrests; Girard also designed the textiles for the upholstery.

Model FD 451 Sofa & Daybed

Peter Hvidt & Orla Mølgaard-Nielsen, *c.* 1956

France & Daverkosen

Danish designers Peter Hvidt and Orla Mølgaard-Nielsen largely favoured natural materials for their furniture, particularly wood but also leather and cane. Woven cane seats and backs feature on lounge chairs and sofas designed by Hvidt and Mølgaard-Nielsen, as well as on the Model FD 451 Sofa & Daybed, where, within a teak framework, braided cane is used for the combined side panels and armrests. These panels can be folded down and a cushion placed on the cane to serve as a pillow when the FD 451 is used as a daybed. A pair of the sofas was sometimes used in a L-shaped formation with a matching coffee table placed at the junction of the two pieces.

Series 3300 Sofa

Arne Jacobsen, 1956 Fritz Hansen

During the late 1950s, Danish architect and designer Arne Jacobsen was invited to work on the architecture and interiors of the SAS Royal Hotel in Copenhagen. Characteristically, Jacobsen involved himself in every aspect of the project including the furniture, designing a series of mid-century icons along the way. The Series 3300 Sofa was influenced by an earlier design created for the architect's own home and features a lightweight but robust tubular steel frame with matching upholstered seat, armrests and back, with an option of a two- or three-seater version. Producer Fritz Hansen also offered a choice of leather or fabric upholstery.

Swan Sofa

Arne Jacobsen, 1958 Fritz Hansen

As with the Egg Chair (1958, see p. 56), the Swan Sofa and Chair –
also designed for the SAS Royal Hotel – combine modern material
with biomorphic form. These designs make the most of the
malleability of injection-moulded polystyrene to create sculptural
shapes, yet the resulting design is almost organic in character
and ergonomic in its seating arrangement. The Swan Sofa features
an aluminium base, a high back and distinctive swan-like wings
that push outward to provide the armrests. Often seen in vibrantly
coloured upholstery, the Swan Sofa was originally designed for
the SAS Royal Hotel's restaurant.

Model 705/FJ41 Poet Sofa

Finn Juhl, 1941 Niels Vodder/House of Finn Juhl

Sofas designed by Danish master Finn Juhl are characterized
by their sculptural forms and, in particular, their distinctive backs
that wrap and envelop the sitter. The Poet Sofa is arguably the
most famous of these pieces, with its soft, rounded, upholstered
form and simple beechwood legs lending the design an elegance
comparable to the work of such contemporaries as Hans Wegner
and Arne Jacobsen. Although designed in 1941, the sofa only
came to prominence during the late 1950s when a well-known
cartoonist used the piece as a suitably refined and comfortable
setting for a poet seeking inspiration.

Baker Sofa

Finn Juhl, 1951 Baker Furniture

Among the many Juhl sofas produced in Denmark by Niels Vodder were the NV45 Sofa of 1945 and a larger version of his famous Chieftain Chair (1949, see p. 62), both with teak frames and upholstered leather seats and backs. Then, during the early 1950s, Juhl began designing pieces for American manufacturer Baker Furniture, including this eye-catching sofa. A lacquered walnut frame supports the seat, which rises to form the lower portion of the backrest as well as the armrests, while a separate and rounded wing comprises the upper portion of the backrest. The curving ends of the upper wing cradle and protect the occupants of the sofa, while adding a dynamic and biomorphic quality to the piece.

↓ Serpentine Sofa

Vladimir Kagan, 1950 Kagan-Dreyfuss

Given his particular love of dynamic, fluid and sculptural forms, Vladimir Kagan was very well suited to the design of sofas. His distinctive and instantly recognizable aesthetic is most famously seen in this Serpentine Sofa, designed as an engaging antidote to straight-backed linear sofas. A focal point in itself, it was originally designed for two art collectors who wanted central seating that would allow the walls of a room to be devoted to art alone. The Serpentine is made with sculpted foam rubber, soft upholstery and recessed hardwood base supports; later variations on the design explore alternative lengths and backrest formations.

Floating Seat & Back Sofa ↑

Vladimir Kagan, c. 1952 Kagan-Dreyfuss

Following on from the Serpentine Sofa (left), Kagan explored ideas for other seating solutions that combined fluid forms and biomorphic influences. One of the most enticing of these subsequent designs is this curvaceous Floating Seat, with a sculptural oak framework reminiscent of the zoomorphic furniture produced by Italian designer Carlo Mollino. The upholstered kidney-shaped seat is complemented by the soft floating pad of the backrest, providing another standalone statement comparable to the Serpentine.

Crescent Sofa

Vladimir Kagan, *c.* **1970** Vladimir Kagan Designs

With the Crescent Sofa of the early 1970s, Kagan stepped toward a
pop-art sensibility, although the love of sinuous dynamism seen in his
earlier work still shines through. Combining a rounded brass plinth
with a lipstick-red padded seat and back, the Crescent Sofa speaks of
glamour and seductive intent. This ruby-red version can be compared
with Studio 65's famous Bocca Sofa, first produced by Gufram in
1970 (see p. 232).

PK31/3 Sofa

Poul Kjaerholm, 1958 E. Kold Christensen/Fritz Hansen

The PK31 series, designed by Poul Kjaerholm, was a unique kind
of modular system where the end user could order a range of seating
options. The foundation of the range was the PK31/1 Lounge Chair,
with its chrome-plated steel frame, down-filled cushions and wood-
framed side panels, upholstered in leather. Kjaerholm designed
the chair in such a way that the panels could simply be omitted as
required and the units locked together to create a two-seater sofa
(PK31/2) or the three-seater version pictured (PK31/3). Special-order
versions by E. Kold Christensen and, later, Fritz Hansen increased
the number of units even further. Kjaerholm's wall-mounted PK26
seating system of 1956 was also designed so that it could be produced
in various sizes and configurations.

Florence Knoll Model 1206 Sofa

Florence Knoll, 1954 Knoll

While Florence Knoll and her husband, Hans, commissioned furniture from many of the figureheads of mid-century design, they sometimes found gaps in their growing collection. Florence Knoll would often design these 'fill-in pieces' herself, including a series of sofas and settees created as staples rather than statements. One of the most successful of these is the Model 1206 Lounge Collection Sofa, now known simply as the Florence Knoll Sofa. With a crisp rectangular chrome-plated steel framework, slim legs and tailored cushions supported by the matching upholstered base and armrests, the sofa remains a much-loved and refined classic, available in three-seater and two-seater versions.

Fredericia Sofa

Børge Mogensen, 1963 Fredericia

Like his mentor, Kaare Klint, Danish designer Børge Mogensen
explored the fusion of modernity and tradition in much of his
elegantly crafted furniture. This was true of his sofas and settees,
such as his Spoke Back Sofa of 1945 for Fritz Hansen and other
post-war designs. His Fredericia sofas, including this 1963 model,
tend to combine oak frames with bases, armrests and cushions
upholstered in leather, offering seating that is comfortable,
practical and also organic in its touch and tone.

Nakai Sofa

Taichiro Nakai, 1954 Esposizione Permanente Mobili

Japanese artist and designer Taichiro Nakai showed his work at
the 'Concorso Internazionale del Mobile' in Cantù, Italy, during
the 1950s with pieces that included bookcases, chairs, coffee
tables and this rare standalone sofa. Awarded a prize by the Cantù
competition jury, the sofa has a sinuous and biomorphic form
comparable to the work of Vladimir Kagan in America. Sculptural
in its intent, such statement pieces have attracted fresh attention
among collectors in recent years.

Conoid Bench

George Nakashima, *c.* 1965 Nakashima Studio

Esteemed woodworker and craftsman George Nakashima designed
a number of sofas and settees during the mid-century period,
including a Model 250 Spindle Sofa for Widdicomb, manufactured
in the late 1960s. One of Nakashima's most engaging designs
produced by his own workshop in New Hope, Pennsylvania, is this
Conoid Bench. The piece is enriched by the striking juxtaposition
of an American black walnut seat slab, floating on slim tapered legs,
and the spindle back reminiscent of more traditional Shaker designs,
as well as a number of other sofas created by Nakashima himself.

Nelson Platform Bench Model 4692

George Nelson, 1947 Herman Miller/Vitra

Prolific, inventive and ambitious, George Nelson sought to develop
a rounded collection of Herman Miller furniture designed 'to meet
fully the requirements for modern living'. His own products for
the firm, for which he was director of design, included many sofas,
settees and benches, such as the Platform Bench (also known as
the Slat Bench). The piece is intentionally multi-purpose, ready
to serve not only as seating but also as a low table or a cabinet
plinth, with a choice of folding legs (Model 4690) or fixed (Model
4692), as well as various lengths. The piece can be compared with
Harry Bertoia's Slat Bench for Knoll (1952, see p. 196) and was
re-introduced to the market by Vitra during the 1990s.

Marshmallow Sofa Model 5670

George Nelson & Irving Harper, 1956 Herman Miller/Vitra

The Marshmallow Sofa has to be one of the most instantly
recognizable pieces of furniture ever created by George Nelson,
who worked on the design in conjunction with associate Irving
Harper. Designed in the mid-1950s, the piece seems to anticipate
the pop-art/op-art culture of the 1960s with its bold use of geometry
and (in most variations) a vivid use of colour. Eighteen round and
padded discs form the seat and back of the sofa, supported on a
lightweight steel frame. As well as coming in multiple colour options,
the Naugahyde-coated marshmallows were originally designed
to be interchangeable so the consumer was given the opportunity to
get involved in the artistic composition of the piece. A larger version,
better suited to commercial or office use, was also produced.

Sling Sofa Model 6833 →

George Nelson, 1964 Herman Miller

During the 1960s Nelson continued working on ranges of sofas, settees and seating systems for Herman Miller, which included his Tandem Shell Seating of 1963 aimed at the office, airport or waiting room. Ideal for the home and one of Nelson's most elegant and refined designs, the Sling Sofa was produced a year later, with options for either a three-seat (Model 6832) or four-seat version (Model 6833). The sofa features a chrome-plated, wrap-around tubular steel frame and sling seats with leather-upholstered cushions, reminiscent of the luxurious bucket seats seen in sports cars of the period.

← Freeform Model IN-70 Sofa & Ottoman

Isamu Noguchi, 1948 Herman Miller/Vitra

While Isamu Noguchi's sculptural IN-50 Coffee Table (1944, see p. 287) might be better known, this sinuous sofa has a similarly dynamic quality. The Freeform Model IN-70 Sofa and matching ottoman (Model IN-71) feature upholstered seats with a kidney-shaped profile and modest birch legs, while the sofa offers a rounded back support that runs along part of its length. The piece is one of a number of biomorphic sofa designs comparable to the work of Vladimir Kagan, Taichiro Nakai and others.

← Living Tower

Verner Panton, 1968 Herman Miller/Fritz Hansen/Vitra

Danish designer Verner Panton repeatedly challenged every convention of furniture design and furniture making. He rejected traditional forms and principles, creating fusion furniture and seating systems that went beyond a chair or a sofa. There were modular systems for Verpan, such as Easy (1963), Cloverleaf (1969) and Welle (1969), yet it was the Living Tower of 1968, originally produced by Herman Miller and then Fritz Hansen, that provided a piece of pop-art abstraction that also functioned as a stage for sitting, reclining and relaxing. The piece is made from two conjoined parts: a birch plywood border forms a rectangular frame around moulded and upholstered sinuous foam shapes that create platforms for perching and sitting.

Model 865 Sofa

Ico & Luisa Parisi, 1955 Cassina

Italian designer Ico Parisi was a polymath who worked, variously, as an architect, artist, photographer, film-maker and stage designer. During the 1950s and 1960s he, along with his wife Luisa, concentrated on furniture design and produced a series of pieces for Cassina in particular. Among them was the elegant Model 812 Sofa of 1953, followed by this, the Model 865, with its distinctive framework of overlapping steel rods forming a base and back support for the rounded seat and backrest, upholstered here in mohair.

ABCD Sofa →

Pierre Paulin, 1968 Artifort

French designer Pierre Paulin initially trained as a sculptor at the Ecole Camondo in Paris. Many of his most famous furniture designs have a decidedly sculptural quality, exploring rounded forms, dynamic shapes and ergonomic curves. As well as his iconic chairs (see p. 82), Paulin created a series of sofas for Dutch company Artifort during the 1960s and 1970s, including the ABCD Sofa, with its undulating, wave-like seat and back defining sunken seating positions within the outline of the piece. Characteristically, the ABCD was produced in vivid colours, often expressed in upholstered stripes of complementary tones for the elongated front, middle and back sections of the sofa.

← Multimo Sofa Model 282

Pierre Paulin, 1969 Artifort

Like his Danish contemporary Verner Panton (see p. 223), Paulin combined sculptural forms, an experimental approach to structure and pop-art influences. Among Paulin's colourful and eye-catching designs for Artifort were the Nest Sofa (1962), a more angular sofa version of his famous Mushroom Chair (1962), and the Multimo of 1969, featuring a combination of polyurethane foam and a metal substructure to create a crescent-shaped seat and a set of six fingers that form four backrests and two armrests. Artifort also produced a rare elongated version of the Multimo with a snake-like twist, seven backrests and armrests at either end.

Cité Cansado Bench

Charlotte Perriand, 1958 Négroni and Métal Meuble for
Galerie Steph Simon

The Cité Cansado in Mauritania was a new mining town, developed
using prefabricated houses by Maison LWD with assistance from
Jean Prouvé. Charlotte Perriand was asked to design the interiors
of these 'Maisons du Sahara' and created a number of pieces
of furniture especially for the project, including this elegant bench
with a slatted mahogany platform on a shallow steel frame and
legs. The bench features one long seat cushion and two backrest
cushions; an integrated drawer at one end floats upon the platform.
Other Cité Cansado pieces included the Bloc Bahut (see p. 329).

Diamond Sofa →

Gio Ponti, 1953 Cassina

For an architect, designer and editor with such a rich and varied
portfolio of work, it is extraordinary that Gio Ponti also managed to
design such a broad range of furniture, including a selection of sofas
and benches. One of the most characterful of Ponti's seating solutions
is the Diamond Sofa, with its distinctive almost triangular armrests
that bookend the piece. With tapered brass legs and upholstered in
faux leather, this piece is from the Milanese home of Ponti's daughter,
Lisa, an artist, critic and editor. The Diamond Sofa featured in the
interiors of Gio Ponti's Villa Arreaza in Caracas, Venezuela, while
a matching armchair was also produced by Cassina.

Parco dei Principi Sofa →

Gio Ponti, 1964 Cassina

A number of Ponti's furniture designs emerged from specific
architectural and interiors commissions, including hotels such as the
Parco dei Principi in Sorrento and its sister hotel in Rome. The Rome
project, completed in 1964 and where Ponti worked with an existing
building, encompassed 200 guest rooms, bars, restaurants and other
amenities that required a range of furniture and furnishings, including
this sofa. With its splayed legs and triangular armrests, the piece
can be seen as an evolution of ideas explored in Ponti's Diamond Sofa
(opposite top), designed a decade earlier. Here, white faux leather
is used for the armrests while the seat and back are in a moss-green
fabric, tying in with the original colour scheme of the interiors.

620 Chair Programme

Dieter Rams, 1962 Vitsoe

Dieter Rams's interest in modular systems carried through to his
work on product design for Braun and his furniture for Vitsoe,
including his 606 Universal Shelving System (1960, see p. 385).
Similarly, the 620 Chair Programme sought to provide a standardized
set of components that could be used to assemble a single chair
or to create longer sofas made up of two or three combined seating
units. The base of the chair is made with birch ply overlaid with
rubberized-coir moulding, while the arms and backs are in fibreglass
and the cushions upholstered in leather. The system is still available,
but in a wider choice of upholstery and colourways.

Tonico Sofa

Sergio Rodrigues, 1963 Oca

Along with a number of Sergio Rodrigues's other instantly
recognizable chairs, his Tonico Lounge Chair has a throne-like
quality. This impression is, naturally, multiplied in the Tonico
Sofa, which also features a jacaranda frame and a high back with
vertical supports topped by roundels. Made in both two- and
three-seater versions, the Tonico has three substantial types of
cushions: the seat cushions, a line of chunky round bolsters and
an elongated ribbon bolster serving as a headrest and held in place
by loops wrapped around the roundels. The upholstery came in
various options, including a choice of colourful fabric or leather.

← Womb Settee & Ottoman

Eero Saarinen, 1950 Knoll

'A great number of people have never really felt comfortable and secure since they left the womb', said Eero Saarinen, developing one of his most famous designs, the Womb Chair, to reassure them. Using polyester reinforced with fibreglass, Saarinen created a 'cup-like' shell seat coated with soft padding and supported on tubular steel legs. The chair was launched by Florence and Hans Knoll in 1948. Two years later, while working on the vast campus of the General Motors Technical Center in Warren, Michigan, Saarinen developed the Womb Settee and a matching ottoman. Like its predecessor, the sofa combines comfort, security and a sculptural form.

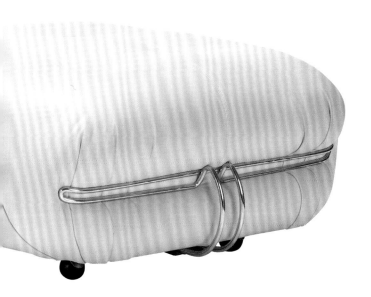

Soriana Sofa & Ottoman

Afra & Tobia Scarpa, 1969 Cassina

Husband and wife design team Afra and Tobia Scarpa developed a number of sofas during the 1960s and 1970s, including the Bastiano Sofa (1962) for Gavina/Knoll. Seven years later, the Scarpas created this distinctive Soriana Sofa (and matching lounge chair and ottoman), which won a prestigious Compasso d'Oro award for design in 1970. Low-slung, rounded and most commonly upholstered in leather, the Soriana features bands of chrome-plated tubular steel that pinch and hold the leather in place. Viewed from the front, the steelwork of the Soriana – which was produced in various lengths – has the look of a car grille or bumper. The piece has been reissued with a fresh choice of upholstery materials and colours.

Bocca Sofa

Studio 65, 1970 Gufram/Edra

A number of artists and designers explored the idea of a lipped
sofa over the course of the 20th century. Salvador Dalí's Mae West
Lips Sofa of 1936 was originally designed for artist Edward James,
while Jean-Michel Frank designed a 'Schiaparelli pink' version for
the Paris-based fashion designer. Studio 65 purposefully referenced
and reworked these earlier lip, or 'bocca', sofas in their superlight
polyurethane version coated in a vivid red jersey fabric, released
by Gufram. The Bocca became a pop-art classic in its own right,
sitting well with the rise of abstract imagery and iconography seen
during the period.

Cane Sofa

Joaquim Tenreiro, *c.* 1958 Tenreiro Móveis e Decorações

Brazilian master designer and craftsman Joaquim Tenreiro famously combined a love of indigenous hardwoods with a lightness of touch. This can be seen at its height in a loosely related collection of jacaranda and cane chairs and sofas of the 1950s and 1960s, which feature beautifully finished timber frames and woven cane seats and backs. Prime among them is this Cane Sofa from around 1958, seating three; there was also a matching armchair produced at the same time. Tenreiro created a series of pleasing variations on this thematic combination of jacaranda and cane, including dining chairs and bedroom chairs.

Model AP34/3 Sofa

Hans Wegner, 1957 A. P. Stolen

Danish master Hans Wegner is well known for his iconic mid-century chairs (see pp. 105–11), but he also designed a number of sofas for a handful of producers during the mid-century period. They included the Model GE236/3 Sofa for Getama (*c*. 1960), the Model JH803 Sofa (1970) for Johannes Hansen and this Model AP34/3 Sofa manufactured by A. P. Stolen. Six slim chrome-plated steel legs support the slanted base and seat cushions, with the armrests echoing this angular form, while a triptych of three high cushions support the back; upholstery options included leather or fabric. The Model JH800 sofa and chairs also used an angular profile.

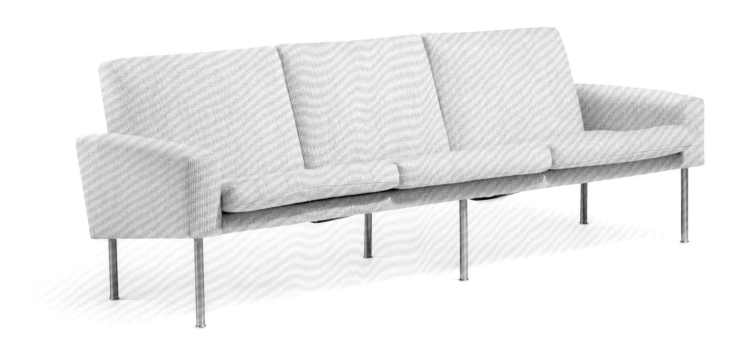

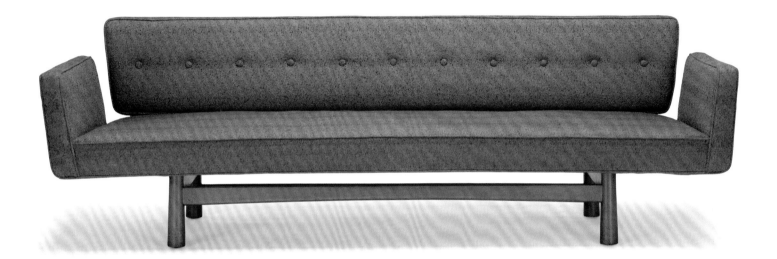

Model 5316 Sofa

Edward Wormley, 1953 Dunbar

Edward Wormley's long relationship with Dunbar, for whom he served as chief designer and director of design, resulted in sofas of all kinds. There were sectional sofas, 'Tête-à-Tête' settees and updates of traditional designs, such as the Model 5407 Sofa (1954) that suggested a pared-down, modern version of a Chesterfield. In terms of composition, one of Wormley's most delightful designs is the Model 5316 Sofa, in which a modest mahogany framed plinth supports an elongated, upholstered seat and back that cantilevers away from the plinth to give the impression of a floating form. Visually, the way that the armrests at either end splay outward slightly to create a subtle sense of separation from the long backrest enhances the sense of lightness.

Presidencial Sofa ↓

Jorge Zalszupin, 1959 L'Atelier

Polish-born, São Paulo–based designer Jorge Zalszupin created
a number of distinctive sofas and benches for L'Atelier, his Brazilian
furniture company. The most famous of these is the Presidencial
Sofa, with its rounded plywood base and matching vertical strips
of rosewood forming the backrest, all supported by a steel frame.
The slatted back of the sofa (and the matching lounge chair) is a
particular delight but often covered by an enveloping set of cushions
and padding that can disguise the sculptural beauty of the piece.

Lady Sofa ↑

Marco Zanuso, 1951 Arflex

During the 1950s, Milanese designer Marco Zanuso worked with Arflex on the design of a series of chairs and sofas, including the Martingala Settee (c. 1954) and the Sleep-O-Matic Sofa (1951), which transformed into a double bed. One of Zanuso's greatest successes with Arflex was the Lady Lounge Chair and Sofa of 1951, using foam rubber to help create the rounded forms of the upholstered seats, backs and kidney-shaped armrests, sitting on splayed metal legs. The Lady Chair won a Gold Medal at the Milan Triennale of 1951, while the sofa was introduced that same year, offering three seats within a crescent-shaped arrangement; a matching ottoman was also produced by Arflex.

TABLES

DINING TABLES
COFFEE TABLES
OCCASIONAL TABLES

One of the most striking aspects of mid-century modern furniture, and tables in particular, is the depth and breadth of design innovation. The 1950s to 1960s was an era of extraordinary evolution and change, with consumers offered an enticing array of choices when it came to shape and form, function and finish. The table was radically reinvented during the mid-century period with every aspect of traditional furniture making questioned and re-evaluated. Modern materials such as plywood, bentwood, tubular steel and Plexiglas were widely drawn upon to create fresh and original designs, yet at the same time natural materials – especially wood and stone – were also explored to the full within a decidedly mid-century aesthetic, which was dynamic, playful and sculptural.

Looking at table design in more detail, as seen over the following pages, a number of key themes begin to emerge, and one of the most important of these is flexibility. Producers such as Knoll, Herman Miller, Fritz Hansen and others began offering consumers a growing number of choices in terms of size and finish, while designers also developed ideas for tables that could grow or shrink, extend and retract, fold or nest, according to the needs of the end user.

Adaptable table designs of one kind or another were explored by mid-century designers in many different parts of the world, but particularly in Scandinavia and the USA, as evidenced by pieces by Alvar Aalto, Arne Jacobsen, Mogens Koch, Børge Mogensen, George Nelson and Florence Knoll. Similarly, nesting tables became a mid-century favourite, seen here in designs by Poul Kjaerholm, Grete Jalk, Gianfranco Frattini and others. Such pieces offered flexibility in the way they might be used in a space yet could also easily be collected up and stored away.

Partly with flexibility in mind, many mid-century designers explored the theme of lightness, or weightlessness, which helped to make tables more portable. Yet, just as importantly, there was also a desire to reduce the overall visual impact of such pieces of furniture in comparison with their 19th-century counterparts, with mid-century tables offering a degree of discretion as well as elegance and practicality. This connects with the way that designers such as Eero Saarinen sought to reduce the familiar clutter of multiple table legs through an intelligent process of simplification that sometimes resulted in a single supporting stem, as in his famous Pedestal Table (1957, see p. 293). Others opted for two legs, or three, as seen in the profusion of tripod tables during the period.

Certainly, the structure, form and function of bases, legs and pedestals were a key focus of innovation during the post-war era for Jean Prouvé, Pierre Jeanneret, Isamu Noguchi and many more. In some cases, as seen in Noguchi's Model IN-50 Coffee Table (1944, see p. 287) or Carlo Mollino's Arabesco Table (1949) and Model 1114 Coffee Table (*c.* 1950, see p. 281), glass tabletops allowed the sculptural form of the base to remain visible.

While glass was widely used for tabletops during the 1950s and 1960s, enhancing their sense of lightness, there was also a counter movement of more monumental designs, often by architects. Among these are Gae Aulenti's Jumbo Coffee Table produced by Knoll (1965, see p. 248) and Angelo Mangiarotti's famous Eros series of marble tables (1971 onward, see p. 277), still produced today by Agapecasa.

FOLLOWING SPREAD The Strick House, Santa Monica, California, USA, by Oscar Niemeyer (restoration: Michael Boyd), 1964

X-Legs Table (Model X800)

Alvar Aalto, 1954 Artek

The majority of Alvar Aalto's furniture designs were produced by Artek, the company that the architect co-founded in 1935 and which still manufactures many of his best-known pieces today. The range of Artek tables includes this X-Legs Table originally designed in 1954 and made of laminated birch and beech. The rounded profile of the legs as they meet the tabletop softens the piece while avoiding sharp corners. Also known as the Fan-Legged Table, it was produced in a choice of sizes, and a matching stool (see p. 159) was designed around the same time.

H-Leg Dining Table (Model H90)

Alvar Aalto, 1956 Artek

Many pieces of furniture created by Finnish master architect and designer Alvar Aalto feature a degree of flexibility, allowing them to be used in various ways. This was true, in particular, of the dining and occasional tables Aalto designed from the 1930s onward. Among his many table designs are a number of circular pieces, including the Model 91 Table of 1933 with an integrated lazy Susan at its centre. The H-Leg design of 1956 came in both rectangular and circular versions, with the Model H90 produced by Artek in birch. The table has an additional central leaf that extends the piece, creating an elongated oval and offering another example of the malleability of many of Aalto's designs.

Model TL2 Table

Franco Albini, *c.* 1950 Poggi

The coffin-lid shape of the Model TL2 tabletop is highly distinctive, and Franco Albini's ingenious design for Ezio and Roberto Poggi is also demountable. Sometimes known as the Cavaletto Table, the piece features X-shaped legs at either end that allow it to be folded down, while lightweight steel struts add extra support. The TL2 was produced in mahogany, rosewood or walnut, while the TL3 manufactured at around the same time features a similar tabletop but with a fixed set of four tapered legs; a circular version of the TL3 was also made available.

Cicognino Model TN6 Tables

Franco Albini, *c.* 1952 Poggi

The birdlike and biomorphic profile of Albini's Cicognino ('little stork') Table makes it one of the designer's most playful and expressive pieces. Yet this lightweight occasional table was also designed with function in mind, and the long bird's-neck handle makes it a simple matter to move the table from place to place. Made of oak, the piece has three legs, with the tripod solution somewhat reminiscent of Albini's Mitragliera ('machine gun') Floor Lamp of 1938, while his Model CR20 Cart (1958, see p. 307) also features three supports with castors, rather than four.

Jumbo Coffee Table

Gae Aulenti, 1965 Knoll

As well as designing buildings such as the Musée d'Orsay in Paris, Italian architect Gae Aulenti created interiors, furniture and lighting over the course of a long and successful career. One of her most famous and enduring designs is the Jumbo Coffee Table produced by Knoll in the mid-1960s and made of stone with a set of elephantine cluster legs. Produced in a choice of three different marbles, the Jumbo is a monumental anchor piece, creating a strong foundation for room settings. The rigid architectural character of the piece contrasts with the relative simplicity of Aulenti's own Tavolo Con Ruote (1980) produced by Fontana Arte and consisting of only a transparent plate of glass and four castors.

Model 103 Tripod Tables

Hans Bellmann, 1947 Knoll

Swiss architect and designer Hans Bellmann began experimenting with designs for a demountable Colonial Table during the early 1940s, initially produced by Möbelfabrik Horgenglarus in Switzerland. A few years later, in 1947, Knoll began producing two versions of what was now known as the Tripod Table, with a detachable round top in birch or white laminate supported by folding tripod legs. The smaller and more popular version of the Tripod was known as the Model 103 occasional table, with a diameter of 61 cm (24 in.), while the Model 114 was slightly larger at 91.5 cm (36 in.).

Model 302 Popsicle Dining Table

Hans Bellmann, 1947 Knoll

The beauty of Bellmann's Tripod Table design (see p. 249) lay in the fact that it was portable, lightweight and easy to fold down and store away. But Bellmann also developed a variation on the theme in his Model 302 Popsicle Dining Table, which features a fixed three-legged base and a tabletop in birch or white laminate. The distinctive tripartite base can be compared with other mid-century designs in a similar vein, such as Jean Prouvé's Guéridon Table designed in *c.* 1941.

Model 1000 Dining Table

Hans Bellmann, *c.* 1947 Wohnbedarf

Bellmann's predilection for unusual and sculptural table bases was
not only expressed in his circular tables but also in this rectangular
table produced in the designer's native Switzerland and marketed
by Wohnbedarf. The table was made of either a naturally finished
oak timber top or a dark laminate, in an ash surround. In either case,
the chief aesthetic and structural interest lies in the base, where a
splayed quartet of tapered legs and struts are supported by a central
cross brace.

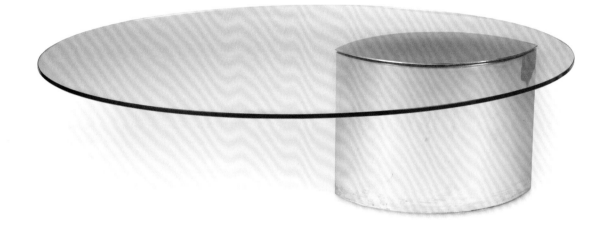

Lunario Table

Cini Boeri, 1972 Knoll

The Lunario Table by Italian architect and designer Cini Boeri is one
of many futuristic mid-century pieces that references, one way or
another, the space race and the final frontier. Her pared-down design
concept for the Lunario juxtaposed two elements: a polished steel
base – which looks like a disjointed stage, or segment, from a rocket
– supporting a cantilevered sheet of moon-shaped glass. The tables
come in a range of heights and dimensions. Boeri was also asked
to design several sofas for Knoll and create the interiors for a number
of the company's showrooms.

Spider-Leg Coffee Table

Carlo de Carli, *c.* 1955 Limited edition

Like his chairs, sofas, beds and other pieces of furniture, the tables
devised by Milanese architect and designer Carlo de Carli are
characteristically expressive and sculptural. One of his most striking
and biomorphic designs is this coffee table, with three legs and a
set of spindle arms reaching upward to support a circular glass top.
Often referred to as the Spider Table or Spider-Leg Table, the
much-imitated design comes in a variety of wooden finishes and
with varying degrees of decoration, which sometimes detract from
the striking form of the piece itself.

Model 180 Dining Table

Carlo de Carli, *c.* 1963 Sormani

Among the larger tables created by Carlo de Carli, this design,
produced by Sormani, is one of the most seductive and engaging.
The Model 180 is commonly described as a dining table, but can
also be used as an elegant centrepiece with its circular rosewood top.
The most expressive element is the base, with a sculpted profile that
resembles a layered vase made on a potter's wheel, narrowing as it
ascends but then expanding slightly outward to offer a secure anchor
for the crafted wooden tabletop. Variations on the theme include
the Round Table in rosewood with a base reminiscent of a tree trunk
emerging from a forest floor.

Leonardo Table

Achille Castiglioni, 1969 Zanotta

Along with a number of other successful and engaging mid-century pieces of furniture, Achille Castiglioni's Leonardo Table fuses tradition and modernity in one intelligent design. The two beechwood supports at either end of the table, which was originally conceived as a prototype in 1950, are modelled on the familiar trestles used for centuries by artists and artisans and can easily be adjusted to five different heights. The minimal tabletop, on the other hand, is made either of tempered glass or a white plastic laminate that provides a distinctly modern element. Zanotta, which has produced the Leonardo since the late 1960s, describes the piece as a 'working table', but it is also commonly used for dining.

Poker Table

Joe Colombo, 1968 Zanotta

As a designer, Joe Colombo was known for his imaginative ingenuity while as a larger-than-life character he was also renowned for a somewhat hedonistic pursuit of pleasure. These two aspects of his personality converge and collide in the form of the Poker Table, which features a distinctive double-layered tabletop and a quartet of fold-out corner leaves holding integrated ashtray holders but also just large enough to accommodate a drink. With substantial circular steel legs and a plastic laminate for the surfaces, the table comes with a removable green baize suited to gaming.

CTM (Coffee Table Metal)

Charles & Ray Eames, 1946 Evans Products/Herman Miller

Charles & Ray Eames's pioneering work on plywood furniture during
the 1940s included early experiments with a number of plywood
tables. Among them were designs initially developed in conjunction
with Evans Products in California and then put into wider production
by Herman Miller. One of the most famous of these early pieces is
the CTM, or Coffee Table Metal, completed around 1946 and then
picked up by Herman Miller from 1949 onward. The earliest CTMs
feature a thin, tray-style top in ash plywood, with a chrome-plated
steel base and three legs. Later versions have four legs (as shown
here) and multiple variations to the tabletop, depending on the kind
of ply used and the finish.

LTR (Low Table Rod) ↑

Charles & Ray Eames, 1950 Herman Miller

During the late 1940s, Charles & Ray Eames noted the proliferation of utilitarian objects, such as shopping trolleys, made of steel wire. They realized that such an affordable, easily available, lightweight and super-strong material offered many possibilities in terms of furniture design. One of the earliest pieces to emerge from their experiments with steel wire rods was the LTR, or Low Table Rod, produced by Herman Miller from 1950 onward, comprising a base of zinc-plated steel wire and a white laminate-over-plywood top. An alternative version of the piece has a rosewood tabletop.

← ETR (Elliptical Table Rod)

Charles & Ray Eames, 1951 Herman Miller

One of the most distinctive and recognizable tables designed by
Charles & Ray Eames resulted from their pioneering work combining
steel wire-rod bases with plywood surfaces. The ETR, or Elliptical
Table Rod, was developed around the same time as the LTR (opposite
top) and put into production one year later than it. Sometimes
known as the Surfboard Table, the piece features two steel cages
supporting the ends of the laminated ply board, with the discretion
of these twin bases allowing the sculptural form and curving lines
of the floating tabletop to be fully appreciated.

La Fonda Table

Charles & Ray Eames, 1961 Herman Miller

In 1960 Alexander Girard, who was also director of Herman Miller's
textile division, was asked to design the interiors of La Fonda del
Sol restaurant in the Time & Life Building, New York. Girard, in
turn, asked Charles & Ray Eames to design chairs and tables for the
restaurant. The resulting La Fonda Chair and Armchair featured
a fibreglass shell seat coated in synthetic leather, along with a
distinctive aluminium base consisting of a four-pronged star and
a vertical support made of two parallel struts of polished aluminium.
A similar base appears on the circular La Fonda Table, which can
be compared to the Eames's Aluminium Group, but is distinguished
by its elegant marble or grey slate top.

Scimitar Coffee Table

Preben Fabricius & Jørgen Kastholm, *c.* 1968 Ivan Schlechter

As well as a number of distinctive and distinguished chairs, the Danish
design partnership formed by Preben Fabricius and Jørgen Kastholm
also resulted in a series of dining and coffee tables. Many of these
employed glass tabletops that allowed the artistry of the bases to be
seen and appreciated fully. Chief among this category of designs is the
Scimitar Coffee Table, with a base made up of three legs connected by
curving bands, or 'scimitars', of stainless steel. The piece is a cousin of
the Scimitar Chair, designed by the same partnership and also produced
in Denmark by Ivan Schlechter (see p. 49).

Model 780 Nesting Tables

Gianfranco Frattini, 1966 Cassina

Milanese architect and designer Gianfranco Frattini designed
a number of original tables over the course of his career, including
the characterful Kyoto Coffee Table of 1974, distributed by Knoll.
Yet one of his most inventive designs is the Model 780 nest of four
matching tables produced by Cassina in dark lacquered wood with
a white laminate top. The individual pieces are elegant in themselves,
but also made to specific dimensions that allow them to form a drum
while nesting. The drum is, in itself, aesthetically seductive as well
as endearingly neat and tidy.

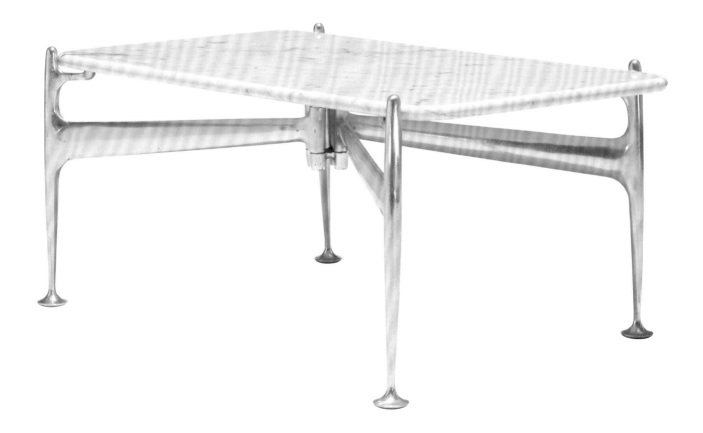

← Snake Occasional Table

Alexander Girard, *c.* 1965 Herman Miller

During the mid-1960s, Alexander Girard was asked to rebrand Braniff Airways in a major commission that embraced everything from its corporate graphic design identity to the interiors of its lounges, including the furniture and furnishings (see pp. 52, 204, 308 and below). One of the more unusual results of this ambitious project is this Snake Occasional Table, featuring a sculptural aluminium base with four legs and an enamelled steel top with a spiralling snake motif. The base has much in common with a number of other Girard occasional table designs from the same period, but this particular prototype is a rarity, given that the tabletop itself was never put into production.

Superellipse Table

Piet Hein & Bruno Mathsson, 1964 Mathsson International/Fritz Hansen

A mathematician, inventor and designer, Piet Hein took a highly logical approach to problem solving. One problem that he was presented with as a consultant town planner during the late 1950s was how to manage complex traffic junctions. His solution was a 'super-ellipse', a shape that fused a rectangular form with rounded, oval ends. This mathematically precise but pleasing variant on a 'roundabout' was then adapted by Hein and applied to other products and designs including, most famously, the Superellipse Table of 1964 featuring lightweight legs made of sculpted sheaves of steel rods designed by Bruno Mathsson. Still in production, the table comes with a choice of laminate, veneer or linoleum for the tabletop; some sources also credit Arne Jacobsen's involvement in the design process.

← Model 66350/66351 Coffee Table

Alexander Girard, 1967 Herman Miller

Girard's extensive collection for Braniff ultimately encompassed a wide range of furniture, including tables and ottomans of various sizes, a number of which were put into a short-lived range produced by Herman Miller known as The Girard Group (see pp. 52, 204, 308). One of the most engaging of these pieces is this coffee table featuring a cast aluminium frame made up of a quartet of interlocking legs supporting a marble tabletop. Variations on the design include a circular version and a variant with a glass tabletop instead of marble.

← Model 6810 AX Coffee Table

Peter Hvidt & Orla Mølgaard-Nielsen, 1948 Fritz Hansen

Having joined forces to establish an architectural and design studio in 1944, Peter Hvidt and Orla Mølgaard-Nielsen created the highly successful AX Armchair in 1947 (see p. 54), manufactured by Fritz Hansen. Around the same time they also designed the complementary AX Coffee Table in both a circular version (Model 6810) and a rectangular shape (Model 6950). Both are made of teak and beech and are partly defined by their distinctive shooting-stick-style legs, strengthened by cross braces.

← Model 523 Table

Peter Hvidt & Orla Mølgaard-Nielsen, 1952 France & Søn

Following on from the AX Coffee Table (opposite top), Hvidt and Mølgaard-Nielsen designed a number of other elegant and distinctive pieces for Fritz Hansen, including the Model 6743 X-Table of 1960. Adaptability was also a familiar theme in their designs, as seen in their drop-leaf tables and in this sculptural design for France & Søn. The Model 523 Table was generally produced as a set of six interlocking pieces, featuring teak tops and brass legs, with each one forming a neat segment within a larger circular formation. Yet the user is free to split the segments and arrange them as they wish, with multiple possibilities to explore.

Custom Ant Table

Arne Jacobsen, 1952/c. 1965 Fritz Hansen

In 1952 Fritz Hansen began producing Arne Jacobsen's famous Model 3100 Ant Chair (see p. 54) with its unforgettable plywood seat and back combined with three chrome-plated steel legs. At the same time Jacobsen designed a table with a similar aesthetic, again featuring three slim and light steel legs combined with an oval tabletop in teak plywood. In around 1965, a custom version of the Ant Table was produced by Fritz Hansen, featuring three recessed oval leaves that pivot outward from their hiding place under the tabletop to extend the surface area. These ingenious satellites are perfect for holding drinks while freeing up the centre of the table for other uses.

Model 3605 Drop-Leaf Table

Arne Jacobsen, 1955 Fritz Hansen

Architect and designer Arne Jacobsen was one of the most influential mid-century pioneers to experiment with drop-leaf and folding tables. The Model 3605 Drop-Leaf Table is characteristically light but also malleable, with rosewood leaves at either end, which are raised to extend the table to a full 233.5 cm (92 in.). The chrome-plated steel legs and struts are strong but discreet, allowing the focus to remain on the tone and texture of the tabletop and leaves; similar but smaller versions of Jacobsen's drop-leaf designs were also produced by Fritz Hansen.

Nesting Tables

Grete Jalk, 1963 Poul Jeppesen

Along with Mogens Koch and a number of her contemporaries, Danish designer Grete Jalk studied with Kaare Klint at the Royal Danish Academy of Fine Arts. Many of her designs use timber and natural materials, but her best-known pieces feature teak plywood, as in her Laminated Chair produced by Poul Jeppesen (1963, see p. 58). These complementary Nesting Tables employ not only the same choice of material but also a similarly sculptural form. The tables possess both simplicity and elegance in equal measure, while the warmth of the single piece of teak laminate needed for each one lifts them far above the ordinary. When nesting together, the tables offer the neat outline of wooden staples tucked one inside the other.

Chandigarh Committee Table ↓

Pierre Jeanneret, *c.* 1963 Limited edition

Pierre Jeanneret's and Le Corbusier's extraordinary commission to create a new state capital and administrative centre for the Punjab, known as Chandigarh, embraced architecture and interiors as well as furniture for a wide range of buildings and uses. Alongside chairs (see p. 59) and desks (see p. 360), there were also a number of tables, including coffee tables, occasional tables, dining tables and this substantial committee or conference table. The table features Pierre Jeanneret's distinctive open scissor legs, but paired here with a vertical V-shaped support to create an X-shaped profile at each end holding the teak tabletop. Rare originals of this kind are much in demand among collectors and aficionados.

Tri-Symmetric Coffee Table

Vladimir Kagan, *c.* 1955 Kagan-Dreyfuss

While Vladimir Kagan is best known for the sinuous shapes and
curvaceous lines of his sofas and chairs (see pp. 63 and 210–12), a
number of his tables also adopt sculptural forms. Chief among them
is his series of interrelated Tri-Symmetric Tables, with their tripod
legs morphing into three outstretched arms that support a glass
tabletop. These pieces include a circular dining table, occasional
tables and the Tri-Symmetric Coffee Table with its biomorphic
walnut base and kidney-shaped transparent glass top that allows
the base to be read from all angles. Kagan also designed and produced
a Tri-Symmetric Chair in the 1950s.

Model 3403 Occasional Tables

Vladimir Kagan, 1956 Kagan-Dreyfuss

Like Kagan's Tri-Symmetric designs (see p. 269), these Model
3403 Occasional Tables showcase a triptych of sculpted and fused
legs. But the similarity ends there, with the 3403 adopting a very
different aesthetic for the upper section of the table. Circular storage
compartments, made of walnut, feature either twin tambour doors
or a combination of a single tambour plus two integrated drawers.
Marble-topped, the piece makes an elegant coffee table but might
equally serve as a bedside unit. As with most of Kagan's designs,
it was produced by his own manufacturing company.

PK61 Coffee Table

Poul Kjaerholm, 1956 E. Kold Christensen/Fritz Hansen

While so many of Poul Kjaerholm's chairs adopt fluid lines and ergonomic forms, the defining characteristic of the Danish master's tables is their strict geometrical precision combined with pared-down detailing. Such is the case with the PK61 Coffee Table, originally produced by E. Kold Christensen and then Fritz Hansen, featuring a chrome-plated steel frame that forms a neat central square with horizontal supports that push out from the centre at right angles to meet the legs, which rise slightly higher than the rest of the frame to help secure the tabletop. Initially, the tabletop was made of either slate or basalt, with glass and granite introduced from 1957 onward; more recently Fritz Hansen began producing a larger variant of the table known as the PK61A.

← PK71 Nesting Tables

Poul Kjaerholm, 1957 E. Kold Christensen/Fritz Hansen

The architectural precision and minimalist character of Kjaerholm's tables came to the fore with the design of the PK71 Nesting Tables, first produced by E. Kold Christensen just one year after the PK61 Coffee Table (see p. 271). Kjaerholm created a nest of three tables with lightweight steel frames that formed a precise cube. Unusually for Kjaerholm, the tops – or lids – of the tables are made of acrylic (rather than stone or glass) and are easily removable, which means that the tables can be slotted one inside the other to create a nest. Simple and seductive, offering pared-down structures that have the look of elegant building blocks, the PK71 Nesting Tables are still produced by Fritz Hansen.

Table Bleue

Yves Klein, 1961 Limited edition

One of the most memorable tables of the mid-century period was created not by a designer, nor an architect, but by an artist. During the late 1950s Yves Klein began experimenting with a rich ultramarine colour that was registered in France, in 1960, as International Klein Blue (IKB). While the French artist used the pigment in his paintings and performance art, he also applied it to objects and furniture, including screens and tables. The most famous of these designs is the Table Bleue: a Plexiglas case containing the blue pigment sitting on a steel base. It was originally produced in small numbers in 1961 and then as a later edition authorized by his widow following Klein's untimely death in 1962 after inhaling toxic fumes at work. Although the Table Bleue is the best known of the Klein tables, there is also a Table d'Or and a Table Rose, again produced in limited authorized editions.

← PK54 Dining Table

Poul Kjaerholm, 1963 E. Kold Christensen/Fritz Hansen

For his most engaging and successful dining table, the PK54, Kjaerholm stepped away from the rectangular forms of comparable pieces such as the PK55. This piece contrasts a cube and a circle to great effect, with the two different elements working in concert while any superfluous distractions are stripped away. The base is a chrome-plated steel cube frame, somewhat similar to the cubes used to create the PK71 Nesting Tables (opposite top), supporting a circular tabletop of flint-rolled Cipollino marble – a material much favoured by Kjaerholm for its colour and texture. Kjaerholm also designed a set of extension leaves for the PK54 made of maple, offering a set of petals that neatly slots onto the stone surface to seat twelve rather than six.

T Angle Coffee Tables

Florence Knoll, 1952 Knoll International

During the 1950s and 1960s Florence Knoll designed a number
of tables for the firm that she built with her husband, Hans Knoll,
and then managed after his death in 1955. In 1952 she launched
her T Angle series of tables, using a standardized steel base and
a laminate top, usually in white or black. The collection includes
a dining table, coffee tables, end tables and occasional tables, as
well as an extending table and an outdoor dining table with a slatted
redwood top. Knoll's Pedestal Table Desk, part of her Executive
series (see p. 365), is also commonly used as a dining table.

Folding Table

Mogens Koch, *c.* 1960 Rud Rasmussens Snedkerier

One of Danish designer Mogens Koch's earliest and most famous designs of the 1930s was his MK-16 Folding Chair, or Safari Chair, based on the idea of a traditional, lightweight and portable campaign chair. Flexibility was a common theme in Koch's work, with the idea of compact furniture explored again in this elegant Folding Table in teak and brass, which could be used in a multitude of settings and situations. Koch's bookshelf system of the early 1960s, with its set of interlocking wooden cases and cabinets, could also be arranged in many different configurations (see p. 367).

Caori Coffee Table

Vico Magistretti, 1961 Gavina

The Caori Coffee Table, designed by Milanese architect and designer Vico Magistretti, doubles as an ingenious storage unit. In its resting position, the Caori provides a hard-wearing stainless-steel tabletop framed by a rectangle of dark lacquered wood resting on a smaller box-like plinth. Yet the unit also offers hidden storage compartments concealed behind fold-down doors and pull-out drawers at either end. Added to this, a pull-up lid set into the surface of the table conceals another useful compartment with slots for storing magazines or books. The Caori was also produced in white and red.

Eros Tables

Angelo Mangiarotti, 1971 Fratelli Brambilla Arredamenti/
Skipper/Cappellini/Agapecasa

The Eros series of tables, developed by Milanese mid-century master
Angelo Mangiarotti, reflects the close and sometimes symbiotic
relationship between architecture and furniture design. This ambitious
series evolved, in part, from Mangiarotti's pioneering work in the
borderland between architecture and structural engineering, as well
as his fascination with gravity joints. His experiments with marble
surfaces and supports led to the evolution of closed and semi-open
'eyelets' carved into the Eros tabletops that are then held securely
in place upon corresponding marble columns and supports by the
weight of the stone itself. The Eros table collection, still produced by
Agapecasa, eventually embraced a wide choice of sculptural shapes
and various uses.

Domino Tables

Mathieu Matégot, 1953 Atelier Matégot

Hungarian-born designer Mathieu Matégot began experimenting with perforated and sculpted steel during the late 1940s after settling in France. Many of the tables produced by his atelier during the 1940s and 1950s are light but robust and biomorphic at times, with spindle legs that look as though they might carry the piece away. One of the most distinctive Matégot designs of the period is his Domino Table, made in black and white, with an L-shaped perforated steel top and three legs; like dominoes the tables could be slotted together to create a larger surface area. Other engaging mid-century Matégot tables include the Elysée Magazine Table (1954) and the Java Table (1955), produced by Artimeta.

Linda Dining Table

Bruno Mathsson, *c.* 1945 Firma Karl Mathsson

As well as his successful collaboration with Piet Hein on the
Superellipse Table (1964, see p. 263), Bruno Mathsson designed
a number of other tables from the 1930s onward, mostly produced
by the family firm in Värnamo, Sweden. These include the
Maria Folding Table (1937), which can be arranged in multiple
configurations and then reduces down to a neat and compact form
for storage, and the circular Annika Table (1936). One of his most
elegant designs is the Linda Dining Table, comprising a teak surface
supported by four laminated birch legs that feature a steam-bent
splay where they meet the tabletop.

Model 162 Dining Table

Børge Mogensen, 1953 Søborg Møbelfabrik

Rather like his Nordic contemporary Bruno Mathsson (see p. 279), who designed the Maria Folding Table in the late 1930s, Børge Mogensen was interested in the idea of flexible furniture. Made of teak, his Model 162 Dining Table, which came in a choice of sizes, features drop leaves at either end that substantially increase the surface area. During the 1950s Mogensen also designed a table for Karl Andersson & Söner that could be massively extended by up to a total of four additional leaves.

Model 1114 Coffee Table ↑

Carlo Mollino, *c.* 1950 Apelli & Varesio for Singer & Sons

Carlo Mollino's love of sinuous biomorphic forms was not only expressed in his seating designs (see pp. 74–75), but also in a number of his tables. One of the most striking is the Model 1114 Coffee Table commissioned by Joseph Singer at the start of the 1950s and produced by Apelli & Varesio in small numbers. Made of Italian walnut, the base feels as though it has grown from the ground itself seeking the light, while the two horizontal planes of glass help strengthen the table as well as providing surfaces. The piece can be compared with Mollino's Arabesco Table (1949), originally produced by Apelli & Varesio at around the same time, which uses moulded plywood instead of walnut while also adopting fluid shapes and similar structural principles.

← Conoid Dining Table

George Nakashima, 1970 Nakashima Studio

Given George Nakashima's deep-rooted respect for the character of the timbers that he used in his work, the dining table was arguably one of the best matches for his design philosophy. The scale and purpose of such pieces created the opportunity to select choice cuts of wood and allow them the opportunity to express themselves to the full, as seen in this Conoid Dining Table. Here, the distinctive Conoid base combines with a surface made up of two broad planks of American black walnut tied together with four rosewood butterfly joints, made at Nakashima's farmstead in Pennsylvania.

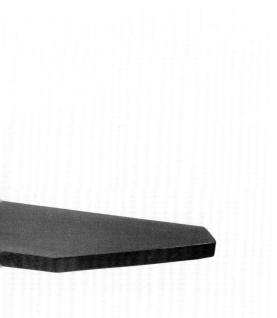

Minguren II Coffee Table

George Nakashima, 1973 Nakashima Studio

The tables designed and made by George Nakashima at his New Hope workshops were each identified by their characterful bases, including the Conoid (opposite top), Frenchman's Cove and Minguren, while the tabletops were partly defined by the intrinsic shape and character of the woods chosen for the task in hand. This particular Minguren II Coffee Table was commissioned for Nelson Rockefeller's Japanese-style garden pavilion, designed by architect Junzo Yoshimura, at his Pocantico Hills estate in Westchester County, New York. The base is combined with a long cantilevered slab of American black walnut, with a natural fissure in the wood on one side.

Tray Table Model 4950

George Nelson, 1950 Herman Miller/Vitra

As design director of Herman Miller from 1945, Nelson devised
a large number of tables serving a variety of uses. One of the
simplest but most pleasing of Nelson's designs is this Tray Table
Model 4950, or 'Tray-table', consisting of a minimal U-shaped
tubular-steel base with a single slim stem supporting the tray top
in moulded ash plywood. The height of the stem is easily adjusted
and the table is very light, making it highly versatile and suited
to use in many different settings, such as the living room or at the
bedside. When the table was launched in 1950 it retailed at just
$12.50 making this elegant and multi-purpose piece an affordable
and tempting purchase.

← Catenary Coffee Table Model 6371

George Nelson, 1963 Herman Miller

During the 1950s and 1960s Nelson designed a series of coffee tables, including the Extension Coffee Table Model 4652 and another with an integrated planter at its centre point (Model 4757). In 1963 Nelson and Herman Miller launched the Catenary Group that consisted of the Coffee Table Model 6371, a chair and an ottoman, defined by their 'catenary' bases made up of two sets of back-to-back steel bows at top and bottom held together by angled steel rods. In the case of the Catenary Coffee Table, the surface is in translucent or smoked glass, which means that the geometry of the base can still be understood even when looking down upon the piece of furniture.

Bronze Group Table Model 64115-6

George Nelson, 1966 Herman Miller

While a number of the pieces designed by George Nelson for Herman Miller, such as his Tray Table (opposite top), are defined by a sense of lightness or weightlessness, this is not always the case. Rather than receding into the background, the Bronze Group Table is purposefully dramatic and eye-catching with its twin X-shaped bronze legs recalling the work of a sculptor's foundry, while the tabletop is in warm rosewood. The piece might be compared with the earlier X-Legs Table Model 8430-X of 1950, where the X-legs are chrome-plated tubular steel, lending the design a very different character.

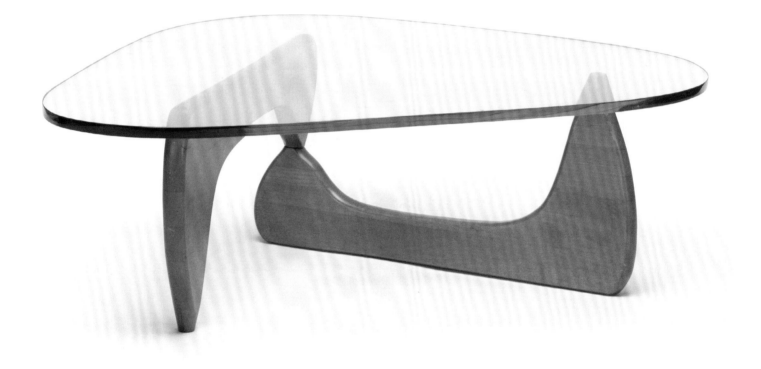

← Model IN-50 Coffee Table

Isamu Noguchi, 1944 Herman Miller/Vitra

Japanese-American designer Isamu Noguchi was also a renowned sculptor and always applied an artist's eye to his designs for lighting, products and furniture. Certainly, the series of distinctive tables that Noguchi created during the 1940s and 1950s has a truly dynamic and sculptural character, beginning with the Model IN-50 Coffee Table for Herman Miller. The piece is composed of two identical and conjoined pieces of either walnut or dark poplar, with one perched upon the other to create a base while the kidney-shaped glass top allows the fluid lines of these timber twins to remain visible. Noguchi's IN-52 Rudder Coffee Table (1944) and IN-62 Coffee Table (c. 1945), also produced by Herman Miller, explore similarly organic, biomorphic and sculptural forms.

Model 312 Cyclone Dining Table

Isamu Noguchi, 1955 Knoll

During the 1950s, Noguchi began to step away from the more organic shapes and materials of his earlier tables, such as the IN-50 (opposite), and explore fresh ideas. These included his Cyclone tables for Knoll, featuring a tornado of circling steel rods connected to a small circular base plate and also a laminate tabletop in white or black. The Model 312 Cyclone Dining Table is the largest piece in the series, with a smaller version (Model 311, 1955) and a Children's Cyclone Table (Model 87, 1955) also produced. The Prismatic Table, designed in 1957 but only produced by Vitra from 2001, makes use of folded pieces of aluminium, a material that was also employed in a number of Noguchi's sculptures from the same period.

Maison de la Tunisie Table

Charlotte Perriand, 1952 Ateliers Jean Prouvé

During the 1950s Charlotte Perriand designed the interiors and
furnishings for a number of student dormitory buildings at the Cité
Internationale Universitaire de Paris. They included student rooms
in the Maison de la Tunisie, where Perriand's ideas comprised a
wall-mounted bibliothèque, a compact bed and this small side table,
designed to sit alongside and just underneath a longer, fitted desk
at one end of the space. Made of ash and with three steel legs, the
lozenge-shaped table could be put to many different uses. Among
other pieces, Perriand also designed a student's table with integrated
drawers for the Maison du Brésil (1959).

Les Arcs Dining Table

Charlotte Perriand, *c.* 1968 Limited edition

During the late 1960s, mountain-loving Perriand dedicated herself
to the design of Les Arcs, a new winter resort in the French Alps,
widely seen as the designer's most rounded and ambitious
achievement. The project encompassed architecture, interiors
and furniture (see pp. 82, 180 and 329), which offered – like the
resort itself – a modern take on Alpine tradition. Largely made
of timber, the collection featured chairs, benches, stools and tables,
including this crafted, rustic design made of pine. Such pieces
formed an important part of the social life of Les Arcs, where
generous communal spaces balanced the relatively modest scale
of the rooms and apartments.

Platner Collection Coffee Table

Warren Platner, 1966 Knoll

As well as the iconic Lounge Chair (see p. 86), produced by Knoll as part of the Platner Collection of 1966, the architect and designer created a range of tables using the same distinctive 'wheatsheaf' bases made up of a series of vertical steel rods held in place by slim circular bands. The Platner tables included a dining table, occasional tables and this coffee table, which comes in a choice of tabletops: a glass version, a rosewood timber surface and also a special-order green marble top. The fact that the seemingly light and translucent base supports such a selection of different materials, with varying weight loads, is testament to the ingenuity of the design and its engineering.

S.A.M. Model 503 Tropique Table

Jean Prouvé, 1951 Ateliers Jean Prouvé

The great French 'constructeur', Jean Prouvé, designed a number
of original tables during the 1940s and 1950s, including the Compas
Table and matching Compas Desk (1953, see p. 383). Such pieces
were elegant and practical, often featuring a distinctive set of splayed
and tapered legs. The origins of Prouve's S.A.M. ('salle à manger')
series of tables dates back to the late 1930s, but the sequence
was developed further during the 1940s and 1950s. This all-metal
Tropique Table – suited to warm and humid environments – was
produced in 1951 using aluminium and steel. The S.A.M. Model 502,
which appeared in the same year, was almost identical in its shape
and form but constructed with wooden legs and a matching tabletop.

← Model T539 Magazine Table

Jens Risom, 1949 Jens Risom Design

Danish–American designer Jens Risom created an elegant set of tables for Hans Knoll during the 1940s, but in 1946 decided to strike out on his own and founded his eponymous firm. There were coffee tables and occasional tables in the collection, but one of the most unusual and inventive Risom designs is this Model T539 Magazine Table made of walnut. The piece has one splayed, fin-shaped leg complemented by a second broader support that doubles as a magazine rack, with a neat cut-out in the rounded tabletop for slotting in a choice of journals. It was a modest example of a new typology, comparable to George Nelson's inventive, fusion furniture designs with integrated televisions or radios.

Pedestal Table

Eero Saarinen, 1957 Knoll

'I wanted to clear up the slum of legs', declared architect and designer Eero Saarinen as he perfected the idea of a table with a single, elegant stem. Launched in 1957, Saarinen's Pedestal Table, generally referred to as the Tulip Table or Saarinen Table, became one of the most recognizable and successful pieces of furniture of the mid-century period, with its minimal yet sculptural support like the base of a wine glass but of cast metal. The Pedestal Collection encompassed a range of sizes and options from the start, including a dining table (shown here), coffee table and occasional tables, with a choice of marble or laminate tabletops. Hugely influential, Saarinen's tables and matching chairs (see p. 98) helped to initiate a rethink around the structural foundations of furniture design.

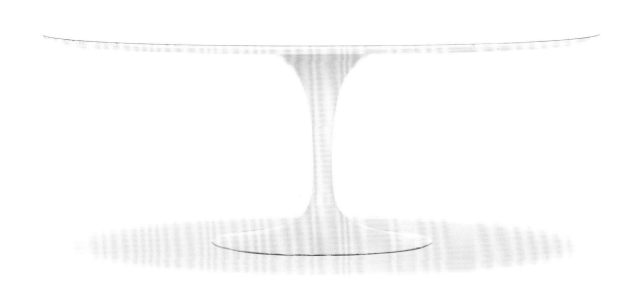

Petal Dining Table Model P320

Richard Schultz, 1960 Knoll

Designer Richard Schultz and his work are intimately associated
with Knoll. He joined the firm in 1951, after studying engineering
and design, and began working with Harry Bertoia on the
development of his wire chair collection, including the Diamond
Chair (1952, see p. 20). Around this time Schultz began thinking
about complementary ideas for a set of tables, but it was only
in 1960 that he came up with the concept for the Petal Collection
using rounded segments of timber fixed to a slim, unobtrusive
and lightweight single-stem base with a radiating series of support
legs in cast aluminium. Schultz wanted the base itself to become
invisible to those seated at the table, with the focus remaining
on the crafted petals. Tables also formed part of Schultz's Outdoor
or Leisure Collection for Knoll, designed in 1966 (see p. 145).

Model 50 Tray Tables

Abel Sorenson, 1946 Knoll

Along with Jens Risom, Ralph Rapson and others, Abel Sorenson
was one of the designers who contributed ideas for furniture in
the early years of the Knoll furniture company during the 1940s.
Among these Sorenson designs was a number of light and portable
pieces, including nesting tables (Model 56), a two-tier plywood
table (Model 55) and this Model 50 Tray Table with a detachable
birch plywood top that when removed revealed a stool with a canvas
webbed seat below. A double version (Model 52) was also produced,
with two trays and a bench.

← Lotrosso Table

Ettore Sottsass, 1963 Poltronova

Designer and architect Ettore Sottsass is best known as a principal
figure in the Italian postmodern movement, and Memphis in
particular. Much of his furniture is playful, expressive, colourful
and sometimes radical or irreverent. Yet his Lotrosso Table of 1963
exhibits a degree of purity and restraint within an aesthetic that
has much more of a mid-century feel than the majority of Sottsass's
later work. The 'Loto' table features a graphic combination of
a steel column in black enamel with a white marble top, as well
as a marble base plate. An alternative version has a black marble
top and a light, chrome-plated steel support.

Ovalette Coffee Table

Ilmari Tapiovaara, 1954 Artek

Finnish designer Ilmari Tapiovaara famously combined a love
of crafted natural materials with a quest for weightlessness and
simplicity. The Ovalette Coffee Table is a prime example of
Tapiovaara's fusion of the organic and the ergonomic, with its
gently rounded birch top and elegant, tapering cross legs with
additional bracing. The table is still produced by Artek, in either
walnut or oak, suggesting the enduring allure of this easily
portable and adaptable design.

Octagonal Coffee Table ↓

Joaquim Tenreiro, *c.* 1960 Limited edition

Often described as the father of Brazilian furniture design, Joaquim Tenreiro explored distinctive geometrical forms in a series of mid-century tables. During the 1960s, he produced distinctive round and triangular dining tables, as well as this Octagonal Coffee Table with four rectangular wooden supports in jacaranda cradling the thick, eight-sided marble tabletop. The combination of four and eight creates a rigorous composition with a sense of mathematical purity, as well as juxtaposing two characterful and natural materials.

Model 9016 Coffee Table ↓ ↓

Tapio Wirkkala, 1958 Asko

Finnish polymath Tapio Wirkkala argued that 'the designer should always be in harmony with his material'. Wirkkala worked successfully in many different mediums, including glass, but achieved fame with his laminate wooden dishes and platters of the 1950s, which used the grain and colour of the timber to provide natural decoration. Similar principles applied to his coffee tables for Asko, for which he used a choice of laminated timber to create natural swirls and patterns in the tabletops, while the slimline legs were in tapered chrome-plated steel. The Model 9016 Coffee Table features a combination of rosewood, teak and birch.

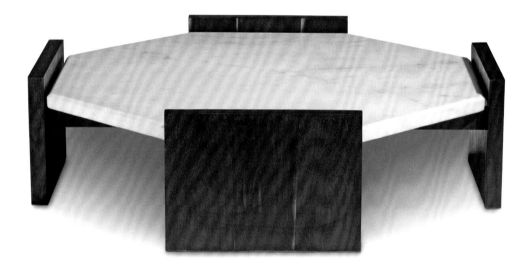

Marcuso Dining Table

Marco Zanuso, 1969 Zanotta

The Marcuso Table, designed by Milanese architect Marco Zanuso, has often been compared to a pared-down modernist building. The form and structure of the table has been reduced to four steel legs, in the shape of circular columns, and a clear glass top. The challenge for Zanuso and Zanotta was how to secure these elements to one another while maintaining the simplicity and elegance of the overall design. The solution was a set of four neat discs carefully but firmly glued to the underside of the glass, with the steel legs then attached to the discs. The table, in a choice of sizes and finishes, is still produced by Zanotta.

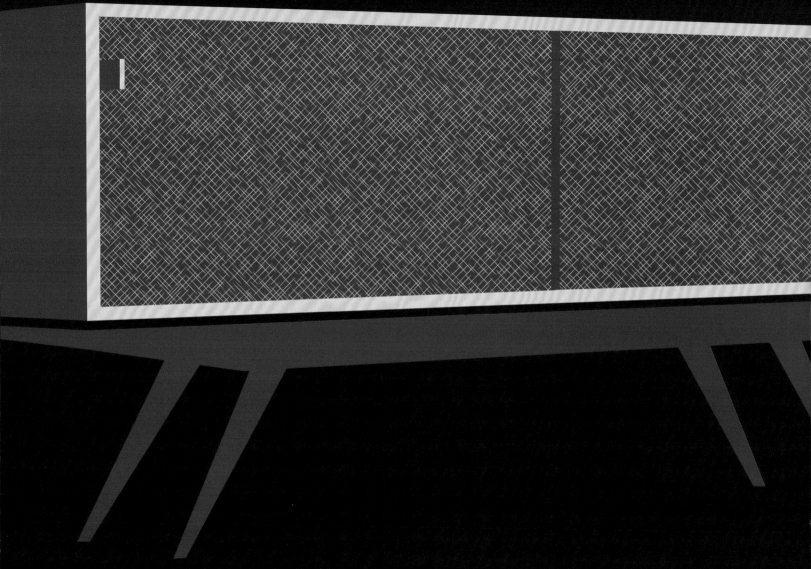

CONSOLES &
CREDENZAS

CONSOLES
CREDENZAS
CABINETS
SIDEBOARDS
BARS

The post-World War II period was undoubtedly a dynamic era for furniture design of all kinds. Yet, for many, one of the most emblematic ingredients of the mid-century interior was the credenza, cabinet or console with the sideboard serving as a staple in countless homes during the 1950s and 1960s. Such pieces were elegant statements in themselves, generally combining an imaginative design approach with characterful materials, fine craftsmanship and a welcome degree of flexible utility.

In many respects mid-century consoles and cabinets referenced both the past and the present. They drew on a long tradition of sideboards and chests within the home, used to store precious family treasures, whether in a great room or a dining room where a credenza might hold the best dinnerware but also double as a serving counter. Similarly, traditional kitchen dressers and cabinets met a need for storage solutions but also offered opportunities for displaying china, ceramics and glassware.

The cabinets and consoles of the post-war period referenced these widespread traditions, yet adopted a fresh aesthetic and, in many instances, were intended to create focal points in a space. There was a grandeur of scale to many of the credenzas created by designers such as Joaquim Tenreiro, Florence Knoll, Sergio Rodrigues and others, with cabinets stretching two metres or more in length and often becoming the dominant elements within a room.

Such engaging pieces tended to be made of hardwoods and other natural materials, with the grain and pattern of these long planes of oak, jacaranda, rosewood, teak or cherry wood playing an important part in defining the character of the cabinet itself. Designers such as Edward Wormley and Vladimir Kagan also used textural and decorative elements to further enrich and enliven their designs. At the same time, credenzas and consoles offered tempting surfaces for display and prime opportunities for creating the kind of 'tablescapes' favoured by David Hicks and other interior designers of the period.

As well as looking to historical precedents, designers also embraced 'contemporary' trends within the design of consoles and cabinets, particularly the growing emphasis on home entertainment and leisure time. George Nelson, for example, designed cabinets that could accommodate hi-fis and speakers, as well as televisions. Others, such as Franco Albini and Franca Helg, devised bar carts and buffets that offered stylish and often portable aids for entertaining.

Above all, it was the flexibility and malleability of mid-century cabinets and credenzas that made them so popular. Given their elegance and ingenuity, they provided welcome additions to many areas of the house and fulfilled a wide variety of functions. The provision of sliding or fold-out doors meant that many household sins could be neatly hidden away, and integrated drawers and adjustable shelving accommodated all kinds of odds and ends while adapting to the needs of the user. For these reasons and many others, such consoles and cabinets remain great favourites today within 21st-century homes and interiors.

FOLLOWING SPREAD Villa Fornasetti, Milan, Italy, interiors by Piero Fornasetti, *c.* 1955

MB15 Cabinet

Franco Albini, 1957 Poggi

As suggested by innovative pieces such as his LB7 storage and
shelving system (1957, see p. 347), storage solutions were one of the
many areas of expertise explored by the Milan-based architect and
designer Franco Albini. This elegant teak cabinet, produced by Poggi,
hosts five hidden shelves plus a removable tray, making it well suited
to office or home use; the slim profile of the sculpted pedestal legs
contrasts neatly with the rectangular mass of the cabinet itself.
Other Albini designs suited to the office or study include his Stadera
and Model 80 Desks (both 1958, see pp. 347 and 348).

Model CR20 Carts

Franco Albini & Franca Helg, 1958 Poggi

Milanese architect, curator and designer Franca Helg joined Albini's office in the early 1950s and continued the practice after Albini's death in 1977. Many key architectural products from the intervening period, as well as furniture and product designs, are credited to Albini and Helg, including this elegant cart produced by Poggi in both mahogany and rosewood. The cart, well suited for use as a portable bar cart, features twin trays supported by a triptych of legs with brass castors and rounded handles. Albini and Helg also designed the Model TL22 Cart (1958, Poggi), which trundled along on three legs as well but featured four integrated drawers and a single pull handle, making it suitable for office use.

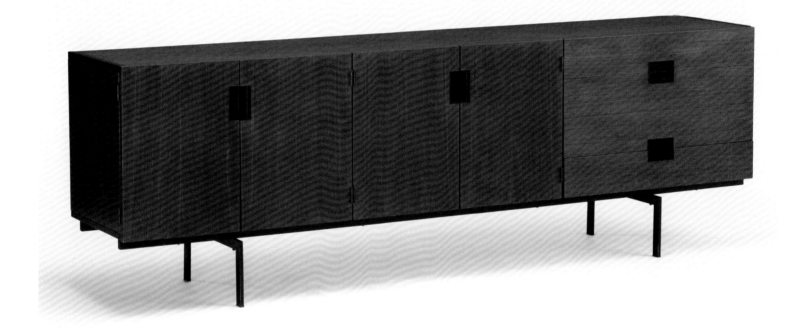

Model DU03 Credenza

Cees Braakman, 1958 UMS Pastoe

Dutch designer Cees Braakman initiated the merger that created
UMS Pastoe in 1955 and then became the manufacturer's head of
design. As well as chairs, including the SB02 birch plywood chair
(1950), one of Braakman's greatest strengths during the 1950s and
1960s lay in the design of storage units, bookcases and credenzas.
A prime example is the Model DU03 Credenza, a long cabinet
made of teak with slim enamelled steel legs and matching detailing.
Four drawers sit at one end of the piece and the remaining four
doors conceal integrated shelves within.

Prototype Cabinet →

Alexander Girard, *c.* 1965 Herman Miller

While designer Alexander Girard's association with Herman Miller
pivoted upon his key role as director of design of the company's
textile division (1952–73), there were many other aspects to his work.
They included the 1967 release of The Girard Group, a collection
of furniture based on a number of designs originally created for
Braniff Airways (see pp. 52, 204 and 263). Among these pieces was
this Prototype Cabinet with a white laminate body floating upon
cast aluminium legs; the four white doors conceal both shelving
and drawers. Unlike the designer's textile division, The Girard Group
was short lived and discontinued after just one year.

Rosewood Sideboard ↑

Finn Juhl, *c.* 1949 Niels Vodder

The partnership between Danish architect and designer Finn Juhl
and master cabinetmaker and craftsman Niels Vodder led to pieces
of furniture that were not just distinctly modern but beautifully
made and finely detailed. One prime example from the late 1940s is
this sideboard made of rosewood, with the warm grain of the timber
bringing added depth and character to the design and composition
of the piece. A quartet of four sliding panel doors to the front
of the cabinet disguise three adjustable shelves and a sequence of
drawers within the sideboard. Other collaborations embraced chairs,
sofas and tables.

Walnut Cabinet

Finn Juhl, *c.* 1951 Baker Furniture

While Juhl is best known for his many masterful chair designs, storage solutions and sideboards formed a significant segment of his portfolio. As well as pieces for Niels Vodder, there were cabinets, cupboards and shelving systems for Bovirke, Søren Willadsen Møbelfabrik and American manufacturer Baker Furniture, based in Michigan. In 1950, Hollis S. Baker flew to Copenhagen and persuaded Juhl to allow him to manufacture a series of his designs in the USA. They included this double cabinet in walnut, with a range of four drawers to one side, becoming deeper as the sequence descends, and a double-doored section to the other, concealing integrated drawers and shelving. Baker produced a number of variations on this design during the early 1950s.

Glove Cabinet

Finn Juhl, 1961 Ludvig Pontoppidan/Niels Roth Andersen/
House of Juhl

The first prototypes for this innovative, hinged cabinet were
developed for Juhl's own house in Charlottenlund, Copenhagen,
and then modified for the Danish Cabinetmakers' Guild of 1961
and produced by Ludvig Pontoppidan. In its closed position, the
cabinet reads as a rectangular piece in crafted cherry wood with
brass detailing, but as it opens ten drawers in a spectrum of colours
reveal themselves, rather like a Wunderkammer or sophisticated
portmanteau unveiling its hidden contents. The cabinet was reissued
by Niels Roth Andersen in the 1980s and then, from 2015 onward,
produced by the House of Juhl.

Chest-on-Chest Buffet

Vladimir Kagan, *c.* 1952 Grosfeld House

As well as chairs, sofas and tables, Vladimir Kagan designed a series
of distinctive cabinets and credenzas during the 1950s and 1960s.
A number of these pieces, such as this extraordinary Chest-on-Chest
Buffet, explored the use of splayed and tapered legs to create a sense
of dynamism comparable to Kagan's seating. This double cabinet
was made by Grosfeld House, using walnut and cane along with brass
detailing, with storage compartments, drawers and adjustable shelves
contained within the two elements.

Credenza ↓

Vladimir Kagan, *c.* 1960 Vladimir Kagan Designs

A number of Kagan's cabinets were designed for specific functional purposes, such as hosting concealed bars or serving as hi-fi units. Others fused general storage use with more decorative elements, as seen in this walnut credenza featuring a band of glazed ceramic tiles with a colourful biomorphic pattern. Kagan collaborated with a number of artists to develop ceramic patterns for such pieces, including the Lithuanian–American artist Aleksandra Kasuba, but also used glass mosaic tiles to add another layer of character to cabinets and tables.

Wenge Credenza

Jørgen Kastholm, *c.* 1968 Limited edition

Danish designer Jørgen Kastholm, who studied under Arne
Jacobsen, was best known for his collaborations with colleague
Preben Fabricius, particularly their sequence of sculptural chairs
such as the Bird, Scimitar and Grasshopper (see pp. 48–9 and 129,
respectively). But there were also elegant solo pieces, such as
this beautifully crafted Wenge Credenza with stainless-steel legs
and detailing. Unusually, the three doors are drop-front and reveal
a collection of five slim drawers and adjustable shelves.

Pedersen Cabinet

Bodil Kjaer, 1959 E. Pedersen & Søn

Danish architect and designer Bodil Kjaer trained in Copenhagen
but spent much of her career working in the UK (with Arup's
architectural unit) and then in the USA. As well as her celebrated
desk and office furniture designs (see p. 362), Kjaer designed a
number of elegant cabinets and credenzas produced by the Danish
firm E. Pedersen & Søn. Chief among them was this characterful
piece in rosewood, with chrome-plated steel supports and seven
drawers, as well as a drop-front drawer that opens to reveal a
pull-out tray.

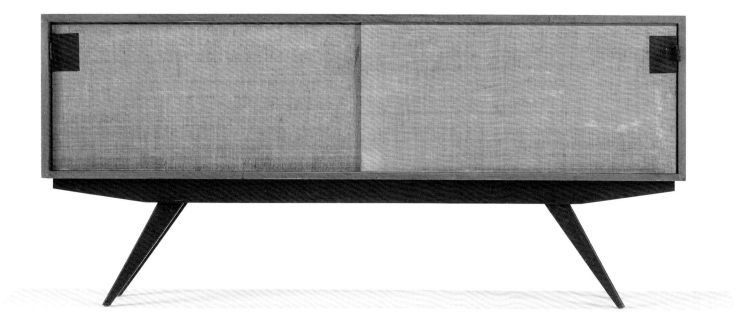

Model 122 Cabinet

Florence Knoll, 1947 Knoll

Cabinets formed part of Florence Knoll's famous Executive Office collection of the early 1960s (see p. 364), but Knoll also created a number of other elegant designs suited to home or office use. One of the earliest and most distinctive of these is the splay-legged Model 122 Cabinet of 1947, made of mahogany and birch, while the sliding doors that disguise the shelves behind are made of grass cloth with leather detailing. Knoll's Model 116 Cabinet, designed a year later, also made use of grass cloth and leather, offering a vivid textural contrast with the smooth finish of the wooden carcass.

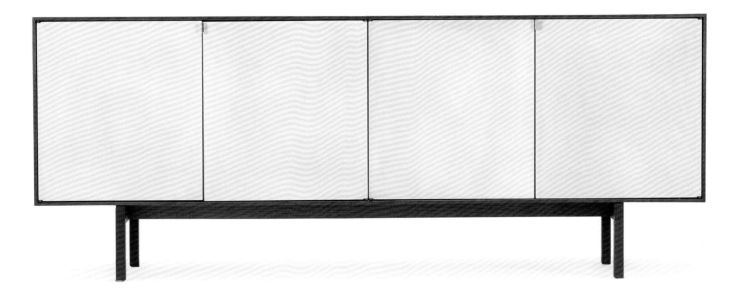

Model 541 Cabinet

Florence Knoll, 1952 Knoll

Designed in 1952, Knoll's Model 541 long cabinet comprises a walnut body and matching legs. Featuring four lacquered doors protecting a combination of drawers and adjustable shelving, it measures nearly two metres in length (1.92 m; 6 ft 4 in.), making it one of a number of Florence Knoll pieces that stretched the proportions of the credenza to fresh extremes. The cabinet remained in production during the 1960s and 1970s and was one of the key designs in a 1972 exhibition in Paris entitled 'Knoll au Louvre'.

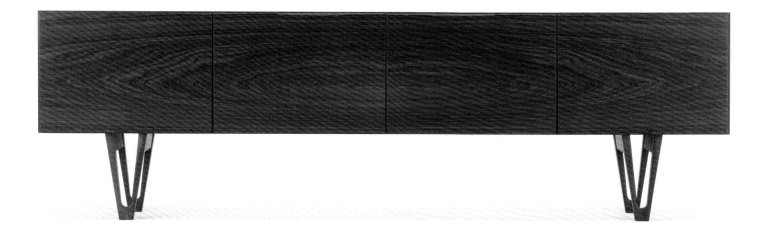

Trol Cabinet

Ib Kofod-Larsen, 1958 Seffle Møbelfabrik

Although Ib Kofod-Larsen designed a number of elegant chairs,
including the Elizabeth (1956) and Seal (1960), it is the Danish
designer's cabinets, consoles and credenzas that truly suggest the
hand of a master at work. Many of the cabinets were super-sized
at over two metres in length, creating a sense of visual drama and
impact, yet the compositions were also delightful, as seen in the
rosewood Trol Cabinet made in Sweden by Seffle Møbelfabrik.
Four doors disguise a blend of shelving and drawers within, but
it is the quartet of V-shaped legs that makes the piece stand apart.

Rosewood Credenza

Ib Kofod-Larsen, *c.* 1960 Faarup Møbelfabrik

Defining features of many of Kofod-Larsen's most engaging pieces are the choice of wood and the inherent sense of craftsmanship. These can be seen, in particular, in pieces made by Danish producer Faarup Møbelfabrik, including this credenza where the extraordinary grain of the rosewood serves as a decorative pattern enriching the doors. During the early 1960s, Kofod-Larsen was also commissioned to design cabinets and other furniture for British company E. Gomme's affordable G-Plan range, although only a relatively small fraction of these pieces were produced, partly because of the challenging costs involved in turning them into reality.

Irwin Collection Cabinet Buffet & Top, Models C8506/C8006 →

Paul McCobb, 1952 Calvin Furniture

As well as his extensive Planner Group collection of modular furniture (see p. 367), prolific American designer Paul McCobb created a wide variety of storage solutions within ambitious ranges for other manufacturers. They include the Irwin Collection produced by Calvin Furniture in Grand Rapids, with cabinets, chests of drawers and sideboards sitting within the line. This C8506 Cabinet Buffet, or 'highboard', was one of McCobb's most substantial Irwin designs, with five drawers and a triptych of folding doors for the base (C8506), and a mix of drawers, shelves and a storage cabinet for the upper section (C8006). The piece was made of mahogany and offered in a choice of two finishes.

Model BM57 Cabinet

Børge Mogensen, 1957 P. Lauritsen & Søn

Danish furniture designer Børge Mogensen created multiple designs
for cabinets, credenzas and chests of drawers after establishing his
own design studio near Copenhagen in 1950. One of his most elegant
storage solutions, this piece was produced in 1957 by P. Lauritsen
& Søn, and is shown here in oak but was also made in a darker teak
version. Unusually, the BM57 features two bifold doors, which can
be locked and secured, with hinges and other detailing in brass.
Internally, there are slim drawers toward the top of the unit, with
shelves below.

Teak Cabinet →

Børge Mogensen, *c.* 1960 Fredericia

Founded in the Danish town of the same name in the early 20th
century, Fredericia initially forged a relationship with Børge
Mogensen during the 1940s, with the alliance deepening during
the 1950s and 1960s. This relationship resulted not only in some
of Mogensen's most famous chairs and sofas (see p. 215) but also
in a number of cabinets and other pieces. Among them was this
unusual double cabinet, or 'highboard', in teak and oak with
brass detailing. The combination of air gaps in the four doors and
adjustable shelves behind makes the piece well suited to kitchen use.

Model OH-212-L Cabinet ↑

George Nakashima, *c.* 1950 Widdicomb

While George Nakashima is best known for the pieces produced
in his own workshops in Pennsylvania, he maintained a relationship
with American manufacturer Widdicomb that spanned the 1950s.
The collaboration led to the production of, among other pieces,
a number of cabinets including designs for the Origins collection
(*c.* 1959) and this substantial twelve-drawer piece, which was produced
in walnut with brass for the drawer pulls. The combination of the
cantilevered top and the unusual fin formation of the legs sets the
piece apart; an eight-drawer cabinet (Model OH-207-L) in laurel
wood and walnut was produced at around the same time.

Free-Edge Sliding Door Cabinet

George Nakashima, *c.* **1965** Nakashima Studio

George Nakashima's own woodworking studios at his New Hope farmstead in Pennsylvania created an exceptional range of cabinets, chests of drawers and credenzas during the mid-century period. There were many themes and variations within the collection, but American black walnut was often used, as seen in this monumental triple-door cabinet, which is over two metres in length with a single plank board used for the characterful timber top. The sliding doors, protecting adjustable shelves within, feature textural panels of pale pandanus cloth, which contrasts pleasingly with the dark grain of the wood.

Thin Edge Cabinet Model 5723

George Nelson, 1952 Herman Miller

Herman Miller's legendary design director George Nelson designed an extraordinarily rich and varied range of furniture for the company, with storage solutions always forming an important strand. Among the most finely detailed and crafted Nelson designs was a collection of 'thin edge' cabinets and credenzas, which included small four-drawer pieces and this Model 5723 Cabinet with a grand total of ten drawers in three sizes. Made of walnut, with white enamelled aluminium handles and slender aluminium feet, the rectangular mass of the cabinet appears to float magically above the ground plane.

Stereo & TV Cabinet Model 4743

George Nelson, *c.* 1955 Herman Miller

Among the many Herman Miller storage systems designed by George
Nelson & Associates for both home and office use (see p. 377) was a
subgroup of pieces devoted to entertainment. These included television
cabinets, such as the Model 4601-TV Cabinet and Thin Edge TV
Cabinet Model 5718, and hi-fi cabinets, such as the Thin Edge Hi-Fi
Cabinet Model 5722. This piece, mounted on a slat bench, features
both an integrated television monitor and stereo storage with a pull-
out turntable, a drop-front door concealing a radio tuner and, lastly,
a speaker cabinet. Materials used include oak, lacquered wood and
linen for the circular speaker cloth; the origins of the design stretch
back to the 1940s, with the piece itself produced during the mid-1950s.

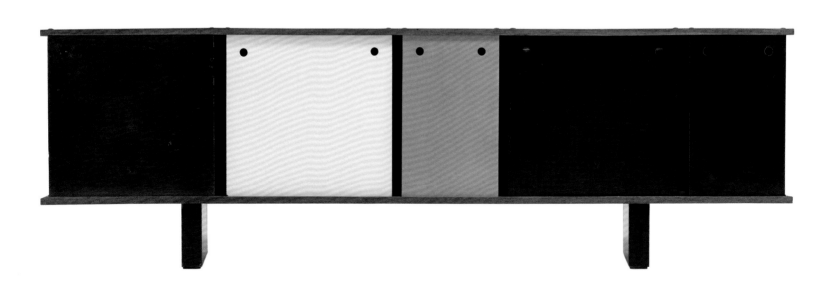

← Unité d'Habitation Air France Wall-Mounted Cabinet

Charlotte Perriand, 1952 Ateliers Jean Prouvé

During the early 1950s, Charlotte Perriand was asked to design the interiors and furniture for a collection of apartments in a dedicated modern building in Brazzaville, Republic of Congo, used by Air France employees. There were around sixty compact apartments arranged across the four-storey building, with a requirement to maximize the amount of available living space through the provision of intelligent storage solutions. Among these was a series of cupboards (Placard Brazza) and these wall-mounted cabinets, produced by Ateliers Jean Prouvé using teak, aluminium, steel and lacquered wood; twin sliding doors conceal shelves within, while an integrated hanging rail is suspended just below the main body of the cabinet.

Les Arcs Wall Mounted Cabinet

Charlotte Perriand, c. 1968 Limited edition

Perriand's extensive collection of furniture for the ski resort of Les Arcs in Savoie, France, included stools (see p. 180), benches, chairs (see p. 82), tables (see p. 289) and storage solutions. Among the latter was a free-standing console unit and also this wall-mounted cabinet from the late 1960s, made of a mixture of pine and laminated timber. This unit features three doors and concealed shelving, while there was also a smaller matching cabinet with twin doors. In addition, Perriand designed wall-mounted shelves and wall hooks for this epic project that spanned over twenty years and encompassed multiple phases and buildings.

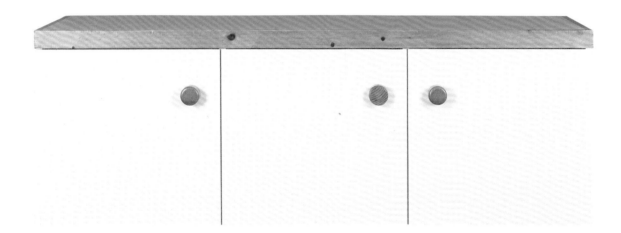

← Bloc Bahut from Cité Cansado

Charlotte Perriand, 1958 Négroni and Métal Meuble/Galerie Steph Simon

Over the course of her career, Perriand designed a number of elegant and innovative bahuts, or sideboards, including pieces created in conjunction with Pierre Jeanneret and master cabinetmaker André Chetaille. In 1958, she was asked to design the interiors for the 750 residences and communal buildings that formed the new mining town of Cité Cansado in Mauritania, constructed using prefabricated 'Maisons du Sahara' designed by Maison LWD with Jean Prouvé. One of the most substantial pieces from the Cansado collection is this Bloc Bahut in ash, steel, aluminium and Masonite, made by Négroni and Métal Meuble, with sliding doors concealing storage compartments and fitted drawers. Galerie Steph Simon in Paris also produced an edition of the design.

Model R-11 Cabinet

Jens Risom, *c.* **1955** Jens Risom Design

Danish–American designer Jens Risom designed a series of cabinets and credenzas during the 1950s and 1960s, produced by his own firm that he launched in 1946 and which grew rapidly during the mid-century period. One of the most unusual pieces is this walnut and mahogany cabinet sitting on a quartet of slim brass legs. The cabinet is divided into two distinct parts: a standard door on one side and a larger storage section with a roll-up tambour front. It was one of a number of pieces suited to a study or office, as were Risom's Executive cabinets and desks (see p. 385) produced at around the same time.

Credenza

Jens Risom, *c.* 1960 Jens Risom Design

Risom's American-made cabinets and sideboards possessed a crafted
quality and made good use of characterful natural materials – as one
might expect of a Danish-born designer who trained in Copenhagen
under Kaare Klint and Ole Wanscher. Risom's own firm, based in
New England, produced chests of drawers and cabinets in walnut,
as well as primavera and rosewood. One of his most substantial
and elegant pieces is this credenza in rosewood, juxtaposed with a
gleaming aluminium frame and legs, holding a total of nine drawers
and a single door concealing a storage compartment with an
adjustable shelf.

Tupã Cabinet

Sergio Rodrigues, 1973 Limited edition

As seen in many of Sergio Rodrigues's most famous seating designs, such as his Sheriff Armchair (see p. 96), the Brazilian designer enjoyed combining crafted timber with pads of leather, contrasting the hard and the soft while retaining a natural palette of materials. Similarly, Rodrigues also introduced textural leather surfaces to a number of cabinets and credenzas during the 1960s and early 1970s, including pieces produced by Oca in rosewood and this Tupã Cabinet made of imbuia. Integrated drawers sit at either end of the piece, while a pair of sliding leather-faced doors are placed centrally, protecting the storage compartment within.

Bar Cart

Sergio Rodrigues, *c.* 1960 Oca

With both flexibility and portability in mind, Rodrigues designed
a number of variations on rolling tables and carts during the mid-
century period. There were occasional tables that could be moved
around on castors and a choice of bar carts produced by Oca during
the 1960s. These included an open-sided design with twin trays
and an integrated handle, and also this design in rosewood with
an enclosed cabinet protected by a sliding leather-faced door.
On the top is a removable serving tray with handles at either side,
made of a wooden frame and a practical laminated surface.

Monumental Cabinet ↑

Joaquim Tenreiro, *c.* 1950 Tenreiro Móveis e Decorações

Cabinets and credenzas designed by Brazilian master Joaquim
Tenreiro were characterized by their ambitious scale, serving as
dramatic anchor pieces in a room. At the same time, they made
use of fine hardwoods with distinctive grains and finishes, adding
to the unique quality of the piece. Chief among these extraordinary
designs is the Monumental Cabinet, made of jacaranda, which is
just over three and a half metres in length (3.51 m; 11½ ft).
The cabinet features a sequence of six doors with embossed leather
fronts and brass detailing, offering subtle pattern and patina, yet
maintaining a focus on natural textures.

Credenza

Arne Vodder, *c.* 1960 Sibast Furniture

During the 1950s and 1960s, Danish architect and designer Arne Vodder collaborated with Sibast Furniture on an extensive collection of furniture. Among the most striking fruits of this long relationship were distinctive and imaginative cabinets and credenzas, combining rich natural materials and playful touches and motifs. This 2.5 m (8 ft 2 in.) rosewood credenza is one of the most substantial of these designs, featuring a combination of storage elements, including seven drawers, a drop-front compartment with an adjustable shelf behind it and two sliding doors in lacquered wood with adjustable shelving beyond.

Cabinet

Hans Wegner, 1952 Andreas Tuck

By the early 1950s, Hans Wegner had secured an international reputation built largely on the back of some of his most iconic chair designs. But he was also working on many other types of furniture by this point, including a number of cabinets and credenzas. One of the most engaging of these early designs is this piece, in teak and oak, produced in Denmark by Andreas Tuck and featuring distinctive bow legs with additional brass supports. This elegant and compact cabinet holds six drawers to one side and twin sliding doors to the other, protecting internal shelving and an additional set of drawers.

Model RY24 Cabinet

Hans Wegner, 1958 RY Møbler

By the time Wegner retired in 1993 around five hundred different
furniture designs had gone into production with a range of Danish
manufacturers. Among these pieces was an extensive collection of
storage solutions, including a number of different cabinets produced
by RY Møbler, such as the Model RY25 Credenza in rosewood and
this double-decker Model RY24 Cabinet in teak. The lower section
holds six drawers, while the top compartment features two sliding
doors with shelving behind. Other RY Møbler/Wegner designs
include the Model RY31 Chest of Drawers, usually made in oak.

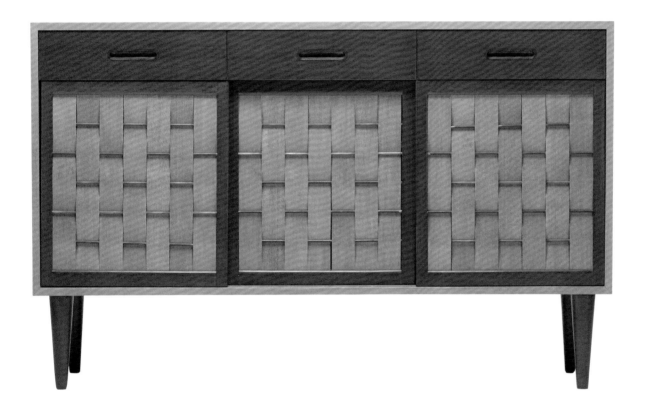

Model 5665 Cabinet

Edward Wormley, *c.* 1956 Dunbar

During Edward Wormley's four-decade tenure as design director
of Dunbar, he created a rounded collection of cabinets suited to
a variety of uses. A common theme within this range of pieces was
Wormley's combination of natural materials with textural elements
that sometimes edged toward the decorative. This Model 5665
Cabinet is one of a micro collection of interrelated designs (also
including models 5666 and 5667) that feature sliding doors made
of woven strips of timber, seen here in bleached mahogany combined
with darker mahogany for the drawers, legs and other elements.
The doors conceal shelving and pull-out trays.

Cross-Legged Cabinet

Jorge Zalszupin, *c.* 1965 L'Atelier

Like the work of his Brazilian contemporary, Joaquim Tenreiro
(see p. 334), the cabinets and buffets designed by Jorge Zalszupin
combine high craftsmanship with a monumental sense of proportion
and scale. From 1959 onward, these pieces were produced in
Zalszupin's own São Paulo workshop, known as L'Atelier. This eye-
catching piece in jacaranda from the mid-1960s combines the mass
and substance seen in many of the designer's cabinets with seemingly
delicate and lightweight cross legs, made of chrome-plated steel,
which give the impression that the entire piece is floating implausibly
above the floor.

DESKS & STORAGE

DESKS
STORAGE
SHELVES
BOOKCASES

Like so many other spheres of life, the world of work began to shift and change rapidly during the post-World War II period. Along with the consumer boom of the 1950s and 1960s, companies of all kinds began to expand their office space while paying more attention not only to the design of corporate buildings but also to their interiors. Increasingly, corporate giants saw the importance of presenting a sophisticated face to the public, with more of a focus on the design of office lobbies and public areas, as well as on the layout and aesthetics of working spaces themselves.

By the 1960s, more offices were going open plan, requiring a shift in mindset but also in the kinds of furniture and furnishings used to punctuate these spaces. The notion of a 'work station' began to develop along with shelving systems that doubled as partitions to delineate these stations, as seen in Franco Albini's LB7 Storage Unit (1957, see p. 347) and Paolo Tilche's Giraffa Bookcase (1960, see p. 388). There was a growing interest in ergonomics related to questions of both productivity and creativity, with furniture companies like Knoll and Herman Miller developing collections of desks and storage solutions targeted at the fast-growing corporate marketplace. Charles & Ray Eames, for example, developed a catalogue of storage options for Herman Miller during the 1950s, known as the ESU collection (see p. 355), in a range of sizes and a choice of integrated elements, such as shelves, drawers and storage cupboards. Again, these units could double as partitions to help define spaces within an open-plan working environment. Florence Knoll also identified the corporate world as a key marketplace, designing a number of Knoll desks, cabinets and other pieces (see pp. 364–5) suited for office use.

Another important marketplace was the education sector. Given that many architects and designers were also teaching at colleges and universities, there was a natural interest in how these environments were furnished. Examples include Poul Kjaerholm's Academy Desk of 1955 for the Royal Academy in Copenhagen (see p. 363), where the designer worked as a tutor, and Arne Jacobsen's Teacher's Desk for Munkegård School (1952, see p. 359), near Copenhagen, where the architect's remit extended from the buildings themselves to the interiors and the furniture. During the 1960s, Jacobsen took a similar approach to the design of St Catherine's College in Oxford. Similarly, the evolution of the Cité Internationale Universitaire in Paris spurred a wave of fresh and important designs, including Charlotte Perriand, Jean Prouvé and Sonia Delaunay's famous Maison du Mexique Bibliothèque (1952, see p. 379).

Importantly, there was also an increased demand for desks, bookshelves and storage for the home as working patterns began to become more informal during the 1960s and 1970s. With growing acceptance of the idea of working from home, particularly within the more creative sectors, the idea of a home office or study gradually became more relevant. This drove, in turn, the creation of elegantly designed office furniture that also sat well in the context of residential interiors. Hans Wegner's Model JH563 Desk (1950, see p. 390), for instance, is a piece that looks perfectly 'at home' in a private study, and the same can be said of the beautifully crafted designs by Jorge Zalszupin, Sergio Rodrigues and other South American masters.

FOLLOWING SPREAD The Farnsworth House, Plano, Illinois, USA, by Ludwig Mies van der Rohe, 1951

← LB7 Storage Unit

Franco Albini, 1957 Poggi/Cassina

Italian architect and designer Franco Albini created a highly adaptable, modular shelving system during the mid-1950s, which has since been reissued by Cassina (under the name Infinito). Originally made of walnut or rosewood, the LB7 library system features elegant vertical struts that can be used to support open shelves and/or drop-front cabinets. The system, which can be easily varied and multiplied, either stands against a wall or – when it is connected to the floor and ceiling with adjustable fixings – serves as a room partition accessible from either side. The LB10 variant featured wider and more substantial leg supports and could be entirely self-standing.

Stadera Desk

Franco Albini, 1958 Poggi/Cassina

With his highly rational, logical and disciplined approach to design, Albini was well suited to creating office furniture that was both elegant and functional. As well as his LB7 (opposite) and LB10 shelving systems, Albini designed desks, such as the TL22 (1958, designed in association with Franca Helg) and the distinctive Stadera Desk, both produced by Poggi. The Stadera Desk consists of two staggered, overlapping trapezoidal planes of wood resting on a single steel stem and base. The formation of the two planes offers two complementary and easily accessible working surfaces. The Stadera has been reissued by Cassina.

Model 80 Desk

Franco Albini, 1958 Gavina/Knoll

Albini's Model 80 Desk represents a process of reduction with the elements of a work station pared down to the essentials, which are then expressed with imagination and precision. The desk consists of a lightweight sawhorse frame in enamelled or chrome steel with a transparent glass tabletop perched upon it. To this, Albini adds a two-drawer lacquered wood storage box that floats on the cross bar of the sawhorse and just under the glass surface; the gap between the top of the drawers and the glass top can also be used for storing papers. The desk was originally produced by Gavina, but was then distributed more widely after Knoll acquired Gavina in 1968.

Model 1625 Desk

Milo Baughman, *c.* 1955 Glenn of California

As well as chairs, sofas and tables, Californian designer Milo Baughman designed a number of pieces suited to the study or office, such as bookshelves, storage units and desks. The Model 1625 Desk was produced by Glenn of California, one of many manufacturers with whom Baughman collaborated over the years. Made of walnut, the desk features a two-tiered working surface along with drawers arranged either side of an ergonomic indent at the centre of the piece that allows the user to bring his or her chair close to the writing surface. The depth of the overall design permitted Baughman to incorporate a hidden bookshelf at the rear of the desk.

Arco Desk

BBPR Studio Architetti, 1963 Olivetti

Milanese design partnership BBPR (founded by Gian Luigi Banfi, Lodovico Barbiano di Belgiojoso, Enrico Peressutti and Ernesto Nathan Rogers) was best known for its architecture, such as the Torre Velasca in Milan (1958). But the practice also worked with Olivetti, which began life as a typewriter manufacturer before expanding into other business and computing products, including an extensive range of office furniture. The Arco Desk, from the group's modular Spazio Collection, comprises a robust steel frame on splayed adjustable feet, a plywood top and a set of plastic drawers suspended on the frame; the system is easily expanded with a return to create an L-shaped work station.

Stillman Desk

Marcel Breuer, 1958/*c.* 1975 James Evangelisti Woodworking

During the 1960s and 1970s, businessman Rufus Stillman became one
of Marcel Breuer's greatest American patrons. Stillman asked Breuer
to design three private family homes in New England as well as playing
an important part in generating many other commissions. This walnut
desk for Stillman, made in the early 1970s, is based on a design dating
back to 1958, when Breuer first designed the piece for his own home
in New Canaan, Connecticut. A variant of the design, known as Desk
Canaan II, was also put into production by Gavina and then Knoll
during the 1960s.

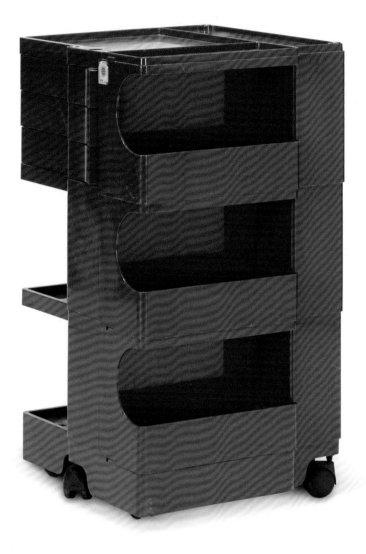

← Boby Trolley

Joe Colombo, 1970 B-Line/Bieffeplast

The Boby Trolley represents Joe Colombo's most successful and influential storage solution design, meeting his own clear ambition to create products that were affordable and flexible enough to adapt to a wide range of users and settings. Originally designed for use alongside a drawing table and made of ABS plastic, the Boby features a collection of different shelves and compartments, including a triptych of swivel-out trays. The lightweight trolley is given added dexterity by being set on castors, which means it is easily wheeled from place to place. Like Colombo's Robot Storage Trolley (1969), the Boby has been put to all sorts of uses in the home and office.

Søren Willadsen Desk

Nanna & Jørgen Ditzel, c. 1958 Søren Willadsen

Designer Nanna Ditzel and her husband, Jørgen, began designing pieces together in the 1940s and went on to establish a joint atelier, as well as write a book on Danish furniture. This elegant and finely crafted writing desk, manufactured by mid-century furniture makers Søren Willadsen, was one of their final collaborations before Jørgen's early death in 1961 at the age of forty. Graced with tapered golf-tee legs, the desk features three drawers with neatly inset handles, which preserve the clean lines of the piece.

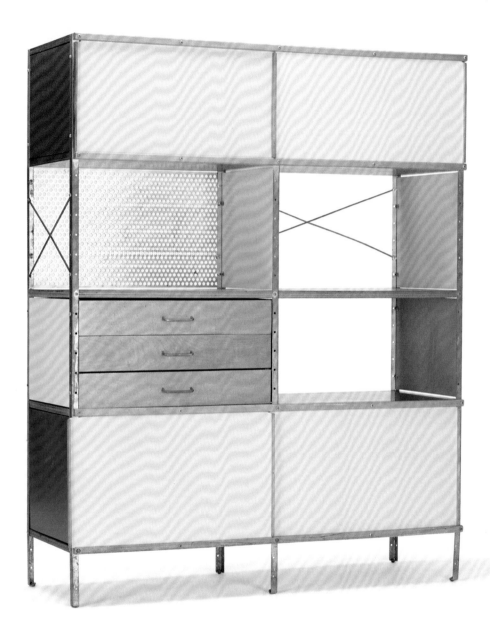

← ESU 400-C

Charles & Ray Eames, 1950 Herman Miller

The Eames Storage Unit (ESU) collection encompassed an extensive range of modular storage units of many different sizes and configurations. Drawing on experiments with storage systems dating as far back as the early 1940s, Charles & Ray Eames developed a full catalogue of options, including the 100, 200 and 400 series, plus a smaller family of desks. Designed to be free-standing and potentially doubling as partitions, pieces such as the 400-C are made of a combination of steel frames, plywood and Masonite, with a mix of drawers, open shelves and storage units protected by sliding doors. A choice of brightly coloured panels was offered as an option within the range, adding a playful touch to a serious, workhorse system.

Bookcase

Piero Fornasetti & Gio Ponti, c. 1955 Giordano Chiesa

Piero Fornasetti and Gio Ponti collaborated periodically from the 1930s onward on furniture and larger projects, including architectural and interior commissions. For their furniture, Ponti tended to define the form and function of the piece, while Fornasetti added layers of decoration and storytelling. Their designs include this substantial bookcase, almost a work of architecture in itself, and largely made of ash. As well as open shelves, the unit features four cabinets protected by hinged or drop-front drawers decorated with *trompe l'oeil* panels of Fornasetti's 'Libri' motif. The shelves of books depicted within the motif offer a kind of meta-referential echo of the purpose of the overall design.

Executive Desk

Herbert Hirche, 1967 Christian Holzäpfel

German architect and designer Herbert Hirche is best known
for his post-war designs for Braun, including his multifaceted hi-fi
cabinets. Yet Hirche's work was wide-ranging and included office
buildings, factories and houses, as well as furniture designs for a
number of producers, such as Christian Holzäpfel. This Executive
Desk, made largely in rosewood with an aluminium base, is part
of a related series produced during the 1960s. Elegant, well detailed
and beautifully crafted, this version features a pair of boxed storage
drawers, along with two writing or drawing surfaces that pull out
from a recessed position set into the edge of the desktop.

Pontoppidan Desk

Peter Hvidt & Orla Mølgaard-Nielsen, 1959
Ludvig Pontoppidan

The creative collaboration between Danish designers Peter Hvidt and Orla Mølgaard-Nielsen, which continued for around thirty years from the mid-1940s, produced many successful, innovative and exquisitely crafted designs. Among these were chairs for Fritz Hansen and Søborg Møbelfabrik, as well as tables and desks, including this rosewood desk produced by Ludvig Pontoppidan. Two pivoting drawer units, or 'secretaries', are positioned under the desktop, toward either end of the desk. One of these holds three locking drawers and the other just two, with recessed handles preserving the sense of crafted, ergonomic simplicity.

Extendable Desk

Arne Jacobsen, 1952 Rud Rasmussens Snedkerier

As an architect and designer who worked on a number of educational projects, including schools and universities, Arne Jacobsen created multiple collections of desks, desk chairs and desk lights during his career. This innovative and flexible desk design, made with a lightweight chrome-plated tubular steel frame, features a plywood top finished in leather plus a set of six suspended plywood drawers to one side floating lightly upon the frame. The desk is easily extended by swinging round a pivoting typewriter/writing surface at one end of the unit to sit at right angles to the main body of the desk.

Munkegård Teacher's Desk

Arne Jacobsen, 1952 Fritz Hansen

Situated in Gentofte, just north of Copenhagen, Munkegård School, a collection of single-storey classrooms interspersed with courtyards, is a prime example of one of Jacobsen's all-encompassing commissions, which fused architecture, interiors and furniture design. Jacobsen's remit extended to every detail, including desks for teachers and pupils. This distinctive and sculptural teacher's desk features a plane of moulded teak plywood wrapped around a chrome-plated tubular steel frame. Two drawers are tucked under the desktop, with a simple pencil store slot recessed into the writing surface. The success of Munkegård helped Jacobsen to secure the commission to design St Catherine's College in Oxford during the 1960s.

Chandigarh Administrative Desk

Pierre Jeanneret, *c.* 1960 Limited edition

As part of Le Corbusier's and Pierre Jeanneret's epic commission
to design a new state capital and administrative centre in the Punjab,
Jeanneret designed a vast collection of furniture to serve the various
buildings at Chandigarh. Within the collection was a wide range
of desks and desk chairs, including designs for the city's college
of architecture as well as its judicial and administration centres.
One of the most pleasing of these designs is this desk from the early
1960s, made largely in teak with a leather writing surface on the
desktop. The desk, used in the administrative buildings, features
a set of four drawers on one side and a distinctive X-shaped support
on the other.

Diplomat Desk

Finn Juhl, *c.* 1961 France & Søn

During the early 1950s Finn Juhl began collaborating with Danish
manufacturer France & Søn, founded by British entrepreneur
Charles France and his Danish business partner Eric Daverkosen.
Together, the designer and manufacturer developed pieces that
could be produced on an industrial scale. The majority of these
pieces were chairs and sofas, but there was also the elegant
Diplomat Desk made of teak. The Diplomat features a matching
pair of slim drawers slung under the worktop, plus two pull-out
work surfaces. A variant known as the Technocrat Desk featured
five more substantial drawers arranged in two bays at each end
of the desk.

Office Suite

Bodil Kjaer, 1959 E. Pedersen & Son

Bodil Kjaer's 'working table' was originally designed during the
late 1950s for offices at the Massachusetts Institute of Technology.
However it became better known as the 'James Bond Desk' after
famously featuring in three Bond films during the 1960s, including
You Only Live Twice (Lewis Gilbert, 1967). The distinctive design
features a slim profile, rosewood top with four integrated and
locking drawers supported by lightweight chrome-plated steel legs
and frame. This suite comprises not only the desk itself but also two
matching cabinets on castors, which tuck neatly under the two ends
of the worktop. Kjaer also designed a rosewood cabinet at around
the same time (see p. 316).

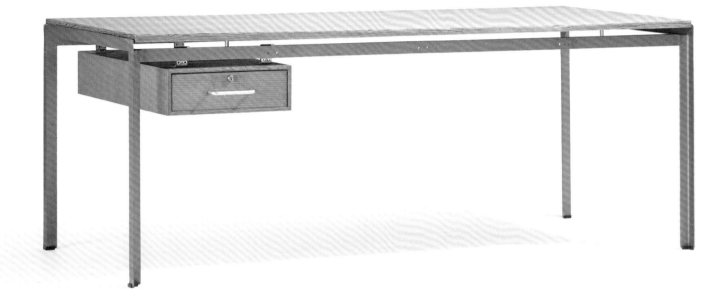

Academy Desk

Poul Kjaerholm, 1955 Rud Rasmussens Snedkerier

Given their purity, elegance and flexibility, a number of Poul
Kjaerholm's tables, such as the PK51 (1957, produced by E. Kold
Christensen), have served not only as dining tables but also as desks.
However, in 1955, just after his appointment as a tutor within the
Department of Furniture at the Royal Academy in Copenhagen,
Kjaerholm was commissioned to produce a dedicated desk for the
School of Architecture. The standard version of the Academy Desk
features a pine top resting on a slim enamelled steel base, with an
option for a single, lockable draw underneath the desktop. But there
was also a range of options for different lengths and finishes, leading
to subtle variations within the Academy line.

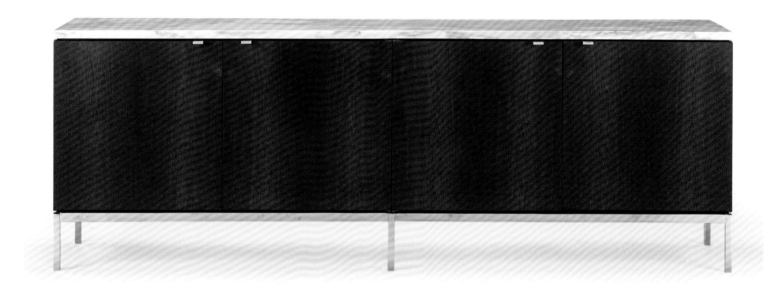

Executive Office Cabinet

Florence Knoll, 1961 Knoll

From the early years of the Knoll furniture company, founded
by Hans Knoll in 1938, office furniture was an important part of
the portfolio. Many of the earliest pieces were designed by Florence
Knoll herself, and her continuing commitment to this arm of the
business culminated in the iconic Executive Office Collection of
1961. A key element of the Executive collection was Knoll's range
of handsome cabinets with chrome-plated steel legs, timber
carcasses, doors and drawers, and marble tops. As well as various
choices for the timber (including rosewood, walnut and ash), there
were also options on length as well as the formation of drawers
and filing drawers.

Executive Desk

Florence Knoll, 1961 Knoll

Arguably, Florence Knoll played an inspirational role in bringing
a true sense of sophistication and elegance to modern office interiors.
As well as careful consideration of ergonomics and planning, Knoll
employed fine materials and finishes to create the kind of furniture
one would be happy to see in the home as well as the office. A key
exemplar is her Executive Desk (also known as the Partner's Desk)
of 1961, with its crafted rosewood top and two slim drawers recessed
within the edge of the desktop. The splayed legs of the slender
chrome-plated steel base match the 2480 Pedestal Table Desk, also
part of the Executive series, which could easily serve as a meeting
or dining table.

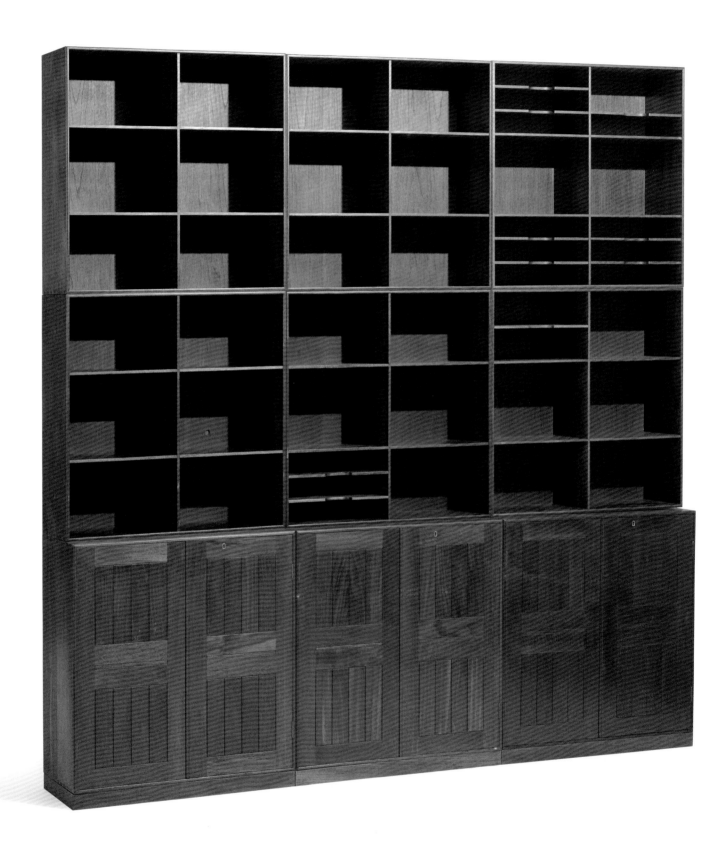

← Bookcases

Mogens Koch, *c.* 1960 Rud Rasmussens Snedkerier

Many of the most successful designs by Danish master Mogens Koch were essentially imaginative reinterpretations of familiar typologies. There was his folding MK Safari Chair of 1932, for instance, and also his famous post-war bookcase and cabinet system of the 1960s. Using pine, mahogany and (as seen here) teak, Koch designed a set of open wooden cases and closed cabinets that could be combined in many different formations. Here, there are six open cases over three closed cabinets, featuring hidden drawers and storage compartments. The cases could also be wall mounted.

Planner Group Desk

Paul McCobb, 1952 Winchendon

The Planner Group by American designer Paul McCobb offered an extensive collection of affordable, modular modern furniture for the home or office. Manufactured by Winchendon, using maple wood in a range of finishes, the collection included a number of designs suited to the study or workplace, including storage units, desk organizers and desks. Typically for McCobb's modular system, this Planner Desk is composed of two complementary units: a Model 1596 Table with a lightweight steel frame and legs, plus two small drawers, and a Model 1562 Cabinet on top, featuring a drop-front work surface as well as additional storage space.

← Glenn Desk

Greta Magnusson Grossman, *c.* 1952 Glenn of California

After moving to the USA from her native Sweden in 1940, Greta Magnusson Grossman began working with a number of American producers, as well as opening her own store in Beverly Hills. These manufacturers included Glenn of California, who produced this eye-catching desk during the 1950s. The piece was made with multiple variations and finishes, but the essential form remained the same: a walnut storage compartment at one end is supported by two small steel legs and a slim, sculptural element at the other, reminiscent of the designer's mid-century floor-light bases. Together, these elements underpin the writing surface, sometimes complemented by an additional, elevated storage compartment floating above the desktop and held aloft by two thin struts.

Mascheroni Desk

Angelo Mangiarotti & Bruno Morassutti, 1955 Mascheroni

During the late 1950s, Italian architect and designer Angelo Mangiarotti formed a five-year collaborative partnership with fellow architect Bruno Morassutti. Much of their work revolved around architectural commissions, but also included some pieces of furniture, such as this elegant walnut desk made by Mascheroni, a manufacturer based near Milan. Made of mahogany, the desk features a triptych of distinctive A-frame legs, supporting the work surface and a set of six drawers. During the early 1970s, Mangiarotti's famous Eros series of marble tables (see p. 277) and consoles (produced by Skipper) also included a desk in a similar style.

Drop-Leaf Desk

Børge Mogensen, *c.* 1950 Søborg Møbelfabrik

The prolific but thoughtful Danish designer Børge Mogensen applied
his research into ergonomics and his passion for both craft and
function to furniture for the workplace as well as for the home.
This elegant, Drop-Leaf Desk produced by Søborg Møbelfabrik
allows for flexibility of use, with the folding extension to the teak
desktop adding nearly a third more surface space. A chrome-plated
tubular steel frame also means that the piece is very light and easy
to move into different positions, while two modest drawers are tucked
under the worktop at the opposite end to the drop leaf.

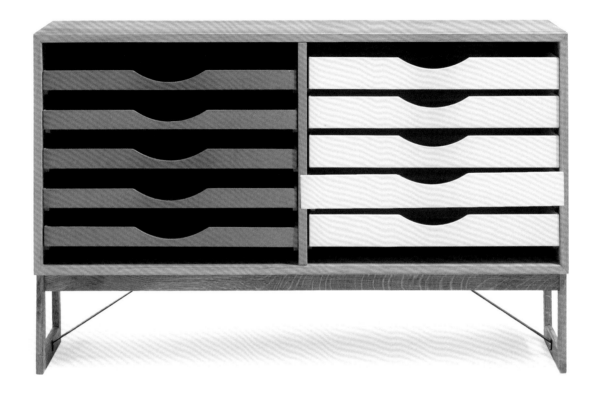

Office Cabinet

Børge Mogensen, *c.* 1955 Karl Andersson & Söner

Along with a number of his mid-century contemporaries, Mogensen
had a particular interest in storage solutions that allowed spaces
to remain uncluttered and ordered within offices and workplaces
as well as the home. There were designs for bookcases for Fredericia,
wall-mounted shelving units for Erhard Rasmussen and a series
of cabinets and filing units for Karl Andersson & Söner. This playful
cabinet in oak and lacquered wood has ten pull-out filing drawers
faced in white and ochre. The same design language and aesthetic
was applied to wall-mounted cabinets and also a desk organizer.

Cross-Leg Desk

George Nakashima, 1959 Nakashima Studio

Like the design of large tables, the creation of desks allowed George Nakashima the golden opportunity to select big slabs of timber suited for use as worktops and writing surfaces. These carefully chosen and lovingly cut pieces of wood were given the chance to fully express their own character in terms of shape and grain. A prime example is this Cross-Leg Desk from 1959, where so much of the piece's identity is defined by the simply finished desktop in American black walnut, while the elegant cross legs are highly crafted yet also subservient to the main event above.

Conoid Desk

George Nakashima, 1964 Nakashima Studio

Among Nakashima's many desk designs from the 1950s and 1960s
was a series of single and double pedestal desks incorporating
drawer units (usually with one deep drawer at the lowermost level
and two shallower drawers above). This 1964 Conoid Desk, named
after Nakashima's self-designed Conoid Studio on his Pennsylvanian
farmstead, is made of American black walnut and features a single
pedestal on one side and a slim cross-leg support on the other.
As is usual for Nakashima, the worktop is formed from one slab
of lovingly curated timber.

Home Office Desk Model 4658

George Nelson, 1946 Herman Miller

From 1945 onward, when George Nelson was appointed design director of the firm, Herman Miller began developing original designs to meet the growing demand for home-office systems. In 1946 Herman Miller released its ingenious Home Office Desk Model 4658, offering a work station that cleverly conceals all the detritus of work when not in use. Tubular steel legs support the walnut or oak worktop, which, in turn, hosts a suspended filing basket in perforated aluminium and a flip-up lid, which disguises a compartment for letters and stationery; a typewriter could also be fixed to the underside of the lid for use when open. An additional storage console floats above the desktop with twin sliding doors. The desk came in different colour options and a leather finish to part of the worktop and the front pieces of the sliding doors.

Swag Leg Desk Model 5850 →

George Nelson, 1958 Herman Miller

During the 1950s George Nelson & Associates continued to explore designs for desks and storage systems that were elegant and appealing enough for home use. One of the most distinctive and characterful of these models is the Swag Leg Desk Model 5850, which forms part of Herman Miller's Swag Leg series, with chairs and a dining table (Model 5853) featuring similarly sculptural chrome-plated steel legs. The desk itself has the look and feel of a keyboard, minus the keys, with the work surface backed by a set of storage compartments featuring colourful dividers in lacquered wood, along with sinuous walnut side panels that bind these elements together. There are some similarities, particularly in terms of the keyboard look, with Nelson's Roll-Top Desk Model 5496 (1955) and Action Office Desk (1964).

Comprehensive Storage System (CSS)

George Nelson, 1959 Herman Miller

As well as serving the home market for desks and storage units, Herman Miller also developed ranges aimed at corporate settings. These collections, designed by George Nelson & Associates, included the Steelframe Series (1954) and the Modern Management Group (1957). There were also storage solution systems aimed primarily at office use, such as the Comprehensive Storage System (CSS) of 1959. The CSS is essentially a shelving system fixed to both the wall and floor, which includes a range of options for storage units within the system, such as drawer cabinets and flip-top or hinge-door consoles. The uprights of the modular system, which can be easily rearranged or expanded, are in metal while the shelves and storage units are usually in walnut; other options include lighting and desks anchored to the wall-based CSS.

← Maison du Mexique Bibliothèque

Charlotte Perriand, Jean Prouvé & Sonia Delaunay, 1952
Ateliers Jean Prouvé

With an interrelated series of mid-century bibliothèques, Charlotte Perriand turned the modern bookshelf into a work of art. Chief among the systems is this innovative design for the Maison du Mexique student dormitory building at Paris's Cité Internationale Universitaire. Working with friend and colleague Jean Prouvé, Perriand designed a substantial, sculptural unit in pine, mahogany and enamelled steel sheets, which create cubist compartments within the bibliothèque. Artist Sonia Delaunay advised on the choice of colours in the resulting montage, which also uses more textural diamond point aluminium. This standalone piece could be employed as a screen, while variations upon the concept include the Maison de la Tunisie Bibliothèque, also for the Cité Universitaire (1952).

Nuage Bibliothèque

Charlotte Perriand & Le Corbusier, *c.* 1956 Ateliers
Jean Prouvé for Galerie Steph Simon/Cassina

During the 1950s, Perriand continued to explore original ideas for bookshelves and storage solutions of various kinds, including multiple versions of her modular Nuage Bibliothèque, initially produced by Ateliers Jean Prouvé for Galerie Steph Simon. These early wall-mounted Nuage, or 'cloud', units come in various configurations, with two or three horizontal layers of ash shelves held together by U-shaped aluminium supports. Perriand's bibliothèques offer graphic 'wallscapes', which invite the participation of the owner in completing the composition through the curation of the books or artworks chosen for display. Later versions of the Nuage, reissued by Cassina, include more substantial, free-standing models and options for sliding doors to protect key compartments.

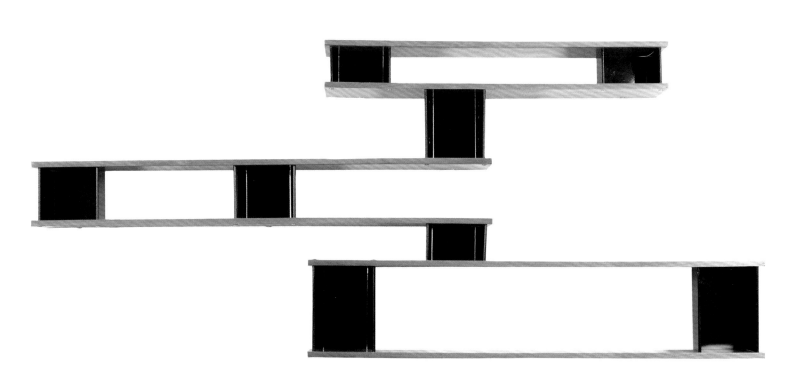

Executive Desk

Warren Platner, 1966 Lehigh Leopold

American architect and designer Warren Platner is best known
for his nine-piece collection of bent steel-wire furniture for Knoll,
commonly known as the Platner Collection (see pp. 86 and 290).
Yet he also designed buildings, interiors and many other pieces
of furniture, including this Executive Desk produced by Lehigh
Leopold. The desk is supported by a dramatic pedestal, made of
stainless steel and composed of a base plate and a vertical support
plate. These hold up the walnut (or rosewood) writing surface above,
finished in leather, while there are two suspended drawers of different
dimensions at each end of the desk. Platner also worked with Lehigh
Leopold on other designs using a similar, distinctive pedestal,
including a credenza, sofa and armchair.

Pirelli Tower Desk

Gio Ponti, 1961 Limited edition

During his long and multifaceted career, Italian master architect
and designer Gio Ponti designed desks for the University of Padua
(1935), the Montecatini office building in Milan (1938) and the Forli
Administrative Offices (c. 1955). This design was created for the
offices situated in Ponti's most famous building: Milan's landmark
Pirelli Tower (designed in association with engineer Pier Luigi
Nervi). The desk itself adopts a simple, sculptural, streamlined form,
with a chrome-plated steel base and a sleek mahogany worktop.
This model features an additional three-drawer unit fixed to one of
the base's steel uprights, as well as a rolling cabinet on four castors.

School Desk

Jean Prouvé, 1946 Ateliers Jean Prouvé

A number of Jean Prouvé's early furniture designs related to education in one way or another. These included desks and other furniture for the Cité Universitaire in Nancy (1931) and a classroom desk for the École Nationale Professionnelle de Metz (1936). The Metz design, created for two pupils sitting next to one another, featured a single worktop and a pair of plywood seats arranged on a steel frame, which was designed as a single supporting element. This idea proved so successful that Prouvé developed multiple variations on the design, including this School Desk from 1946 made with enamelled steel and beech for the desktop and seating.

Compas Desk

Jean Prouvé, 1953 Ateliers Jean Prouvé

Jean Prouvé developed a whole series of desk designs during the
1940s and 1950s, while continuing to receive commissions from
educational institutions such as the Cité Universitaire in Antony
and the Université de Lille. One of the most famous of these designs
is the Compas Desk of 1953, a variation on Prouvé's Compas Table.
The desk features a pair of tapered, enamelled steel legs (each one
reminiscent of a compass) in a trestle-style formation linked with
a cross beam, supporting a simple wooden worktop. The resulting
shape is pleasing in itself, yet there are also versions that offer a
choice of drawers suspended under the worktop, ranging from a pair
of single drawers (one at either end) to a set of three. There is also
a curved version.

← 606 Universal Shelving System

Dieter Rams, 1960 Vitsoe

With his rigorous focus on form, function and elegant minimalism, Dieter Rams played a key part in defining Braun's products from the mid-1950s onward, serving as the electronic giant's head of design for over three decades. In 1959 Rams accepted a rare commission from beyond the Braun family, creating the modular Universal Shelving System for Vitsoe. The foundation of the system is a set of wall-mounted aluminium struts, which support not only shelves, made of the same anodized metal, but also a collection of other component parts, including drawer and storage units, as well as work and display surfaces. Adaptable and flexible, the Universal Shelving System remains a familiar feature in many modern homes (including Rams's own house in Frankfurt) and workplaces.

Risom Desk

Jens Risom, c. 1955 Jens Risom Design

Having created some of Knoll's earliest furniture designs during the 1940s, Danish-born Jens Risom established his own firm in 1946. Risom's furniture adopted a Scandinavian aesthetic with a focus predominantly on crafted timber, as seen in the walnut desktop and drawers of this desk from the mid-1950s. The detailing of the neatly partitioned drawer interiors and handles is finely done, while the writing surface is finished in leather. The frame of the piece is in aluminium, offering a sense of contrast with the timber and creating a sense of lightness.

Clara Desk

Sergio Rodrigues, 1965 Oca

Brazilian designer Sergio Rodrigues was best known for his
expressive, sink-in armchairs and sofas coated in soft leather
cushions. Yet his portfolio was broad and included benches, tables
and desks that explored the beauty and character of native hardwoods.
Among these was a series of desks produced by Rodrigues's own
furniture company, Oca, such as the Itamaraty Desk of 1960 and
the Gordon Desk of 1962. Like its predecessors, the Clara Desk
is made of jacaranda, with the crafted timber lending the piece
warmth and substance. A bank of three drawers sits on either side,
featuring inset circular finger-pulls rather than handles.

Bookshelf →

Joaquim Tenreiro, *c.* 1954 Tenreiro Móveis
e Decorações

There was a lightness of both touch and appearance to Joaquim
Tenreiro's work, which extended into the field of desks, shelves and
storage solutions. With his shelving units, in particular, Tenreiro
created both floor and wall-mounted pieces, usually in Brazilian
hardwoods, that possessed a highly sculptural quality. Made of
jacaranda, this bespoke piece manages to combine a sense of delicacy
with a robust, functional structure. A slim framework, reinforced
by cross bracing, helps to support three integrated storage cabinets,
as well as shelving. One of these cabinets features a drop-down desk
while the other two are devoted to storage. The slimmest cabinet
has sliding doors made of reverse-painted glass.

Giraffa Bookcase

Paolo Tilche, 1960 Arform

Flexibility was a key element in the furniture and products invented by Italian architect and designer Paolo Tilche. His designs for Arform, for instance, included a 1956 desk with an additional pull-out work surface, and a 1963 table with twin leaves that could be demounted and neatly stored away, allowing the piece to serve as a console. This teak bookcase, designed to be fixed to both the floor and ceiling, is also adjustable in terms of the position of its shelves and the potential of the integrated storage cabinet's drop-front door to be used as a work surface. The design can be compared to Franco Albini's LB7 (1957, see p. 347) and LB10 shelving systems for Poggi.

Desk & Return →

Arne Vodder, c. 1955 Sibast Furniture

Danish designer Arne Vodder designed a number of desks and storage cabinets for Sibast during the 1950s and 1960s. Typically, these pieces were made of crafted teak or rosewood (or jacaranda), lending comparison with the work of Jorge Zalszupin and other contemporaries in Brazil, as well as with some designers in Denmark itself. This Desk & Return is one of Vodder's most complex and substantial pieces, featuring a teak desk with two suspended drawers and a side return, with these two elements arranged in an L-shaped formation. As well as an additional writing surface, the return offers extra storage, including a set of colourful, lacquered pull-out filing drawers in the centre, which contrast with the prevailing natural timber finish.

Snedkermester Desk →

Ole Wanscher, c. 1960 A. J. Iversen Snedkermester

Characteristically, the desks designed by Ole Wanscher fuse modern influences, masterful craftsmanship and historical references. During the 1940s the Danish designer created a desk for Fritz Hansen in walnut and brass, followed by pieces for A. J. Iversen Snedkermester in mahogany. This desk from the 1960s has more in the way of a mid-century character, as seen in the expressive detailing of the legs and frame. Made of teak, the desk features three drawers with brass handles and a drop-leaf extension to the writing surface, suggesting an appreciation of the increasing demand for flexible furniture during the period.

Model JH563 Desk ↑

Hans Wegner, 1950 Johannes Hansen

Masterful and prolific Danish furniture designer Hans Wegner
periodically turned his attention to desks and desk chairs. These
included the Model AT325 Desk in teak and steel (*c.* 1960) produced
by Andreas Tuck, and multiple designs for Johannes Hansen, including
the Model JH810 Desk (1960) and this delightful piece, made of
teak and oak, dating from 1950. The delight comes chiefly from the
delicately tapered legs and the frame, including a central V-shaped
support, that connects a cross brace to the worktop, a detail that echoes
the wishbone motif seen in one of Wegner's most famous chairs. The
piece also has two slim drawers, one on either side of the desk, which
do not interfere with the appreciation of the overall composition.

↓ Model 912C Roll-Top Desk

Edward Wormley, *c.* 1957 Dunbar

American designer Edward Wormley created a handful of highly original desks for the Dunbar Furniture Company, where he was director of design for almost forty years. These included two striking designs from the 1950s: the sculptural Model 5735 Desk (*c.* 1957) in walnut and mahogany, and the Model 912C, which spliced the idea of a traditional writing desk with a roll top. Made principally of walnut and rosewood (jacaranda), the desk has a central worktop flanked by two compartments with rolling tambour doors concealing storage beneath; a triptych of slim drawers is also situated beneath the desktop. During the 1970s, Dunbar produced a variation on the design featuring a steel-framed base designed by architect Rex Goode.

Jacaranda Desk ↑

Jorge Zalszupin, *c.* 1965 L'Atelier

The cabinets and credenzas designed by Jorge Zalszupin have a sense of presence and character born of their almost architectural monumentality. The same is true of an interrelated collection of jacaranda (or rosewood) desks produced by L'Atelier during the 1960s. Also known as patchwork desks on account of their characterful collage of conjoined strips of jacaranda, the desks offer subtle variations in their detailing and configuration. This model, from the mid-1960s, features a set of three drawers plus an additional pull-out work surface on one side. Distinctive handles are formed from leather bindings wrapped around rounded batons of timber.

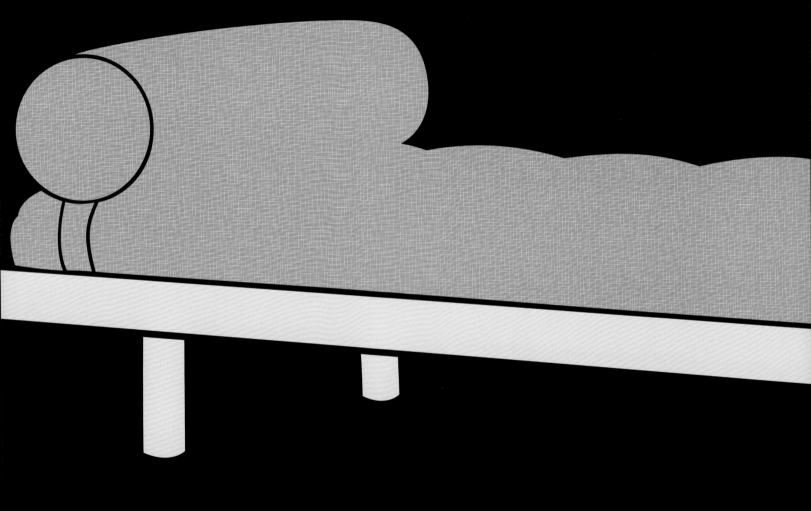

BEDS & BEDSIDE

BEDS

DAYBEDS

NIGHTSTANDS

The design of beds and daybeds offered mid-century designers a number of golden opportunities. First, there was the chance to create an expressive piece of furniture that sat well with the more exuberant strand of mid-century style. Beds by such designers as Carlo de Carli, Ico & Luisa Parisi and Osvaldo Borsani, for example, explored the kind of playful and sculptural forms that were much in evidence in mid-century Italian design in general. Borsani, for instance, collaborated with Italian sculptor Arnaldo Pomodoro to develop a brass bed for Tecno (*c*. 1960, see p. 398) that encapsulated both artistry and delight.

Second, there was the opportunity to place the bed within the context of a wider ergonomic environment. Architect and designer Gio Ponti devised a number of beds that featured integrated headboards, with shelves, lighting, a radio and other elements contained within one cohesive unit. Such an approach was well suited to hotels, as seen in Ponti's beds for the Royal Hotel in Naples (1948, see p. 421), but also to the home. Joe Colombo famously took the notion of a multifaceted living environment even further in his Cabriolet Bed (1969), which featured a radio, fan and ashtray in the headboard, as well as a vanity unit tucked neatly onto the back of it. An integrated canopy could also be folded down to create a room within a room. Colombo expanded on the idea of an experimental 'dwelling machine' in his Total Furnishing Unit (1972), which packed all of the essential elements of the home – including a bed – into one compact installation.

Daybeds also experienced a marked revival during the 1950s and 1960s. The idea of a daybed stretches back to the Romans and Greeks, yet there was something about the flexibility and informality of a daybed that made it a staple of mid-century design. An elegant, well-designed daybed could certainly serve multiple uses within different parts of a home or hotel. Daybeds by Charlotte Perriand, Pierre Jeanneret, Bruno Mathsson, Finn Juhl and others could serve as seating, recliners or lightweight beds. Jean Prouvé's Antony Daybed (1954, see p. 425) was originally designed to do all of these things within students' rooms at the Cité Universitaire in Antony, Paris.

The daybed came complete with a small integrated side table, which could be neatly tucked away under the bed when not in use.

The flexibility and malleability of such pieces of furniture also helped to inform the evolution of the sofa bed. Well suited to occasional use for sleeping, particularly by visiting guests, beautifully crafted sofa beds by Richard Stein, Hans Wegner and others were also elegant enough to serve as desirable focal points in a room. Wegner's ingenious GE 258 Sofa Bed for Getama (*c*. 1954, see p. 430) featured an upholstered, angled backrest that could be simply pushed back and repositioned to free the full width of the mattress for sleeping.

FOLLOWING SPREAD Healy Guest House, Sarasota, Florida, USA, by Ralph Twitchell & Paul Rudolph, 1950

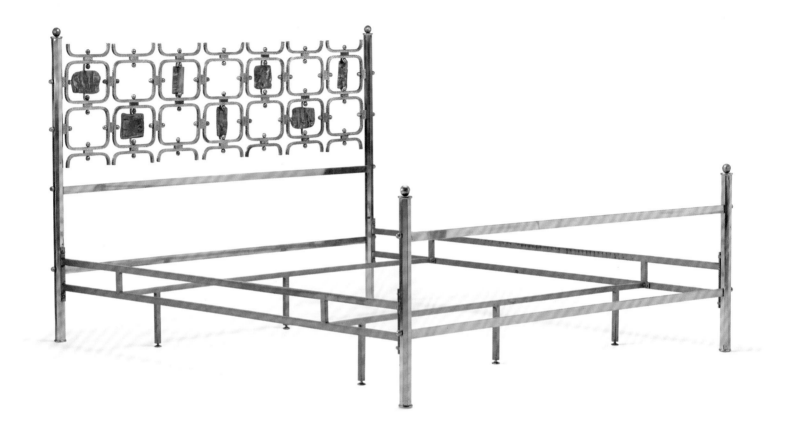

Brass Bed

Osvaldo Borsani & Arnaldo Pomodoro, *c.* 1960 Tecno

Along with his twin brother Fulgenzio, designer and entrepreneur
Osvaldo Borsani was the co-founder of Italian furniture company
Tecno. As well as designing many of Tecno's most famous chairs
and sofas (such as the P40 Folding Lounge Chair and D70 Sofa,
see p. 199), Osvaldo created this bed frame in fire-enamelled brass
and enamelled steel in collaboration with Italian sculptor Arnaldo
Pomodoro, who settled in Milan (where the Borsanis were based)
during the early 1950s. Rich in colour and texture, the bed is
one of Tecno's more expressive and atypical pieces, suggesting
the strength of Pomodoro's influence upon its design.

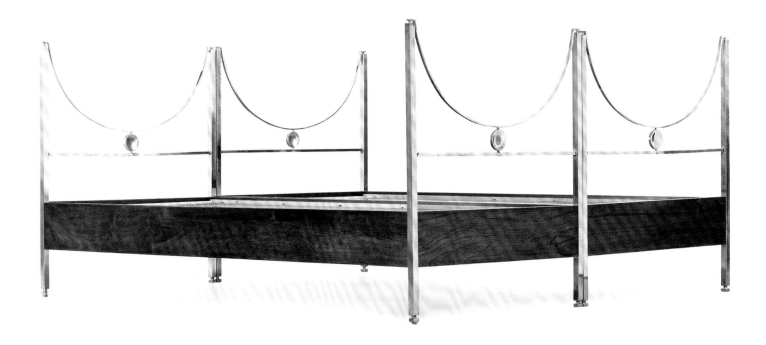

Model D90 Beds

Carlo de Carli, 1963 Sormani

Milanese furniture designer Carlo de Carli began his career working for Gio Ponti before establishing his own atelier, designing for manufacturers such as Cassina and Gubi. This distinctive pair of matching beds, in rosewood and brass, was designed for the Italian furniture company founded in 1961 by Luigi Sormani, which soon established a strong reputation for its focus on fine craftsmanship and imported hardwoods. Later, de Carli became a highly influential academic and writer at the Politecnico di Milano, which he had attended himself as a student.

Camillo Beds

Achille Castiglioni, *c.* 1946 Gavina

Of the three Castiglioni brothers, Achille Castiglioni was the youngest and enjoyed by far the longest career, which took him from the 1940s all the way through to the 1990s (he died in 2002). This matching pair of beds for Gavina, in mahogany and mahogany plywood, was one of his earliest solo commissions after graduating from the Politecnico di Milano in 1944. The use of curvaceous ply for the headboard and footboard softens the outline of the design, while raising it above the ordinary. Around the same time, just after the end of World War II, Achille began collaborating with his middle brother Pier Giacomo, with the two of them co-authoring many of the most famous Castiglioni furniture and lighting designs.

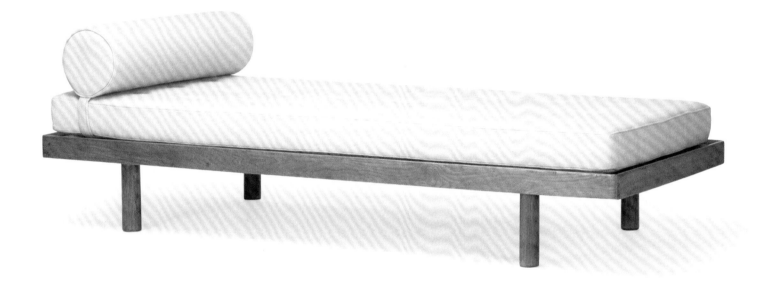

Chapo Daybed

Pierre Chapo, *c.* 1960 Atelier Pierre Chapo

Drawing inspiration from the organic design principles of Frank
Lloyd Wright and a love of natural materials, French designer–
maker Pierre Chapo is best known for his crafted but modern
timber furniture of the 1960s and 1970s. One of Chapo's first private
commissions was a bed, a one-off piece for writer Samuel Beckett
and known as The Godot Bed (1965), while this daybed, in stained
pine (or sometimes oak), is one of his most elegant and successful
designs. With its combination of simplicity, restraint and modernity,
it recalls mid-century daybeds by other French designers such as
Charlotte Perriand and Jean Prouvé.

Jeppesen Daybed

Grete Jalk, *c.* 1965 Poul Jeppesen

Danish designer, writer and editor Grete Jalk is best known for her dynamic and sculptural chairs of the 1960s made of plywood and laminated timber (see p. 58), as well as crafted lounge chairs. But Jalk was also the author of sofas and daybeds, including this piece from the mid-1960s produced by Poul Jeppesen, with whom she collaborated many times. Suitable for sleeping and/or seating, the daybed features a sturdy oak (or teak) frame, comfortable mattress and an ingenious hinged backrest that opens up like a clam shell and can be used for storing sheets and blankets.

Chandigarh Daybed
(private residences)

Pierre Jeanneret, *c.* 1955 Limited edition

Among the many pieces of furniture designed especially for the new city of Chandigarh in northern India, a series of daybeds was created by Pierre Jeanneret, who worked on the epic project in conjunction with his cousin and colleague Le Corbusier. The series included designs featuring splayed legs and thick, heavy-duty mattresses for the Administrative Buildings, as well as lighter pieces created for the private houses and residences. Made in India with teak frames, slim mattresses and roll cushions, the Jeanneret daybeds – along with so many other Chandigarh classics – are now highly collectable.

Baker Twin Beds ↑

Finn Juhl, *c.* 1951 Baker Furniture

During the 1940s and 1950s, celebrated Danish designer Finn Juhl established a reputation for curvaceous, sculptural forms combined with high standards of craftsmanship and fine materials. Such an approach was seen at its height in Juhl's chairs and sofas, from the Pelican Chair of 1940 and the Poet Sofa of 1941 onward (see p. 208), yet the designer also brought his imagination to bear on more prosaic pieces, such as these beds designed for the American manufacturer Baker Furniture. Made of walnut and maple, the picket fence headboard seems familiar but the curving high bar on the footboard – rather like the top of a church pew – is a delightful touch that elevates the design as a whole.

Bovirke Daybed ↑

Finn Juhl, *c.* 1955 Bovirke

Over the course of his career, Finn Juhl worked with a number of manufacturers in Denmark and beyond, including Niels Vodder, France & Søn and Baker Furniture. His relationship with Danish manufacturer Bovirke began in the mid-1940s and included chairs, desks and hybrid pieces such as the Table Bench of 1953, strong enough to serve as a low table, a bench or even a daybed. This dedicated daybed was produced around the same time, and made with a teak frame, slim steel legs and an upholstered mattress. There was also an elegant Cocktail Bench for Baker Furniture (1951) in walnut that shared a similarly multifunctional purpose.

PK80 Daybed ↓

Poul Kjaerholm, 1957 E. Kold Christensen/Fritz Hansen

Poul Kjaerholm's PK80 is one of the most successful and influential examples of mid-century daybed design. Taking some inspiration from Mies van der Rohe and Lilly Reich's Barcelona Daybed of 1929, Kjaerholm created an elegantly crafted piece using lightweight steel legs and frame, a plywood base plate and a neatly upholstered leather-coated mattress. Simple rubber O-rings attach the frame to the plate, while leather tabs are passed through the rings to keep the mattress in place; the clear distinction between these elements allows the PK80 to be easily assembled or disassembled. A square version of the daybed was custom produced for a number of key projects such as Tårnby Town Hall in Denmark.

Nightstands Model 127

Florence Knoll, 1948 Knoll

As a designer, Florence Knoll's extensive portfolio included a wide range of cabinets and storage solutions for both home and office. There was a number of designs for nightstands, with these elegant Model 127 pieces being an early example. Made of birch, each three-drawer cabinet sits upon tapered wooden legs. Later, during the mid-1950s, Florence Knoll designed the Model 227 nightstand in walnut with a laminate top, as well as the wall-mounted Model 575 in teak with an additional steel supporting mono-leg to the front.

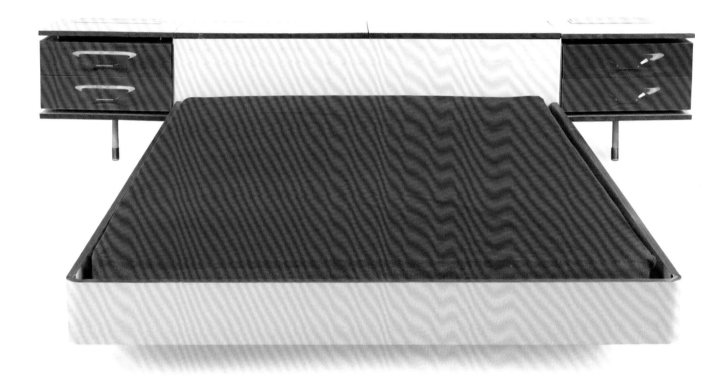

DF-2000 Bed

Raymond Loewy, *c.* 1960 Compagnie de l'esthétique Industrielle/Doubinsky Frères

As one of the most influential industrial and product designers of the 20th century, Raymond Loewy designed everything from trains to cars to refrigerators. His colourful DF-2000 furniture collection of the 1960s included cabinets, nightstands, valet units and this dynamic headboard and bed made from laminates and plastics. The headboard doubles as a storage unit, with twin drawers at either end picked out in a vivid crimson. Rather like contemporaneous designs by Joe Colombo, the headboard – which also includes integrated lighting – is multifunctional.

Kyoto Daybed

Mathieu Matégot, *c.* 1950 Atelier Matégot

Hungarian–French designer Mathieu Matégot balanced two successful
careers in tapestry and furniture. In the field of furniture, Matégot
and his own workshops (in Paris and Casablanca) pioneered the use
of tubular and perforated steel in sculptural chairs, tables and other
lightweight designs. Among these pieces, which were usually given
evocative lyrical names, the Kyoto Daybed was made in France
with a tubular steel frame, a perforated metal base and a mattress
upholstered in leather. In profile, the shape of the combined legs and
side supports creates an elegant 'W' with a flattened, horizontal
centre to the letter formed by the mattress.

Berlin Daybed

Bruno Mathsson, 1950 Firma Karl Mathsson

Within many of his most distinctive and original furniture designs, Swedish designer Bruno Mathsson explored the idea of rest and repose from an ergonomic perspective. These experiments included famous pre-war pieces such as the Pernilla Chaise Longue (1934), produced by Firma Karl Mathsson, the family business run by his father. The Berlin Daybed was designed with comfort and the shape of the reclining body in mind, and features a gently turned end, like the prow of a ship, to support the head and neck. The frame is laminated beech, with the sculpted legs in particular beautifully detailed, while the nearly fitted mattress is upholstered in leather.

Wall-Mounted Nightstands

Børge Mogensen, *c.* 1955 Søborg Møbelfabrik

Rather like his Danish contemporary Finn Juhl, designer Børge Mogensen worked with a range of producers and manufacturers, including Fredericia and Fritz Hansen. During the 1950s, Mogensen designed nightstands and storage cabinets for Karl Andersson & Söner, as well as these wall-mounted nightstands in teak produced by Søborg Møbelfabrik. Each piece features a single, pull-out drawer floating underneath a ledge. The rounded edges and detailing of this shelf soften the piece, making it more ergonomic and enticing as a choice of bedside furniture.

Fredericia Daybed →

Børge Mogensen, 1955 Fredericia

There is an element of the rustic to many of Børge Mogensen's designs, as well as a strong thread of the organic in his choice of predominantly natural materials. This daybed, or sofa bed, is a case in point, featuring a robust oak frame supported by two wooden floor fins positioned at right angles to the base. The rectangular frame holds a thick mattress, complemented by a matching back cushion, meaning that the daybed easily doubles as comfortable seating in the style of a sofa or settee. In this respect, the piece is a good example of simple multi-purpose vernacular seating.

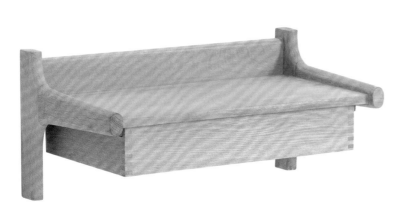

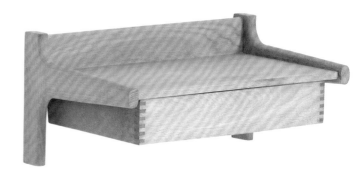

Casa del Sole Bed →

Carlo Mollino, 1954 Ettore Canali

For the mountain-loving Carlo Mollino, Casa del Sole was a golden commission. The architect and multi-talented designer was asked to create a new apartment building in the ski resort of Cervinia in northern Italy near the Swiss border. As part of the commission, Mollino designed custom furniture for the apartments themselves, including these distinctive beds in oak, walnut and brass, with ladder-like head- and footboards that echo the *brise soleil* on the building's façade. The beds can be used as singles or stacked to form bunk beds; some of the beds feature integrated drop-down side tables and coat hangers.

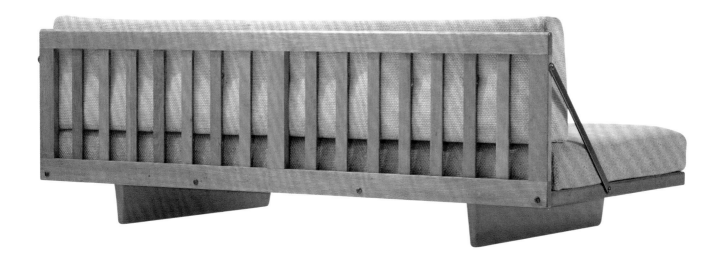

Origins Nightstands Model 215

George Nakashima, 1961 Widdicomb

While George Nakashima produced much of his furniture by hand at his own workshops, the designer and architect also created ranges for Knoll and Widdicomb. The Widdicomb Origins collection of the 1950s and 1960s featured chairs, tables and cabinets, including the elegant Model 214 Gentleman's Cabinet, which was well suited to a bedroom or dressing room. Nakashima's Model 215 nightstand is made of walnut and combines an open cabinet topped by a single drawer; the rectangular composition sits upon four tapered legs.

King-size Bed with Plank Sculpture Headboard →

George Nakashima, 1971 Nakashima Studio

The flat plane of a bed headboard offered Nakashima a tempting opportunity to present an expanse of cut timber in a way that allowed the character of the wood itself to sing out. King-size beds were generally made to order for specific clients and featured a substantial platform, usually in American black walnut. Nakashima selected a single, large slab of oak burr for the headboard in this striking example from 1971. The fissures are joined together by four 'butterflies' made of laurel; such butterflies were commonly used by George Nakashima Woodworkers to strengthen larger planks of timber.

Plank Daybed →

George Nakashima, 1965 Nakashima Studio

Working at his studios in New Hope, Pennsylvania, Nakashima developed a number of closely related variants on a daybed design from the early 1950s onward. The basis of these designs is a robust wooden platform (supporting a mattress), usually in American black walnut, with four rounded dowel legs positioned toward the corners but inset from them. Many Nakashima daybeds also feature a distinctive plank back using a wide slab of characterful timber, which means that the piece can also function as a sofa; some versions have an armrest at one end.

Daybed Model 5088

George Nelson, *c.* 1950 Herman Miller

Having succeeded Gilbert Rohde as director of design at Herman Miller in 1946, George Nelson designed a small number of daybeds over the following years as part of his debut collections for the firm. They included the 5087–5090 group, which were variants on a theme, with a sprung base supported by a birch frame resting on legs that were usually in tubular steel but sometimes wood. The Model 5088 comes with a back support, formed by a thick plank of birch held in place by tubular steel rods anchored to the base, with both a mattress and thick cushions; it also had the option of armrests at each end.

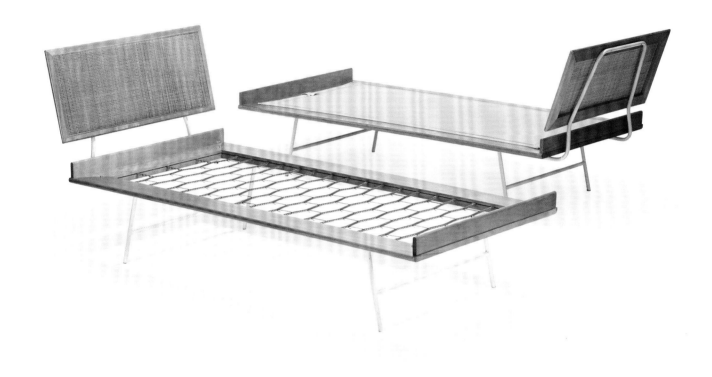

Thin Edge Beds Model 5491

George Nelson, 1955 Herman Miller

In 1952 George Nelson designed the 5200 Rosewood Case series
of cabinets and chests of drawers featuring super thin and finely
detailed casings. A few years later these pieces became the
foundation of the Thin Edge collection (see p. 326), which grew
to include nightstands, desks and the Thin Edge Bed of 1955.
Light and versatile, the Model 5491 single bed has a suitably
thin wooden base (in birch or ash) supported by two pairs of
steel legs, strengthened with horizontal struts, and a headboard
made of cane; Model 5492 is the double version of the design.

Walnut Bed

Ico & Luisa Parisi, 1954 Limited edition

Architect, furniture designer, artist, film-maker and photographer
Ico Parisi was born in Palermo but based in Como near Milan for most
of his working life. From around 1948 onward, Parisi collaborated on
his design work with his wife Luisa. Their pieces include some highly
expressive and sculptural beds, such as this one in bleached walnut
with tapered brass legs. The legs double as support rods for the head-
and footboards, which share the same poetic vocabulary of rounded
edges and punctured handle-like ends. An earlier variant on the design,
in lacquered wood with chrome legs, featured in the couple's interior
for the Bini Residence in Milan (1950).

Palisander Bed

Ico & Luisa Parisi, 1964 Limited edition

Ico and Luisa Parisi's work on bedroom furniture, like so much
of their other furniture, was characterful and finely detailed. Their
commissions included, for example, the interiors of the Hotel Lorena
(c. 1960) in Grosseto, Tuscany, where they placed vanity units and
nightstands with integrated lighting. Just a few years later, in 1964,
the couple designed this bed in palisander (rosewood) with brass
legs and detailing. Despite the limitations of form and function, the
design was typically original and defined by a combination of fine
craftsmanship and a playful aesthetic.

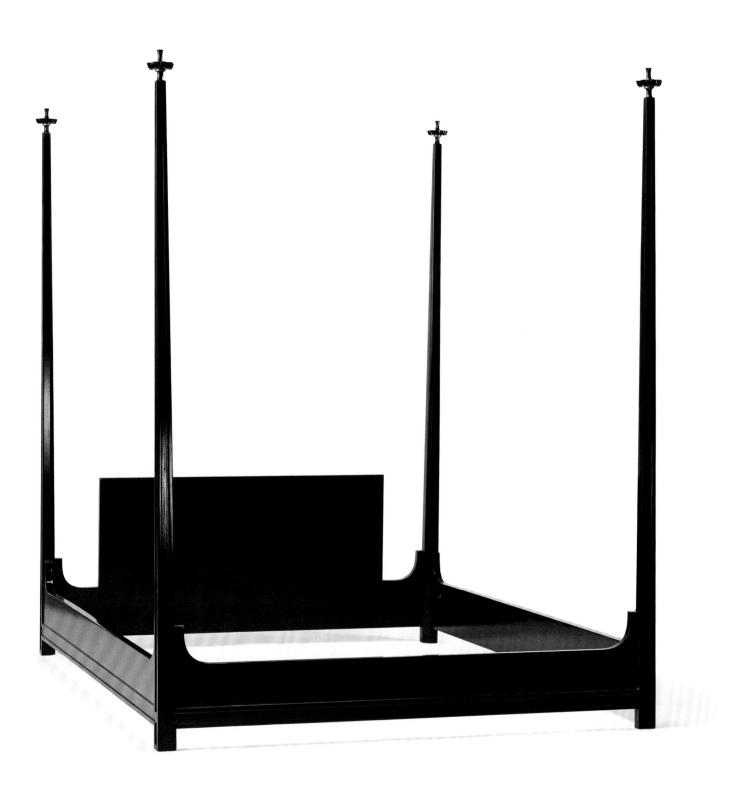

← Parzinger Bed

Tommi Parzinger, *c.* 1952 Parzinger Originals

German-born Tommi Parzinger, the son of a sculptor, settled in the USA during the early 1930s and took a sculptural approach to form. A fine case in point is this limited-edition bed, produced by Parzinger's own atelier in New York, made of lacquered wood and brass detailing. The bed is Parzinger's imaginative reworking of a four-poster, with the corner columns topped with floral-like finials. Together with the monolithic headboard, the columns frame the piece and provide a modest sense of security and enclosure. Parzinger also designed daybeds and nightstands, as well as a range of other furniture types, mirrors and lighting.

Fondation franco-brésilienne/ Maison du Brésil Daybed

Charlotte Perriand, 1959 Galerie Steph Simon

The Fondation franco-brésilienne and the Maison du Brésil formed part of the ambitious Cité Internationale Universitaire de Paris campus. Brazil House was designed by Le Corbusier with Brazilian modernist architect Lúcio Costa and completed in 1959. The project represented a fresh opportunity for Le Corbusier and Charlotte Perriand to work together again, collaborating on the interiors of the student rooms. This Perriand daybed with an oak frame, an upholstered mattress and a round bolster cushion, was well suited to these modestly sized rooms, doubling as a bed and seating. Galerie Steph Simon also produced a double version of the design.

X Selettiva Bed →

Gio Ponti, 1947/1973 Brugnoli Mobili

Multi-talented Italian architect and designer Gio Ponti created a number of beds and daybeds during his long and highly productive career. This design for a bed and integrated headboard was first created in 1947 as a prototype. Later, Ponti developed the design (in lacquered wood with bronze detailing) for a 1973 exhibition held in Cantù, near Como, in northern Italy. The headboard features integrated shelves, lights, a radio and a picture frame, echoing the multifaceted furniture systems and installations developed during the 1970s by other Italian designers such as Joe Colombo.

← Royal Hotel Bed

Gio Ponti, 1948 Giordano Chiesa

Ponti's work in the field of hotel design provided him with the
impetus to develop his ideas for 'systems of living' that combined
a range of functions within one unit. During the late 1940s and
early 1950s, Ponti worked on the Royal Hotel in Naples (now known
as the Royal Continental), within a commission that included the
rooftop seawater swimming pool on the tenth floor and the hotel
furniture. This bed and headboard for the Royal Hotel is made
of Italian walnut and – like the X Selettiva Bed (above) – features
integrated shelves, a cup holder and lighting, as well as a distinctive
Safar radio.

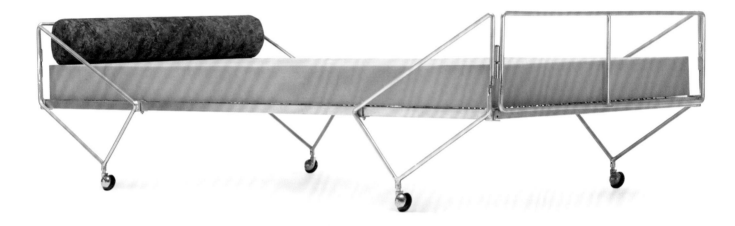

Apta Daybed

Gio Ponti, 1970 Walter Ponti

The Apta collection of furniture was designed by Ponti in 1970
and first presented at the 'Eurodomus 3' exhibition in Milan devoted
to new concepts in modern residential living. The pieces, which
included a folding dining table and a folding console table, were
designed to be flexible enough for compact apartments or small
homes, but were also characterized by a bold use of colour within
a seaside palette of blues and whites. The Apta Daybed has a
lightweight galvanized and tubular steel frame, mounted on castors
so that the bed can be easily moved around. The foam mattress is
complemented by a round bolster cushion at one end.

Unité d'Habitation Air France
Double Bed

Jean Prouvé, 1942/1951 Ateliers Jean Prouvé

Around 1950, Air France commissioned a new four-storey apartment building in Brazzaville, capital of the Republic of the Congo, to house their employees. Charlotte Perriand was asked to work on the interiors and furnishings (see p. 329) and began collaborating on designs with Jean Prouvé, who was commissioned to provide beds (both single and double) for these residences. Basing his Unité d'Habitation designs on earlier models from the 1930s and 1940s, Prouvé and his atelier created this design with an enamelled steel frame, a simple oak headboard, a mattress and a round bolster cushion. Prouvé also completed and delivered three prefabricated 'Maisons Tropicales' to Brazzaville in 1951.

SCAL Model 458 Bed

Jean Prouvé, *c.* 1952 Ateliers Jean Prouvé & Galerie
Steph Simon

Ateliers Jean Prouvé developed a series of bed designs, both pre- and
post-war, focused on use within hospitals, campus buildings and the
dormitories of the SCAL factory in Issoire, France. By the early 1950s,
Prouvé recognized the potential of the general residential market and
made a small number of key designs available to private buyers. Chief
among these, sold through Galerie Steph Simon, was the SCAL series.
SCAL Model 458 has an enamelled steel frame and a rounded head-
and footboard in oak. A variant on this design featured an integrated,
swivelling side table designed by Charlotte Perriand.

Antony Daybed

Jean Prouvé, 1954 Ateliers Jean Prouvé

The Antony Daybed forms an important part of one of Prouvé's final collections. Designed for the residences of the Cité Universitaire at Antony, Paris, the range also included the Antony Chair and Desk (see pp. 91 and 383). Like so many of Prouvé's designs, the daybed combines simplicity with ingenuity and elegance. An enamelled steel base, with sprung support, cradles the upholstered mattress, with its round matching cushion, while an oak outrigger forms a neat platform for a drink or book; this outrigger could be neatly folded away under the unit, which could serve as seating or sleeping. The daybed was also known as the SCAL 450, which was distributed by Galerie Steph Simon from 1956 onward.

Twin Bed

Ladislav Rado, *c.* 1955 Knoll + Drake

At the invitation of Walter Gropius, Czech architect and designer
Ladislav Rado emigrated to the USA to study at Harvard University,
completing his postgraduate studies in 1940. After the end of
World War II, in 1945, he co-founded an architectural practice
with Antonin Raymond. Rado's furniture designs comprised chairs,
storage cabinets and this twin bed with a mahogany frame, steel legs
and an upholstered headboard finished in vinyl. The combination
of these elements, including the thin wooden base, can be compared
with George Nelson's Thin Edge Bed for Herman Miller (see p. 415).

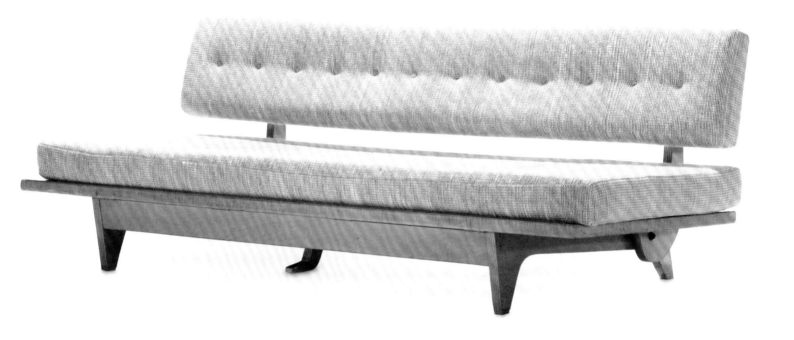

Model 700 Sofa Daybed

Richard Stein, 1947 Knoll

Like Ladislav Rado, architect Richard Stein studied at Harvard
Unversity under Walter Gropius and worked with Gropius and Marcel
Breuer after his postgraduate studies. Stein was one of a prestigious
group of American and European designers and architects invited
by Hans and Florence Knoll to contribute furniture designs during
the late 1940s; a Knoll advertising image shows Stein alongside Harry
Bertoia, George Nakashima, Isamu Noguchi and others. The Model
700 Sofa Daybed was a one-off collaboration and features a birch and
birch plywood frame with a mattress and an upholstered backrest
that folds down flat when the piece is used for sleeping.

Daybed

Joaquim Tenreiro, *c.* 1955 Langenbach & Tenreiro

Together with a business partner, Portuguese–Brazilian master
designer Joaquim Tenreiro launched his own atelier in Rio de Janeiro
in 1943 and a showroom in Copacabana a few years later, followed
by a successful satellite in São Paulo. By the mid-1950s the business
was thriving, and around this time Tenreiro designed and made a
number of daybeds using caviuna, a characterful Brazilian hardwood.
They included this elegant design for a private client in Rio de
Janeiro, which exhibits the lightness and sculptural simplicity of
some of Tenreiro's finest pieces. For the bedroom, Tenreiro also
designed nightstands using rosewood.

Beech Bed

Ole Wanscher, *c.* 1945 Fritz Hansen

Danish designer Ole Wanscher combined an encyclopaedic knowledge of furniture history with a love of craft and an imaginative approach to form. Many of his designs referenced historical precedents, yet Wanscher's most delightful pieces possessed a degree of dynamism that came from a sculptural use of timber. His Beech Bed of the mid-1940s, for example, features distinctive head- and footboards with triptychs of wave-like cross braces between the corner supports. A similar motif featured on the ladder-back of a Wanscher Lounge Chair from 1944, also produced by Fritz Hansen, with a quartet of waves.

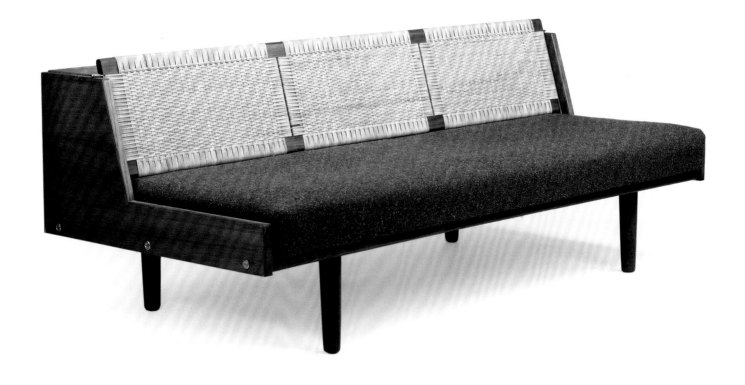

Model GE 258 Sofa Bed

Hans Wegner, *c.* 1954 Getama

During the 1950s and 1960s, master designer Hans Wegner
worked with long-established Jutland manufacturer Getama on
a number of sofa bed and daybed designs. Some of these designs,
such as the GE 258 and GE 259 daybeds, are still manufactured
today in the town of Gedsted, North Jutland. This distinctive sofa
bed features a substantial teak frame and upholstered mattress
in combination with a more delicate cane back, creating a range
of contrasting textures. The backrest can be easily retracted
and repositioned to free the mattress for a night's sleep.

Model GE 701 Bed ↓

Hans Wegner, *c.* 1960 Getama

Wegner and Getama also collaborated on the production of a
number of beds, such as the Model GE 705 Bed with a simple teak
base plus an elongated headboard with integrated wall-mounted
nightstands. Wegner's GE 701 Bed is a more ambitious, free-standing
design with a teak frame and a textural headboard made of cane.
Lightweight shelving units to either side form outriggers. The
footboard, finished in vinyl, has a rounded profile giving the entire
piece the maritime flavour of a low-slung boat.

WOOD

While wood is one of the most natural and traditional materials, it was embraced and reimagined in such a way during the mid-century period that it could also be described as something 'modern'. A number of mid-century designers and makers emerged from a strong craft tradition, which placed particular emphasis on the provenance and intrinsic character of a chosen timber, but wood was also twisted and turned in fresh directions.

Laminates, formed of multiple layers of veneered wood, were widely used in furniture making from the 1930s onward, with plywood (see p. 434) following on soon after. When steamed, shaped and bent, laminated wood offered increasingly sinuous and sculptural shapes, suited to the more expressive furniture that rose to prominence during the post-war era. At the same time, designers such as Nanna Ditzel (see p. 40) and Eero Aarnio (see p. 158) explored other organic materials, for example, cane and rattan, which provided similar opportunities to create characterful pieces that were still infused with natural patina and warmth.

The craft tradition was particularly influential in the rise of Scandinavian furniture design during the 1950s and 1960s. Designers such as Hans Wegner (see pp. 105–7), Bruno Mathsson (see pp. 135 and 409) and Børge Mogensen (see pp. 72–73) emerged from a well-established network of workshop apprenticeships, as well as arts and crafts schools and academies, yet went on to reinvent familiar typologies, such as the Windsor chair or the chaise longue, and experiment with new ideas and ways of making. In doing so, they were greatly assisted by the opportunities for creative collaboration with respected furniture manufacturers across the Nordic countries, including Fritz Hansen, Niels Vodder, Carl Hansen, Fredericia and others. There was a particular fondness for pale and blond woods, such as beech and birch, which gave a sense of lightness to so much Nordic modern furniture.

The region's richness in forestry combined with the commitment of the industry to innovation placed Scandinavia at an advantage in the development of new laminates. Architect and designer Alvar Aalto made the most of such possibilities in his furniture, creating pieces that were light, structurally innovative, sculpturally expressive and ergonomic (see pp. 14 and 120). His designs provided the foundation for the Finnish furniture company, Artek, which he co-founded in 1935 with his wife Aino, patron Maire Gullichsen and art critic Nils-Gustav Hahl, and which went on to work with such designers as Ilmari Tapiovaara (see pp. 100 and 297) during the post-war period.

The Scandinavian mid-century modern aesthetic was hugely influential around the world, particularly in the UK and the USA, where émigré Nordic designers such as Jens Risom (see pp. 95 and 293), Abel Sorenson (see p. 295) and also Finnish–American designer and architect Eero Saarinen (see p. 97) – who settled in Cranbrook,

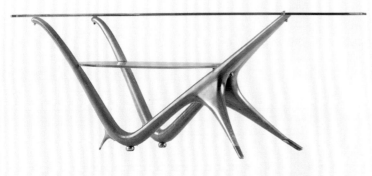

FROM TOP
Carlo Mollino, Model 1114 Coffee Table, c. 1950
Hans Wegner, Cabinet, 1952

Michigan, with his father Eliel and his family as a teenager – made a great impact on the evolution of mid-century furniture. The USA was another epicentre of innovation in laminates and ply, yet also had a powerful craft tradition of its own, as seen in the work of designer-makers such as Wharton Esherick (see p. 164) and particularly master woodworker George Nakashima (see pp. 217 and 283), who fused a range of influences from North America and Japan in his farmstead workshops at New Hope, Pennsylvania.

With ready access to such a rich library of hardwoods and other regional timbers, South American designers also gained a strong reputation during the 1950s and 1960s for furniture that was both crafted and expressive. This was particularly true in Brazil where designers such as Joaquim Tenreiro (see pp. 101 and 428), Jorge Zalszupin (see pp. 339 and 391) and Sergio Rodrigues (see pp. 96 and 386) made use of characterful woods such as jacaranda, imbuia and caviuna. Tenreiro and Zalszupin designed, among other pieces, super-sized credenzas that allowed the patina of the wood to sing out to the full; while Rodrigues was best known for lounge chairs and sofas that combined wooden frames with oversized leather cushions that flowed over the armrests, reinforcing the organic quality of such furniture.

While many mid-century designers recognized the importance of connecting with craft traditions and historic precedents within furniture making, it should be remembered that wood was also used as an experimental material. Some of the early cantilevered chairs, such as Gerrit Rietveld's Zig-Zag Chair of 1932, were made of wood and laminates, and Verner Panton's Model 275/276 S-Chair, designed in 1956 and first manufactured in 1965, was developed with Thonet, who pioneered early bentwood furniture back in the 19th century. In Italy, Carlo Mollino and Gio Ponti saw fresh possibilities that made best use of a familiar friend, with Mollino developing biomorphic pieces with the eye of a sculptor (see pp. 75 and 281), and Ponti creating, among other items, his iconic Superleggera chair (1957, see p. 88) in ash and cane, which was the result of years of work and thoughtful refinement to create an iconic modern design rooted in the vernacular.

FROM TOP
Franco Campo & Carlo Graffi, Lounge Chair, 1951
Grete Jalk, Laminated Chair, 1963
George Nakashima, Long Chair, 1951

PLYWOOD

For many mid-century modern furniture designers, plywood was their material of choice. It was versatile and malleable but also light and strong. Made using a semi-industrial process in a factory setting, plywood became relatively affordable and available during the post-war years, yet given its natural provenance it also offered an organic sense of warmth and character. Not surprisingly, then, it became a key element within the mid-century vocabulary of design, adopted by such designers as Alvar Aalto, Arne Jacobsen, Poul Kjaerholm, Norman Cherner, George Nelson, Ilmari Tapiovaara, Charles & Ray Eames and many others.

Plywood is a kind of laminated timber, with origins that stretch back to the late 18th or early 19th centuries. Laminates are manufactured by gluing together thin layers, or veneers, of wood to create a plank or beam. At first, laminated timbers were used in building construction and architecture, often as a supporting structural element on account of their strength. By the late 19th century, advances in production led to early versions of plywood sheets, where the grain of the timber in each layer sits at right angles to the layers above and below it, greatly increasing the strength of the sheet overall. It also allowed for various thicknesses according to the intended use of the ply, including thinner versions that were more easily shaped and manipulated.

By the 1920s, plywood sheets, as well as laminated beams, were being used in the USA and elsewhere as construction materials. But there was also a growing interest in employing plywood in other ways. Light, strong and malleable, marine ply was increasingly used for boat building alongside special glues and treatments to ensure that the timber remained water resistant. During World War II, moulded plywood was used for producing such aircraft as the de Havilland Mosquito bomber, first manufactured in 1940 and used by the British RAF and the Canadian forces. During the war years, Charles & Ray Eames designed a stackable, lightweight leg splint in plywood for the US Navy (opposite), while recognizing the potential of the material for use in their post-war chairs and furniture designs, including the LCW (Lounge Chair Wood) of 1945 (see p. 42).

For modernist and mid-century furniture designers, plywood offered a golden opportunity to create designs using a combination of natural materials and industrial processes, which meant that they could be factory produced rather than made by hand. A set of standardized component parts could be formed by manipulating plywood to create curved seats, backs and legs within an ordered process that combined lamination with moulding using frames and compression systems, while usually applying heat or steam to help manipulate the laminate. Made in this way, the plywood could be 'sculpted' on the factory floor to offer a range of shapes and to accommodate a multitude of needs and functions.

Pioneering Scandinavian modernists such as Alvar Aalto and Arne Jacobsen were particularly interested in the possibilities offered by the 'plasticity' of moulded ply, which drew on organic local materials that were then transformed by these modern methods of

FROM TOP
Sori Yanagi, Butterfly Stool, 1956
Gio Ponti, Model 2140 Display Cabinet, 1951

manufacturing. Aalto was fascinated by the way in which plywood could be shaped to meet the contours of the human body, developing his Model 41 Paimio Armchair of 1933, for example, with a profile that helped to ease the breathing of tuberculosis patients at the Paimio Sanatorium in Finland, for which he created the architecture, interiors and much of the furniture. Later, Aalto co-founded the furniture company Artek to produce a growing range of ply and bentwood furniture.

A number of Danish designers also explored the opportunities offered by plywood. Arne Jacobsen famously used ply to create the combined seat and back of his Ant Chair (1952, see p. 54), initially designed for a canteen at the offices of Danish pharmaceutical company Novo Nordisk. The Series 7 Chair of 1955 (see p. 54), produced by Fritz Hansen, was an evolution of the Ant and also made of plywood. Jacobsen contemporary Poul Kjaerholm was best known for his steel-framed furniture, yet he too was drawn to ply to create the PK0 Chair of 1952 (see p. 65). Highly sinuous and dynamic, the PK0 feels like a racing car transformed into an extraordinary piece of sculptural furniture. Similarly, Hans Wegner was fascinated by the possibilities provided by ply and developed a number of 'shell chairs', beginning with the Model FH1936 (top left; see p. 105) produced by Fritz Hansen.

Post-war designers built upon these early successes while taking advantage of the additional layers of innovation achieved during World War II. As well as the work of Charles & Ray Eames, one thinks of plywood classics by Norman Cherner, whose Cherner Armchairs (left; see p. 33) were first produced by Plycraft; and Egon Eiermann, who developed a sequence of such affordable plywood chairs as the four-legged SE68 (1950) and the three-legged SE69 (c. 1952, see p. 46). As well as chairs, plywood and super-thin laminates were used to make many other pieces of furniture and product design, including Grete Jalk's Nesting Tables (1963, see p. 267) and Tapio Wirkkala's beautifully crafted leaf dishes made of laminated birch and teak plywood.

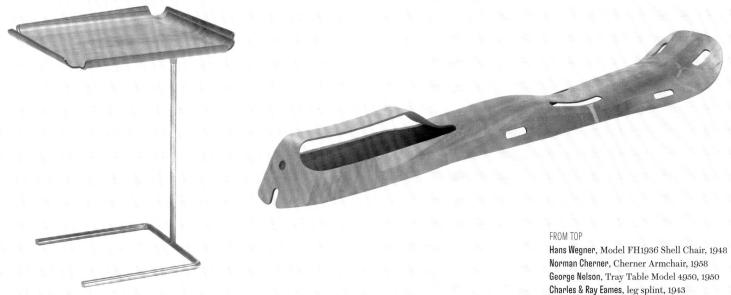

FROM TOP
Hans Wegner, Model FH1936 Shell Chair, 1948
Norman Cherner, Cherner Armchair, 1958
George Nelson, Tray Table Model 4950, 1950
Charles & Ray Eames, leg splint, 1943

PLASTICS

We have a complicated relationship with plastics. They form such an intrinsic part of our daily lives, touching on every aspect of our day-to-day experience within the world of design, yet they have also become highly controversial. Today, seen from the context of the climate emergency, we inevitably consider any material largely made from fossil fuels with suspicion. The rise of disposable plastics, which affect every part of our planet, has irreparably damaged our perception of something revolutionary and which we once viewed with wonder.

It is important to remember that most mid-century designers intended furniture made of plastics to be affordable and durable, but not disposable. Indeed, many of the pioneering pieces that were produced using plastics during the 1950s and 1960s are still with us and are often highly collectable, with a sense of value derived from the level of thought, creativity and ingenuity that went into their design. During the 1960s, in particular, plastics played a key part in the evolution of a fresh generation of furniture that took ideas of abstraction and hybridization to new levels. The possibilities offered by plastics to reinvent furniture also carried through, of course, into many other disciplines of design around the same time, including homeware as well as new generations of consumer products and electrical appliances targeted at the home.

The complex history of naturally derived plastics stretches back many centuries and includes malleable resins and gums such as shellac, used to lacquer furniture and other products. The process of vulcanizing rubber originates from the mid-19th century, but it was not until the early 20th century that the first synthetic plastics, such as Bakelite, came into use. By the 1930s, Bakelite and other synthetic polymers were being used to make new consumer products, particularly such early electrical devices as radios and hairdryers. As was the case with many other 'modern' materials, experimentation with plastics, including Plexiglas and fibreglass, accelerated rapidly during World War II, with mid-century designers increasingly aware of the possibilities offered by plastics in the field of furniture making.

Just as Charles & Ray Eames became fascinated by plywood (see p. 434) during World War II, they were also intrigued by fibreglass, an industrially made material that is composed of a polymer reinforced with thin strands of glass. Fibreglass was first produced during the 1930s and used in boat building as well as in the aircraft industry, initially as radar enclosures known as 'radomes' but then more widely. During the late 1940s and early 1950s, the Eameses worked with Herman Miller and Zenith Plastics on the painstaking development of the first 'shell chairs', which involved not only perfecting the material itself but also developing the moulding presses used to produce the shell seats. The Fiberglass

FROM TOP
Verner Panton, Panton Chairs, 1967
Yrjö Kukkapuro, Karuselli Lounge Chair & Ottoman, 1964

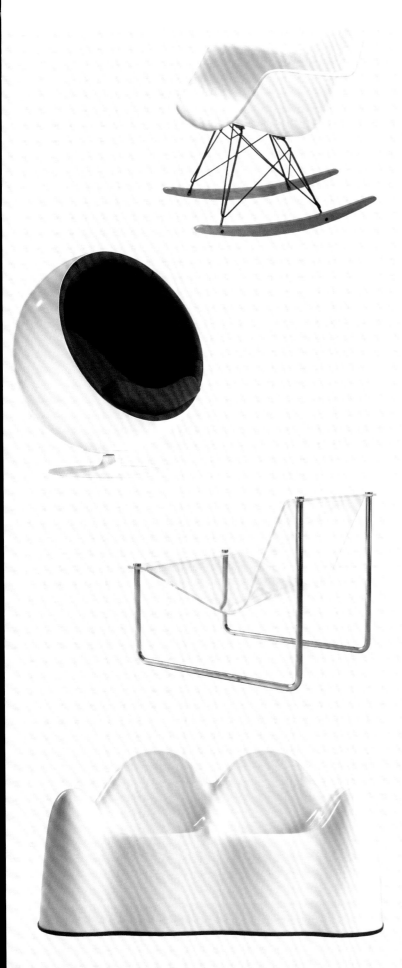

Chair Group, made with glass-reinforced polyester, was initially released in 1951 and included the DAR (Dining Armchair Rod, see p. 43) and the DAX (Dining Height Armchair X-Base), with the idea that a standard shell seat could be fitted with a choice of different bases. Fibreglass was also used to create the experimental La Chaise of 1948 (see p. 127), although the design proved too complex to be mass-produced until the 1990s, when Vitra put the piece into production.

Fibreglass was taken up by a number of other mid-century designers including Eero Aarnio, who used the material to make the futuristic Ball Chair (left; 1966, see p. 15) and Pastilli Chair (1967, see p. 121), and Finnish designer Yrjö Kukkapuro (opposite; see p. 68). French designer Charles Zublena produced a collection of fibreglass recliners seen across Club Med beach resorts during the 1960s and 1970s (see p. 151).

During the late 1950s and early 1960s, designers and manufacturers raced to come up with the first injection-moulded pieces of plastic furniture. They included Joe Colombo, who developed the Universale Chair with Kartell (1967, see p. 35), and Verner Panton, who famously created the first injection-moulded plastic chair made in a single piece and of just one material. The cantilevered Panton Chair (opposite; see p. 81) was produced with Vitra, initially in 1967, with subsequent adjustments and perfections to the choice of plastic and production techniques over the following years. That same year, 1967, Robin Day released his Polypropylene Armchair (see p. 37), with a mass-produced thermoplastic seat sitting on tubular steel legs. Like the Eames's Fiberglass Chair Group, the Polyprop was produced in a range of colours and with a choice of different bases, including stackable versions.

Injection-moulded plastics were soon being put to a wide range of uses across many different furniture typologies, including storage units like Joe Colombo's Boby Trolley (1970, see p. 353) and outdoor furniture, as in Peter Ghyczy's Garden Egg Chair (1968, see p. 50). Such pieces allowed designers to create increasingly abstract and sculptural forms, and the same was true of polyurethane foam, which could be moulded into all kinds of shapes and then neatly upholstered. Hybrid seating systems such as Archizoom's Safari (1967, see p. 194) and Panton's Living Tower (1968, see p. 223) were made possible, at least in part, by the use of sinuous, moulded plastics, even if they were hidden away behind colourful textile coats.

Plastics were also used in other imaginative ways. Erwine & Estelle Laverne (see p. 69), as well as Charles Hollis Jones (left; see p. 61), employed transparent Perspex and acrylic to create chairs and other pieces of furniture that almost disappeared into a space. There were 'transformative' pieces, too, such as DDL Studio and Carla Scolari's inflatable armchair named Blow (1967, see p. 38) and Gaetano Pesce's polyurethane Up5 Chair (1969, see p. 84), which arrived sealed in an airtight package and only expanded into its final shape after opening. In many respects, plastics were radically transformative for designers and architects of the period, allowing the realization of new concepts, compositions and ideas.

FROM TOP
Charles & Ray Eames, RAR (Rocking Armchair Rod), 1951

Eero Aarnio, Ball Chair, 1966
Charles Hollis Jones, Sling Chair, c. 1968
Wendell Castle, Molar Group Settee, c. 1968

STEEL

Industrially produced, light and robust, steel was one of the key materials embraced by pioneering modernist furniture designers during the 1920s and 1930s. It was a material that invited experimentation and innovation, making it a firm favourite of many mid-century designers who built upon the ideas of the early modernists and began using steel in a variety of unexpected ways, making the most of its strength and versatility to create sculptural designs and cantilevered compositions.

Marcel Breuer, who became master of the furniture workshop at Bauhaus Dessau during the mid-1920s, was famously inspired by the example of his own tubular-steel-framed bicycle. Noting its inherent strength and lightness, he began experimenting with tubular-steel chairs and tables, developing prototypes that were then put into production by Thonet. Pieces such as the Cesca Side Chair Model B32 (1928) and its siblings used tubular steel to create cantilevered forms that allowed the occupant to feel as though he or she was floating above the ground. Breuer's iconic B3 Lounge Chair, or Wassily Chair (1925, named in honour of Breuer's colleague, artist Wassily Kandinsky), famously used a combination of a sculpted, tubular-steel frame and an elegant, slung-leather seat and back support. Importantly, such pieces were not only innovative and distinctly fresh but also sat well within the modernist-inspired principles espoused by the Bauhaus, which suggested good design should be made as widely available as possible, with factory-made furniture and industrial processes offering at least the potential to bring down the cost of such pieces.

At the same time, chrome-plated tubular steel was associated with the more glamorous art deco movement, with gleaming steel-framed furniture by Eileen Gray, for example, deftly splicing deco forms and early modernist ideas. Chrome-plated steel not only lent itself to the streamlined forms of deco-influenced furniture but it was also taken up by the car industry and the world of product design, with 'streamlining' intimately associated with the rise of machine-age dynamism, which was eventually translated from trains, planes and automobiles to chairs, fridges and vacuum cleaners.

FROM TOP
Luigi Colani, Lounge Chair, *c.* 1968
Warren Platner, Platner Collection Lounge Chairs, 1966

By the 1950s, steel had thus already proved its credentials and was carried forward by designers such as Jean Prouvé and Charlotte Perriand, whose careers spanned the pre- and post-war periods. Knoll famously began producing and promoting steel-framed furniture by Breuer and his former Bauhaus colleague Ludwig Mies van der Rohe during the mid-century period, reaching a new and much wider audience. In Scandinavia, master designer Poul Kjaerholm treated steel with the kind of reverence that other contemporaries reserved only for wood, creating pieces such as the landmark PK22 Chair (left; 1956, see p. 66), which combined engineered elegance with fine craftsmanship while embracing the nobility of this industrially produced metal alloy.

Light and super-strong steel-framed bases were widely used by mid-century designers, often in combination with other lightweight materials such as plywood (see p. 434) and fibreglass (see p. 436). Simple steel legs and metal lattices were adopted by designers such as Arne Jacobsen, Charles & Ray Eames and George Nelson, partly because they were so light and discreet, allowing the sculptural shape of a chair's seat and back to sing out.

Others were drawn to the sculptural possibilities offered by the use of steel, as seen, for example, in the work of Harry Bertoia and Warren Platner. Both designers began experimenting, in different ways, with thin steel rods, using them to create new forms and structures. For Bertoia, who was also an artist and sculptor, lattices of welded rods were transformed into the Diamond Chair (left; 1952, see p. 20) and other pieces for Knoll produced at the same time and with the same methodology, such as the Bird Chair (1952, see p. 21). Platner, also working with Knoll, created wheatsheaf compositions made up of vertical steel rods, bent into shape and held in place by circular steel ribbons. The Platner Collection, launched in 1966 (opposite; see pp. 86 and 290), included not only chairs but also tables with wheatsheaf bases and glass tops.

For designers such as Bertoia, Platner and others, it was not simply that such ways of making brought about pieces that were original, sculptural and 'modern'; equally as important was the way in which the resulting furniture was so much lighter and more translucent than any period predecessors. Sunlight could pass right through these pieces, which sat gently within a space rather than seeking to dominate. They were hard-wearing enough to adapt to multiple settings and situations, with Bertoia's chairs finding their way into, for example, the new universities of the 1960s, as well as homes and offices.

FROM TOP
Harry Bertoia, Diamond Chair (Model 421), 1952
Poul Kjaerholm, PK22 Chair, 1956
Jean Prouvé, Standard Chair, c. 1934
Gae Aulenti, Sgarsul, 1962

DIRECTORY OF DESIGNERS

Aalto, Alvar (1898–1976)
Architect and designer Alvar Aalto grew up in a rural part of Finland. He studied in Helsinki and established his own practice in 1923. Aalto developed his own unique style drawing upon his love of nature, natural materials and an ergonomic, humanist approach to architecture, interiors and design. Famously, his work formed the cornerstone of Artek, the furniture company that he co-founded in 1935.

Aarnio, Eero (b.1932)
Finnish designer Eero Aarnio studied at the Helsinki Institute of Industrial Arts and established his own design studio in 1962. Aarnio's best-known pieces combine sculptural and colourful pop-art abstraction with the innovative use of such modern materials as fibreglass and acrylic.

Albini, Franco (1905–1977)
Italian architect and designer Franco Albini studied at the Politecnico di Milano before working in the office of Gio Ponti, going on to establish his own architectural and design studio in Milan in 1930. His best-known furniture designs date from the 1950s. During the 1960s, Albini concentrated on larger architectural commissions, including stations for the Milan subway system.

Aulenti, Gae (1927–2012)
Born in Udine, Italy, Aulenti studied architecture at the Politecnico di Milano, while also contributing to design magazines such as *Casabella*. As an architect, furniture and lighting designer, Aulenti found that many of his product pieces emerged or evolved from specific architectural commissions, which included the conversion of the Gare d'Orsay into one of Paris's major art museums.

Baughman, Milo (1923–2003)
American furniture designer Milo Baughman was born in Kansas and grew up in Long Beach, California. He served in the US Air Force during World War II and then studied architectural and product design in Los Angeles. Baughman opened his own design studio in 1947. In 1953 Baughman began a long and highly productive working relationship with furniture manufacturer Thayer Coggin.

Bellini, Mario (b.1935)
Italian furniture and product designer Mario Bellini was born in Milan, where he studied architecture at the Politecnico di Milano, graduating in 1959. He was design director for La Rinascente group of department stores in the early 1960s, before co-founding an architectural practice with Marco Romano and then establishing Studio Bellini in Milan in 1973. Bellini designed furniture in parallel with industrial and product work.

Bellmann, Hans (1911–1990)
Swiss designer Hans Bellmann worked with Ludwig Mies van der Rohe during the 1930s before founding his own design studio in Zurich in 1946. His designs include the Einpunkt plywood dining/side chair produced by Horgenglarus (1951), the Model 1000 Dining Table made by Wohnbedarf (c. 1947) and the Popsicle table for Knoll (1947).

Bertoia, Harry (1915–1978)
Sculptor and designer Harry Bertoia was born in Italy but settled in the USA as a teenager. He studied art in Detroit and then attended Cranbrook Academy of Art, where he first met Florence Knoll and Charles and Ray Eames, with whom he worked in California during the 1940s. The success of his landmark collection of wire-rod chairs for Knoll, released in 1952, allowed Bertoia to devote more of his time to sculpture during the years that followed.

Bill, Max (1908–1994)
After studying at the Bauhaus, Max Bill went on to achieve success in a range of disciplines: architecture, industrial design, furniture design and graphic design. During the 1930s, while based in Zurich, he focused mainly on architecture and graphics. As an educator, Bill began his teaching career in Zurich before co-founding the Ulm School of Design in 1953, based upon the Bauhaus model.

Bo Bardi, Lina (1914–1992)
Architect, furniture designer, writer, journalist and editor, Lina Bo Bardi was born Achillina Bo in Rome and studied at the college of architecture at Rome University. She went to work with Gio Ponti in Milan and then founded her own architectural practice. She moved to Brazil in 1946, becoming a Brazilian citizen in 1951, and designed chairs and other pieces of furniture alongside her work as an architect.

Bonet, Antonio (1913–1989), **Ferrari Hardoy, Jorge** (1914–1977) & **Kurchan, Juan** (1913–1972)
Spanish architect Bonet and his Argentinian colleagues, Ferrari Hardoy and Kurchan, all worked in Le Corbusier's Parisian office during the late 1930s. In 1938, the three moved from France to Argentina where they developed one of their most famous works: the Butterfly Chair.

Borsani, Osvaldo (1911–1985)
In 1953 Italian furniture designer Osvaldo Borsani and his brother founded the Tecno furniture company in Milan. The company was established to market Borsani's own collection of furniture, including the adjustable P40 Folding Lounge Chair and the D70 Sofa (both 1954). Tecno opened its first shop in Milan in 1956.

Breuer, Marcel (1902–1981)
Born in Hungary, Marcel Breuer studied in Vienna and then at the Bauhaus. He later became master of the furniture workshop at the Bauhaus in Dessau, where he began developing innovative and experimental designs using laminates and tubular steel. In 1928 Breuer launched his own architectural practice in Berlin and then, in 1935, emigrated to London. In 1935 Walter Gropius offered him a teaching post at Harvard. In 1941 Breuer founded his own practice, moving it to New York in 1956.

Caldas, José Zanine (1919–2001)
A self-taught designer, Brazilian furniture maker Zanine Caldas began by building architectural models for Oscar Niemeyer and Lúcio Costa in Rio de Janeiro. He started producing furniture in 1948 and later moved to São Paulo. Early pieces explored fluid forms and experimented with timber and plywood; pieces from the 1960s onward adopted a more robust sense of monumentality, using slabs of timber.

Castiglioni, Achille (1918–2002) & **Castiglioni, Pier Giacomo** (1913–1968)
The work of Milanese designers Achille and Pier Giacomo Castiglioni was often avant garde and experimental. They combined innovation and touches of surreal playfulness, as seen in their furniture, lighting and product designs.

Castle, Wendell (1932–2018)
American furniture designer Wendell Castle studied sculpture before moving into furniture design. His work adopted an abstract and sculptural character, whether in wood or fibreglass. Castle's Molar lounge chairs and coffee tables of 1969 were produced in gel-coated fibreglass in vivid reds and yellows, although he increasingly turned to wood for later designs.

Cherner, Norman (1920–1987)
American architect, furniture designer and writer Norman Cherner is best known for his plywood chairs, first designed for Plycraft in 1958. Now known simply as Cherner chairs, the pieces include a side chair and an armchair, with sculptural plywood wings emerging like taut bows from the main body of the chair.

Colani, Luigi (1928–2019)
German designer Luigi Colani took the idea of streamlining to new extremes within a playful design approach that placed great emphasis on dynamic, rounded forms. He studied painting and sculpture in Berlin and aerodynamics in Paris before moving into car design in the 1950s, working for Fiat, Alfa Romeo and BMW as well as producing his own kit car. During the early 1960s, Colani began to design furniture.

Colombini, Gino (b.1915)
Italian furniture and product designer Gino Colombini worked with architect and designer Franco Albini during the late 1930s and the 1940s. From 1949 to 1961, he served as technical director of Italian manufacturer Kartell. Colombini designed a number of early Kartell products during the 1950s, exploring the versatility of plastics in furniture and household products.

Colombo, Joe (1930–1971)
Despite a career cut short by his untimely death, Italian polymath designer Joe Colombo made a huge impact on the world of design and particularly within the field of furniture. He studied art and architecture in Milan and began a career as a painter and ceramicist before opening his own design studio in Milan in 1962. His work over the next decade spanned product design, lighting and furniture.

Day, Robin (1915–2010)
Born in High Wycombe, Robin Day studied in London at the Royal College of Art (where he met his future wife) and went on to found a design office with Lucienne Day in 1948. He focused primarily on furniture as a freelance designer, working with Hille and others. His most famous chair, made by Hille, is the injection-moulded Polypropylene Chair (1963/64), which sold in the millions and still graces countless schools and village halls.

De Pas, D'Urbino & Lomazzi
DDL design studio was founded in Milan by Jonathan De Pas (1932–1991), Donato D'Urbino (b.1935) and Paolo Lomazzi (b.1936). Their furniture designs of the 1960s are associated with the playful pop culture of the period, particularly their inflatable plastic Blow chair (1967) – one of the first 'transformative' pieces of its kind.

Ditzel, Nanna (1923–2005)
Born Nanna Hauberg in Copenhagen, Danish furniture and textile designer Nanna Ditzel married fellow designer Jørgen Ditzel in 1946. Many of Ditzel's designs of the 1950s were collaborations with her husband (who died in 1961). Her rattan and teak, bucket-seated Rattan Lounge Chair (1950) has an organic, endearing warmth that it shares with one of her most famous designs: the cocoon-like Hanging Chair of 1957.

Eames, Charles (1907–1978) & **Eames, Ray** (1912–1988)
Known primarily for their pioneering work of the 1950s and 1960s, Charles and Ray Eames were key innovators in the field of 20th-century furniture design, as well as working in architecture, set design, interiors, textiles, graphics and film. They met at the Cranbrook Academy of Art in 1940 and, in 1942, first began experimenting with plywood. Over the following years, Charles & Ray Eames worked on a landmark series of ply chairs and other designs, followed by groundbreaking work in fibreglass, plastics and aluminium.

Eiermann, Egon (1904–1970)
German architect, interior and furniture designer Egon Eiermann established an architectural practice with Robert Hilgers in 1945. He combined his building commissions with the development of a series of innovative chairs manufactured by Wilde + Spieth, many of which used plywood.

Ekström, Yngve (1913–1988)
Swedish designer Yngve Ekström co-founded furniture manufacturer Swedese in 1945. The company still produces many of Ekström's own designs from the mid-century period, including his most famous piece: the Lamino Lounge Chair (1956).

Ercolani, Lucian (1888-1976)
Born in Tuscany, furniture designer Lucian Ercolani moved to England with his family as a child. In 1910 he joined the furniture company Parker Knoll and later moved to E. Gomme, the maker of G-Plan furniture. In 1920 Ercolani founded his own furniture-making business, Ercol. Government contracts helped see the company through the war years and the business thrived during the 1950s.

Esherick, Wharton (1887-1970)
Sculptor, illustrator, furniture designer and maker Wharton Esherick fused sculpture and craft in his work. His long career also encompassed painting and interiors, including the crafted timber kitchen of his niece's house, designed by Louis Kahn and known as the Esherick House (1961) in Philadelphia. His own house and studio at Paoli, Pennsylvania, evolved organically over many years to become an extraordinary and highly personal 'Gesamtkunstwerk' in the woods.

Evans, Paul (1931-1987)
American furniture designer Paul Evans studied at the Cranbrook Academy of Art. His work fused art, craft, design and sculpture within contemporary pieces handmade either by his own studio or by furniture company Directional. Evans signed and closely supervised the manufacture of his pieces, many of which were custom or limited-edition designs.

Fornasetti, Piero (1913-1988)
One of the most original and distinctive masters of Italian furniture and interior design, Piero Fornasetti was also an artist, illustrator and ceramic designer. He studied at the Accademia di Belle Arti in Milan before becoming a protégé of Gio Ponti. Fornasetti designs were particularly popular during the 1950s and 1960s, when his personal portfolio of motifs and themes were applied to his furniture, ceramics, wallpapers and textiles.

Ghyczy, Peter (b.1940)
Hungarian-born designer Peter Ghyczy studied architecture in Germany and lived and worked in the country before settling in the Netherlands. He helped pioneer the evolution of plastic products and furniture during the 1960s, including his hinged Garden Egg Chair of 1968, a clam-shell design in fibreglass that unfolds to reveal an upholstered seat and backrest.

Girard, Alexander (1907-1993)
Having initially trained and worked as an architect, largely based in Italy, Alexander Girard eventually settled in the USA and was appointed head of Herman Miller's textile division. He balanced this with other projects, including furniture design and interiors. Key commissions included the interiors of the iconic Miller House (1957) in Columbus, Indiana, designed by architect Eero Saarinen; and a major reinvention of Braniff Airways' corporate identity.

Graffi, Carlo (1925-1985) **& Campo, Franco** (b.1926)
Italian designer and architect Carlo Graffi was part of the 'organic school of Turin' and worked with Carlo Mollino before setting up his own design studio with Franco Campo. Graffi and Campo's best-known design is their 1951 Lounge Chair, using a sinuous birch plywood and laminate frame with velvet seat cushions.

Hein, Piet (1905-1996)
Writer, poet, urban planner, mathematician, inventor, and product, lighting and furniture designer Piet Hein was a well-known Danish polymath. Among his best-known designs are his leather-seated steel Bar Stools (1971) and the Superellipse Table (1964), designed with Bruno Matthson.

Hvidt, Peter (1916-1986) **& Mølgaard-Nielsen, Orla** (1907-1993)
Danish designers Hvidt and Mølgaard-Nielsen both studied cabinetmaking in Copenhagen and began working together in the mid-1940s. In 1944 they developed the Portex stacking chair and went on to design furniture for Fritz Hansen, Søborg Møbelfabrik, France & Søn and others. Their Fritz Hansen designs include the AX Armchair (1947) and table (1948).

Jacobsen, Arne (1902-1971)
A multifaceted architect and designer, Arne Jacobsen preferred to take a holistic approach to his projects, creating harmonious fusions of interiors, textiles and furniture. He trained as a stonemason and then studied in Copenhagen, going on to work in the architectural offices of Paul Holsøe before founding his own design practice. His organic and ergonomic version of Scandinavian modernism has proved perennially popular.

Jalk, Grete (1920-2006)
Danish designer Grete Jalk studied joinery and furniture design in Copenhagen, opening her own studio in 1953. She designed furniture for Fritz Hansen, France & Søn, Johannes Hansen and Poul Jeppesen, among others. Jalk edited the *Mobilia* design journal for many years.

Jeanneret, Pierre (1896-1967)
Although overshadowed by the achievements and personality of his famous cousin and collaborator, Le Corbusier, Pierre Jeanneret was an architect and furniture designer of distinction in his own right. Jeanneret worked with his cousin on many key architectural projects and co-designed – with Le Corbusier and Charlotte Perriand – a number of iconic pieces of furniture from the late 1920s. During the post-war period, Jeanneret's furniture assumed a more distinct identity, as seen in his Scissor Chair (1948). Throughout the 1950s and 1960s Jeanneret devised an extraordinary and sought-after range of chairs and other furniture for use in the highly ambitious Indian administrative centre of Chandigarh, in the Punjab, where Jeanneret ultimately became chief architect.

Johnson, Philip (1906-2005)
American architect and designer Philip Johnson's most famous building was undoubtedly his own Glass House (1949) in New Canaan, Connecticut, which was largely based on principles and ideas developed by Ludwig Mies van der Rohe. Johnson worked as an associate architect on Mies's Seagram Building in New York (1958), which included the design of interiors and furniture, as well as developing his own practice and a career that explored a number of aesthetic styles over the years.

Jones, Charles Hollis (b.1945)
American furniture and lighting designer, Charles Hollis Jones is known for his use of Lucite and acrylic, which lends his work a sense of 1920s glamour spliced with a mid-century modern feel. His work from the late 1960s and 1970s attracted celebrity and design-industry clients, including interior designer Arthur Elrod and Frank Sinatra. Among Jones's best-known pieces are his Waterfall series of benches, tables and chairs from the late 1960s and early 1970s.

Juhl, Finn (1912-1989)
Danish architect and furniture designer Finn Juhl worked in both fields during the 1940s before setting up his own design studio in 1945 to concentrate on furniture. He worked with manufacturers such as Niels Vodder, France & Søn and Baker, with his pieces combining sinuous teak frames with rounded, sculpted cushion pads and upholstery, offering both ergonomic comfort and elegance. Juhl also served as a senior tutor at the Frederiksberg Technical School.

Kagan, Vladimir (1927-2016)
German-born designer Vladimir Kagan settled in the USA at a young age and studied architecture at Columbia University. He began designing furniture and interiors in the late 1940s, opening his first furniture store in New York in 1949. Private clients included Marilyn Monroe and Gary Cooper, while he also had a wide range of commercial clients. Many of Kagan's chair designs of the 1950s have a sculptural, sinuous and anthropomorphic quality.

Kjaer, Bodil (b.1932)
Danish architect and designer Bodil Kjaer studied in Copenhagen and London before starting work with Arup during the late 1960s; she has also lectured in the USA, Denmark and the UK. Much of her furniture dates from the mid-century period and includes chairs, outdoor furniture and, particularly, pieces for office use such as desks and storage units.

Kjaerholm, Poul (1929-1980)
Danish furniture designer Poul Kjaerholm studied furniture design in Copenhagen at the School of Arts & Crafts. Although he initially served an apprenticeship as a carpenter, Kjaerholm is best known for precision pieces that juxtapose such modern, industrially made materials as steel with organic elements like rattan seats.

Knoll, Florence (1917-2019) **and Knoll, Hans** (1914-1955)
Son of a German furniture manufacturer, Hans Knoll emigrated to the USA in 1938 and founded the Hans G. Knoll Furniture Company the following year in New York, initially collaborating with designer Jens Risom. In 1941 he met architect and designer Florence Schust, who had trained at the Cranbrook Academy of Art. They married in 1946 and ran the company, which became Knoll Associates, together until Hans's death in 1955, after which Florence continued the business, designing many key pieces herself. The Knoll collection grew rapidly in the post-war period, with iconic designs by a number of architects and designers that Florence had met at Cranbrook, including Eero Saarinen and Harry Bertoia.

Kukkapuro, Yrjö (b.1933)
Finnish furniture designer Yrjö Kukkapuro founded his own design studio in Helsinki in 1959. He worked with fibreglass plastics during the early 1960s, creating the ergonomic and enveloping Karuselli ('Carousel') Lounge Chair of 1964. Kukkapuro developed a number of fibreglass chairs in the 1960s while his interest in ergonomics also fed into his designs.

Laverne, Erwine (1909-2003) **& Laverne, Estelle** (1915-1997)
Husband-and-wife furniture designers and artists Erwine and Estelle Laverne both studied painting at the Art Students League of New York before founding their own design studio in 1938. Laverne Originals (later Laverne International) produced many of their own designs as well as pieces by a small coterie of other designers. Chief among their output is a range of sculptural chairs from the late 1950s, made of clear acrylic, known as the Invisible Group.

Magistretti, Vico (1920-2006)
One of the great mid-century Milanese polymaths, Vico Magistretti combined architecture with furniture and lighting design. His pieces include the injection-moulded plastic Selene Chair (1968) and the Caori Coffee Table (1961).

Magnusson-Grossman, Greta (1906-1999)
Swedish-born lighting and furniture designer Greta Magnusson studied and worked in Stockholm before marrying American Billy Grossman and emigrating to the USA in 1940. Magnusson-Grossman opened her own store in Los Angeles selling her work and soon established a Hollywood following. She produced furniture and lighting designs for a number of companies in the 1950s and 1960s, and also designed a series of houses in Los Angeles during the mid-century period.

Maloof, Sam (1916-2009)
American furniture designer and woodworker Sam Maloof worked from his own Californian workshop in Alta Loma and was a key practitioner of studio furniture making in the post-war period. During the early 1950s, industrial designer Henry Dreyfuss commissioned Maloof to produce pieces for his own home. Maloof's output fused Shaker and Scandinavian influences but retained its own character.

Mangiarotti, Angelo (1921-2012)
Italian architect, furniture and product designer Angelo Mangiarotti studied at the Politecnico di Milano and worked in the USA during the early 1950s. In 1955

he co-founded an architectural practice with Bruno Morassutti in Milan. In 1960 he established his own design studio, which produced a broad body of furniture and product design, as well as lighting.

Matégot, Mathieu (1910–2001)
Born in Hungary, furniture and interior designer Mathieu Matégot moved to Paris in 1931 and started his career as a set designer. After being held as a prisoner of war during World War II, he began designing furniture from the late 1940s onward, focusing on the use of perforated sheet metal ('Rigitulle'), which could be bent and moulded to create seats, chairs and tables supported by a tubular-steel framework.

Mathsson, Bruno (1907–1988)
Swedish furniture designer Bruno Mathsson served an apprenticeship in his father's cabinetmaking workshop and began experimenting with bentwood and laminate furniture during the 1930s. Matthson's pioneering early furniture was made by Karl Matthson's family workshop. The sculptural and organic character of his pieces anticipated the mid-century, soft modernist Scandinavian style. During the 1950s Mathsson concentrated on architectural and interior commissions, but returned to furniture design in the 1960s after taking over leadership of the family company.

McCobb, Paul (1917–1969)
American furniture designer Paul McCobb studied painting in Boston. He established his own design studio in New York in 1945 and began working as a consultant for Modern Age Furniture. His multiple furniture lines of the 1950s included the Directional collection for Custom Craft, the Planner Group made by Winchendon and pieces for Calvin Furniture. McCobb's furniture was well made and modern but also affordable. As his success grew, he also designed wallpapers, lighting, textiles and household products.

Mies van der Rohe, Ludwig (1886–1969)
Born in Germany, Mies van der Rohe worked with Peter Behrens and others before establishing his own practice in Berlin in 1912. He was director of the Bauhaus for three years before its closure in 1933 and emigrated to the USA in 1938, later taking American citizenship. His pioneering houses, skyscrapers and furniture were all to have a huge impact, making him one of the most influential architects and designers of the 20th century. During the late 1940s and 1950s, Knoll began producing a number of his iconic furniture designs, developed in the pre-war period in conjunction with Lilly Reich, including the Barcelona Collection.

Mogensen, Børge (1914–1972)
Danish furniture designer Børge Mogensen trained with Kaare Klint in Copenhagen, establishing his own design practice in the early 1950s. He developed a range of furniture that drew upon his interest in ergonomics, sustainability and traditional furniture forms, as well as contemporary aesthetics. His Spanish Chair of 1958, with an oak frame and slung-leather seat and back, recalls the work of Latin American

contemporaries such as Sergio Rodrigues, while Mogensen also experimented with plywood to great effect.

Mollino, Carlo (1905–1973)
Carlo Mollino studied architecture in his native Turin before embarking on a multilayered career that encompassed architecture, interiors and furniture design, as well as photography, motor racing and downhill skiing. His furniture is famously dynamic and expressive but also beautifully crafted, as seen in his biomorphic tables and chairs. Mollino is commonly referred to as the godfather of Turinese Baroque and was a key influence upon designers such as Franco Campo and Carlo Graffi.

Mourgue, Olivier (b.1939)
French furniture designer Olivier Mourgue studied design in Paris and Scandinavia. He established his own design studio in Paris in the mid-1960s. His colourful, futuristic designs, such as the Djinn Model 8412 Sofa (1965), use steel frames coated in foam upholstery held in place by elasticated fabrics. Mourgue's furniture appeared in Stanley Kubrick's film *2001: A Space Odyssey* in 1968.

Nakashima, George (1905–1990)
Born in Spokane, Washington, to Japanese parents, George Nakashima studied architecture at the University of Washington and MIT. In 1931 he began working in Japan with architect Antonin Raymond. In 1942, after returning to the USA, Nakashima and his family were interned (along with many others of Japanese ancestry) at Camp Minidoka in Idaho, where he worked with master craftsman Gentaro Hikogawa. With Raymond's help, Nakashima and his family were able to leave the camp in 1943 and settled in New Hope, Pennsylvania. Here, Nakashima began creating his own distinctive collections of hand-crafted furniture, balancing designs for Knoll and Widdicomb with his own designs and commissions.

Nelson, George (1908–1986)
George Nelson's first successful career, following on from his studies at Yale and time in Europe, was in architecture. This was later eclipsed by a much better known, post-war period in the world of furniture and product design, having been appointed as Herman Miller's director of design in 1946 and then establishing his own design studio a year later, juggling these two overlapping roles during the 1950s and 1960s. As well as encouraging and commissioning many key Herman Miller designers, including Charles & Ray Eames, Nelson and his studio associates designed an extraordinary portfolio of furniture for the company.

Noguchi, Isamu (1904–1988)
The Japanese–American artist and designer Isamu Noguchi, who was born in Los Angeles to an American mother and a Japanese father, concentrated on sculpture during the early years of his career. He worked with Constantin Brâncuși in Paris and largely concentrated on art after settling in New York. His furniture of the 1940s and 1950s explored sculptural shapes

and forms. Noguchi also made a lasting impression in the world of lighting design through his post-war collaborations with Japanese paper lantern producers Ozeki & Co, developing an extensive collection of Akari 'light sculptures', which are still in production.

Nurmesniemi, Antti (1927–2003)
Finnish product, interior, exhibition and furniture designer Antti Nurmesniemi designed everything from sauna stools to electricity pylons and ferry interiors during a long and highly productive career. From 1951 to 1956 Nurmesniemi worked in the architectural office Viljo Revell, designing interiors and furniture. In 1956 Nurmesniemi founded his own design studio and a year later married textile designer Vuokko Eskolin.

Panton, Verner (1926–1998)
Having trained as an architect, Verner Panton initially worked with Arne Jacobsen in Copenhagen. By 1955 he had established his own studio, combining architecture, interiors and furniture design. Panton's Cone and Heart Cone chairs of the late 1950s earned him international attention. During the early 1960s Panton relocated to Basel to work with Vitra on the development of the iconic Panton Chair (1967), the first single-piece, injection-moulded plastic chair.

Parisi, Ico (1916–1996) & **Parisi, Luisa** (1914–1990)
Italian architect, film-maker, artist and furniture designer Ico Parisi studied in Como before starting work with architect Giuseppe Terragni. During the late 1940s he began working as an independent designer and collaborating with his wife, Luisa. They designed an extensive range of furniture throughout the 1950s and 1960s.

Paulin, Pierre (1927–2009)
Following his studies in art and sculpture at the Ecole Camondo in Paris, Pierre Paulin began concentrating on furniture design. He formed a long, creative collaboration with Dutch manufacturer Artifort, who produced many of his key designs. Colourful, expressive and dynamic, his pieces are infused with a pop-art sensibility.

Perriand, Charlotte (1903–1999)
French architect, interior architect and furniture designer Charlotte Perriand studied at the Ecole de l'Union Centrale des Arts Décoratifs in Paris, graduating in 1925. Soon afterward she joined Le Corbusier's architectural and design studio, collaborating with him and Pierre Jeanneret on a number of iconic furniture designs of the inter-war period. During the 1940s, Perriand lived and worked in Japan and Vietnam before returning to France. In the 1950s she collaborated with Jean Prouvé and designed a number of key pieces for the Steph Simon Gallery in Paris, as well as designing Alpine resorts.

Pesce, Gaetano (b.1939)
Born in La Spezia, Italy, architect and furniture designer Gaetano Pesce studied architecture and design in Venice. Based in Padua in the early 1960s, Pesce later moved

to Paris and then New York. In 1969 Pesce designed his famous Up Series of furniture for B&B Italia (then known as C&B Italia): a collection of abstract and highly sculptural seating and ottoman designs in bright pop-art colours, using stretch-fabric coverings over a moulded polyurethane base.

Platner, Warren (1919–2006)
After studying architecture at Cornell University, Warren Platner went to work with legendary industrial designer Raymond Loewy and then spent 15 years with architect Eero Saarinen. Founding his own practice in 1967, Platner balanced architectural projects with interior commissions and furniture design. He is best known for his collection of steel wire-rod furniture for Knoll, simply known as the Platner Collection (1966).

Pollock, Charles (1930–2013)
American product and furniture designer Charles Pollock worked in the office of George Nelson during the 1950s, where he began designing pieces for Herman Miller. He founded his own design office in 1958, designing for Knoll and Thonet.

Ponti, Gio (1891–1979)
Architect, designer, educator, teacher, writer and more, Gio Ponti was the archetypal mid-century modern polymath whose influence was felt across the world of Italian and international design. Key buildings include the Pirelli Tower (1956) in his native Milan, along with hotels and houses in Italy, Europe and beyond. His glassware for Venini is revered, while his extensive portfolio of furniture features the Diamond Lounge Chair and Sofa (1953) and the iconic Superleggera chair (1957).

Prouvé, Jean (1901–1984)
Designer, manufacturer, entrepreneur, construction consultant, engineering expert and former mayor of Nancy, Jean Prouvé worked in many fields and disciplines. As a designer and producer of furniture and buildings, he was fascinated by prefabrication and factory production techniques. Never formally registered as an architect, he explored many experimental ideas through collaborations with other modernist architects and engineers. His furniture was factory produced using industrially made materials yet is imaginative, inventive and influential.

Quistgaard, Jens (1919–2008)
Danish furniture and product designer Jens Quistgaard studied sculpture and woodwork before serving an apprenticeship with silverware maker Georg Jensen. He co-founded a manufacturing company – Dansk International – in 1954 with American partner Ted Nierenberg. Dansk produced many of Quistgaard's own designs, ranging from stools to teak ice buckets, cutlery and sculptural peppermills.

Race, Ernest (1913–1964)
After studying interior design at the Bartlett in London, Ernest Race worked as a draughtsman and then opened a home-furnishings showroom selling a mixture

of his own designs and pieces produced by others. Just after World War II, Race began working on a fresh furniture collection and soon founded his own manufacturing company, which became Race Furniture.

Rams, Dieter (b.1932)
As a product designer, Dieter Rams has been profoundly influential. His emphasis on a considered combination of beauty, logic and function within pared-down, easy-to-use products has been widely imitated. Rams was born in Wiesbaden, Germany, and was influenced by his grandfather, a carpenter. He studied architecture and interior design at Wiesbaden School of Art before joining the architectural office of Otto Appel in Frankfurt. In 1955 he was first employed by Braun as an architect and interior designer, initially working on Braun showrooms, before moving over to product design. He was appointed director of design at Braun in 1962 and held the post until his retirement in 1995.

Rapson, Ralph (1914–2008)
American architect, academic and furniture designer Ralph Rapson studied at Cranbrook Academy of Art, where he met Florence Knoll. In 1944, Knoll asked Rapson to design a collection of chairs and sofas, which were released the following year. Rapson taught architecture at the University of Minnesota for many years, becoming dean of the architecture school, and designed American embassies in Copenhagen and Stockholm (both 1954).

Risom, Jens (1916–2016)
Danish designer Jens Risom studied with Kaare Klint in Copenhagen before settling in the USA in 1939. He designed a number of innovative chairs and other pieces of furniture during the early 1940s for Hans Knoll, before launching his own eponymous and successful furniture manufacturing and distribution company in 1946.

Robsjohn-Gibbings, T. H. (1905–1976)
English-born furniture and interior designer Robsjohn-Gibbings studied architecture in London before moving to the USA. He opened his own furniture showroom in New York in 1936 and also designed a series of houses for prestigious clients in New York and California. His work combines modernist and neo-classical influences and includes a broad and successful collection for the Widdicomb furniture company, designed between 1943 and 1956.

Rodrigues, Sergio (1927–2014)
Brazilian designer Sergio Rodrigues was born in Rio de Janeiro and studied architecture before deciding to devote himself largely to furniture design. He opened his own furniture store, Oca, in Rio in 1955 and soon began marketing his designs. Following the success of these early pieces, Rodrigues opened a larger furniture-making workshop near São Paulo and later began balancing the furniture business with an architectural practice. Known for his use of native woods and natural materials, Rodrigues's key pieces include the Mole Lounge Chair of 1957, which was renamed the Sheriff for international distribution.

Saarinen, Eero (1910–1961)
Son of Finnish architect Eliel Saarinen and textile designer Loja Saarinen, Eero Saarinen was born in Finland and moved to the USA in 1923 with his family. He studied sculpture in Paris and architecture at Yale. From 1936 onward he collaborated with his father, as well as working with Charles Eames. Following the death of his father, Saarinen established his own practice in Bloomfield Hills, Michigan. As well as his architectural projects, Saarinen designed celebrated ranges of furniture for Knoll, including the iconic Pedestal Collection.

Scarpa, Tobia (b.1935) & Scarpa, Afra (1937–2011)
Son of architect Carlo Scarpa, Tobia and his wife Afra both studied at the Istituto Universitario di Architettura in Venice. During the late 1950s – like Carlo Scarpa before them – they began designing glassware for Venini. Their furniture includes the Bastiano Sofa for Gavina (1962) and the Soriana Lounge Chair for Cassina (1969). Architectural and interior projects include factories for Benetton and B&B Italia, as well as residences and showrooms.

Schultz, Richard (1926–2021)
American furniture designer and sculptor Richard Schultz began his career working with Knoll in the early 1950s, collaborating initially with Harry Bertoia. He went on to design the Petal Collection of tables for Knoll in 1960. This was followed by the Leisure Collection of 1966: hard-wearing but stylish outdoor furniture with aluminium frames and nylon mesh seating, initially intended for the hotel market but eventually becoming a ubiquitous favourite for poolsides and terraces.

Tapiovaara, Ilmari (1914–1999)
Finnish furniture and product designer Ilmari Tapiovaara began his career in the London office of Artek during the 1930s. He briefly worked in the Paris office of Le Corbusier before serving as art director of Finnish furniture company Asko. During the post-war period Tapiovaara's work became more ambitious. He was particularly fascinated with the idea of developing an affordable but well-designed chair staple, creating the Domus birch plywood chair in 1946. Tapiovaara established his own design studio in Helsinki in 1950.

Tenreiro, Joaquim (1906–1992)
Born to a family of furniture makers and artisans in Portugal, Joaquim Tenreiro settled in Brazil in 1928. Assisted by a commission from Oscar Niemeyer to provide furniture for a residential project, Tenreiro founded his own furniture company in 1943 and opened stores in Rio and São Paulo, offering crafted collections that made use of indigenous woods and natural materials. At the height of his success in the late 1960s, Tenreiro decided to close the business and focus on his work as a sculptor.

Wanscher, Ole (1903–1985)
Danish furniture designer Ole Wanscher studied with Kaare Klint and immersed himself in furniture history, drawing lessons and inspiration from a wide spectrum of historical designs. During the 1940s and 1950s Wanscher designed for a number of manufacturers, including Fritz Hansen. Among his most enticing designs are a rosewood and leather rocking chair (1951) and his Colonial Chair (1949).

Wegner, Hans (1914–2007)
One of the best-known and most influential mid-century furniture designers, whose work remains in great demand, Hans Wegner served an apprenticeship to a master cabinetmaker before studying at the Copenhagen School of Arts & Crafts. He worked briefly with Arne Jacobsen before opening his own design studio in 1943. Wegner's early pieces referenced historic precedents, yet his work became increasingly expressive, original and experimental over time. With a focus on craft, largely natural materials and sculptural forms, Wegner is widely regarded as the leading light in the golden era of Danish design.

Wirkkala, Tapio (1915–1985)
Tapio Wirkkala was a Finnish glassware and furniture designer who initially studied sculpture in Helsinki. He began designing glassware for Iittala in 1946 and continued working with the company until his death. Wirkkala also designed ceramics for Rosenthal and furniture for Asko. Wirkkala's Leaf platters for Soinne et Kni (1951), using laminated birch in sinuous striped swirls, became design icons.

Wormley, Edward (1907–1995)
Born in Illinois, Edward Wormley studied at the Art Institute of Chicago before finding work as an interior designer for the Marshall Field's department store. In 1931 he began a long and productive relationship with Dunbar Furniture, eventually becoming director of design. Dunbar produced the majority of Wormley's extensive and original portfolio of furniture in the 1950s and 1960s.

Yanagi, Sori (1915–2011)
Japanese furniture designer Sori Yanagi studied architecture in Tokyo and worked briefly with Charlotte Perriand when she established an office in Japan in the 1940s. He founded his own design studio in 1952.

Zalszupin, Jorge (1922–2020)
Brazilian furniture designer Jorge Zalszupin was born in Poland and studied architecture in Romania before emigrating to Brazil in 1949. Settling in São Paulo, he founded L'Atelier in 1955 and produced, among other pieces, a distinctive series of ribbed-back rosewood or jacaranda sofas supported by steel frames or aluminium rods.

Zanuso, Marco (1916–2001)
Having trained as an architect at the Politecnico di Milano, Marco Zanuso opened his own multidisciplinary design studio in the city in 1945. He combined architectural commissions with, among other things, furniture design, creating expressive pieces for Arflex and others. Zanuso also collaborated with Richard Sapper in the field of product design, including compact televisions and radios for Brionvega.

BIBLIOGRAPHY

Albus, Volker, et al., *Modern Furniture: 150 Years of Design*, H. F. Ullmann, 2011

Auscherman, Amy, Sam Grawe & Leon Ransmeier (eds), *Herman Miller: A Way of Living*, Phaidon, 2019

Berry, John R., *Herman Miller: The Purpose of Design*, Rizzoli, 2009

Breward, Christopher & Ghislaine Wood (eds), *British Design from 1948: Innovation in the Modern Age*, V&A Publishing, 2012

Bo Bardi, Lina, *Lina Bo Bardi*, Instituto Lina Bo e P. M. Bardi/Edizioni Charta, 1994

Bundegaard, Christian, *Finn Juhl: Life, Work, World*, Phaidon, 2019

Byars, Mel, *The Design Encyclopedia*, Laurence King, 2004

Chair: 500 Designs That Matter, Phaidon, 2018

Chen, Aric, *Brazil Modern*, Monacelli, 2016

Cobbers, Arnt, *Marcel Breuer*, Taschen, 2007

Cohen, Jean-Louis, *Le Corbusier*, Taschen, 2006

Czerwinski, Michael, *Fifty Chairs That Changed The World*, Conran Octopus, 2009

Dormer, Peter, *Design Since 1945*, Thames & Hudson, 1993

Droste, Magdalena, *Bauhaus*, Taschen, 2011

Dybdahl, Lars, *Furniture Boom: Mid-Century Modern Danish Furniture 1945–75*, Strandberg Publishing, 2019

Eidelberg, Martin (ed.), *Design 1935–1965: What Modern Was*, Abrams/Le Musée des Arts Décoratifs de Montréal, 1991

Engholm, Ida, & Anders Michelsen, *Verner Panton*, Phaidon, 2018

Falino, Jeannine (ed.), *Crafting Modernism: Midcentury American Art & Design*, Abrams/Museum of Arts & Design, 2012

Ferrari, Fulvio & Napoleone, *The Furniture of Carlo Mollino*, Phaidon, 2010

Fiell, Charlotte & Peter, *1000 Chairs*, Taschen, 2005

––, *Design of the 20th Century*, Taschen, 1999

––, *Industrial Design A–Z*, Taschen, 2000

––, *Masterpieces of British Design*, Goodman Fiell Publishing, 2012

––, *Masterpieces of Italian Design*, Goodman Fiell Publishing, 2013

––, *Plastic Dreams: Synthetic Visions in Design*, Fiell Publishing, 2009

––, *Scandinavian Design*, Taschen, 2005

Girard, Alexander, & Todd Oldham, *Alexander Girard*, AMMO Books, 2012

Godau, Marion, & Bernd Polster (eds), *Design Directory: Germany*, Pavilion, 2000

Gura, Judith, *Scandinavian Furniture: A Sourcebook of Classic Designs for the 21st Century*, Thames & Hudson, 2007

Habegger, Jerryll, & Joseph H. Osman, *Sourcebook of Modern Furniture*, Norton, 2005

Holmsted Olesen, Christian, *Wegner: Just One Good Chair*, Hatje Cantz, 2014

Jackson, Lesley, *Contemporary: Architecture & Interiors of the 1950s*, Phaidon, 1994

––, *Modern British Furniture: Design Since 1945*, V&A Publishing, 2013

––, *Robin & Lucienne Day: Pioneers in Modern Design*, Mitchell Beazley, 2001

––, *The Sixties: Decade of Design Revolution*, Phaidon, 1998

Jean Prouvé: Architect for Better Days, Phaidon, 2017

Julier, Guy, *Design Since 1900*, Thames & Hudson, 1993

Koenig, Gloria, *Charles & Ray Eames*, Taschen, 2005

Kries, Mateo, et al. (eds), *Atlas of Furniture Design*, Vitra Design Museum, 2019

Kries, Mateo, & Jolanthe Kugler (eds), *Eames Furniture Sourcebook*, Vitra Design Museum, 2017

Kries, Mateo, & Alexander von Vegesack (eds), *Joe Colombo*, Vitra Design Museum, 2005

La Pietra, Ugo, *Gio Ponti*, Rizzoli, 2009

Lahti, Louna, *Alvar Aalto*, Taschen, 2004

Lupfer, Gilbert, & Paul Sigel, *Walter Gropius*, Taschen, 2006

Lutz, Brian, *Knoll: A Modernist Universe*, Rizzoli, 2010

Massey, Anne, *Interior Design of the 20th Century*, Thames & Hudson, 1990

McDermott, Catherine, *20th Century Design*, Carlton Books, 1999

Merkel, Jayne, *Eero Saarinen*, Phaidon, 2005

Miller, Judith, *Miller's 20th Century Design*, Miller's/Mitchell Beazley, 2009

Müller, Michael, *Børge Mogensen: Simplicity & Function*, Hatje Cantz, 2016

Neumann, Claudia (ed.), *Design Directory: Italy*, Pavilion, 1999

Oliveira, Olivia de, *Subtle Substances: The Architecture of Lina Bio Bardi*, Gustavo Gili, 2006

Orrom, James, *Chair Anatomy: Design & Construction*, Thames & Hudson, 2018

Peters, Nils, *Jean Prouvé*, Taschen, 2006

Phaidon Design Classics: Volume Two, Phaidon, 2006

Pollock, Naomi, *Japanese Design Since 1945*, Thames & Hudson, 2020

Polster, Bernd (ed.), *Design Directory: Scandinavia*, Pavilion, 1999

Polster, Berd, et al., *The A–Z of Modern Design*, Merrell, 2009

Raizman, David, *History of Modern Design*, Laurence King, 2010

Roccella, Graziella, *Gio Ponti*, Taschen, 2009

Rouland, Steven & Linda, *Knoll Furniture*, Schiffer Publishing, 2005

Ryder Richardson, Lucy, *100 Midcentury Chairs: And Their Stories*, Pavilion, 2016

Sembach, Klaus-Jürgen, *Modern Furniture Designs 1950–1980s*, Schiffer, 1997

Serraino, Pierluigi, *Eero Saarinen*, Taschen, 2006

Sparke, Penny (ed.), *Design Directory: Great Britain*, Pavilion, 2001

Twitchell, Beverly H., *Bertoia*, Phaidon, 2019

Ueki-Polet, Keiko, & Klaus Kemp (eds), *Less Is More: The Design Ethos of Dieter Rams*, Gestalten, 2009

Webb, Michael, *Modernist Paradise*, Rizzoli, 2007

Wilk, Christopher, *Plywood: A Material Story*, Thames & Hudson/V&A Publishing, 2017

Wilkins, Amy (ed.), *The Furniture of Poul Kjaerholm: Catalogue Raisonné*, Gregory R. Miller & Co, 2007

Williamson, Leslie, *Handcrafted Modern*, Rizzoli, 2010

Wright, Russel, *Good Design Is For Everyone*, Manitoga/Russel Wright Design Center/Universe, 2001

Zimmerman, Claire, *Mies van der Rohe*, Taschen, 2006

AUTHOR BIOGRAPHY

Dominic Bradbury is a writer, journalist, lecturer and consultant specializing in architecture and design. He writes for many magazines and newspapers in the UK and internationally, while his many books include *Mid-Century Modern Design*, *The Iconic House*, *The Iconic Interior*, *The Iconic American House* and *New Nordic Houses*, all published by Thames & Hudson.

ACKNOWLEDGMENTS

The author and publishers would like to express their gratitude to the team at Wright20 auction house (www.wright20.com) for their valuable assistance and patience in the making of this book, with particular thanks to Richard Wright, Todd Simeone, Jennifer Mahanay, Jake Watts and their colleagues.

We would also like to thank photographer Richard Powers for the interior pictures, Karolina Prymaka for the graphic design and Catherine Hooper for her expert editing and proofreading skills.

The author would also like to thank Lucas Dietrich and Helen Fanthorpe at Thames & Hudson, along with Evie Tarr, Fleur Jones and the rest of the team. This book would have been an impossible task without the support of all of the above.

Last but not least, thanks are due to Carrie Kania at Conville & Walsh, along with Faith, Florence, Cecily, Noah & Elsie Bradbury.

PICTURE CREDITS

All photographs are from Wright 20 auction house (www.wright20.com), unless otherwise stated below.

pp. 12–13, 118–19, 156–57, 192–93, 242–43, 304–5, 344–45, 396–97: Interiors Images by Richard Powers, © Richard Powers

p. 121: Pastilli Chair Courtesy of Eero Aarnio Originals, www. aarniooriginals.com

p. 203: Loveseat Courtesy of Ercol/Ercol Heritage/© Ercol, www.ercol.com

p. 255: Leonardo Table Courtesy of Zanotta/© Zanotta, www.zanotta.it

p. 256: Poker Table Courtesy of Zanotta/© Zanotta, www.zanotta.it

p. 299: Marcuso Dining Table Courtesy of Zanotta/© Zanotta, www.zanotta.it

p. 352: Boby Trolley Courtesy of B-Line/© B-Line, www.b-line.it Photograph by Claudio Visentin

p. 384: 606 Universal Shelving System Courtesy of Vitsoe /© Vitsoe, www.vitsoe.com

INDEX

First published in the United Kingdom in 2022 by Thames & Hudson Ltd, 181A High Holborn, London WC1V 7QX

First published in the United States of America in 2022 by Thames & Hudson Inc., 500 Fifth Avenue, New York, New York 10110

Mid-Century Modern Furniture © 2022 Thames & Hudson Ltd

Text © 2022 Dominic Bradbury

For a full list of picture credits, see page 444

British Library Cataloguing-in-Publication Data
A catalogue record for this book is available from the British Library

Library of Congress Control Number 2022931537

ISBN 978-0-500-02222-1

Printed and bound in China by C&C Offset Printing Co.Ltd

Be the first to know about our new releases, exclusive content and author events by visiting
thamesandhudson.com
thamesandhudsonusa.com
thamesandhudson.com.au